LATIN AMERICA

PRENTICE HALL
Needham, Massachusetts
Upper Saddle River, New Jersey
Glenview, Illinois

Program Authors

Heidi Hayes Jacobs

Heidi Hayes Jacobs has served as an educational consultant to more than 500 schools across the nation. Dr. Jacobs is an adjunct professor in the Department of Curriculum on Teaching at Teachers College, Columbia University. She completed her undergraduate studies at the University of Utah in her hometown of Salt Lake City. She received an M.A. from the University of Massachusetts, Amherst, and completed her doctoral work at Columbia University's Teachers College in 1981.

The backbone of Dr. Jacobs' experience comes from her years as a teacher of high school, middle school, and elementary school students. As an educational consultant, she works with K–12 schools and districts on curriculum reform and strategic planning.

Brenda Randolph

Brenda Randolph is the former Director of the Outreach Resource Center at the African Studies Program at Howard University, Washington, D.C. She is the Founder and Director of Africa Access, a bibliographic service on Africa for schools. She received her B.A. in history with high honors from North Carolina Central University, Durham, and her M.A. in African studies with honors from Howard University. She completed further graduate studies at the University of Maryland, College Park, where she was awarded a Graduate Fellowship.

Brenda Randolph has published numerous articles in professional journals and bulletins. She currently serves as library media specialist in Montgomery County Public Schools, Maryland.

Michal L. LeVasseur

Michal LeVasseur is an educational consultant in the field of geography. She is an adjunct professor of geography at the University of Alabama, Birmingham, and serves with the Alabama Geographic Alliance. Her undergraduate and graduate work is in the fields of anthropology (B.A.), geography (M.A.), and science education (Ph.D.).

Dr. LeVasseur's specialization has moved increasingly into the area of geography education. In 1996, she served as Director of the National Geographic Society's Summer Geography Workshop. As an educational consultant, she has worked with the National Geographic Society as well as with schools to develop programs and curricula for geography.

Special Program Consultant

Yvonne S. Gentzler, Ph.D.
School of Education
University of Idaho, Moscow, Idaho

Content Consultant on Latin America

Daniel Mugan
Center for Latin American Studies
University of Florida
Gainesville, Florida

PRENTICE HALL
Needham, Massachusetts
Upper Saddle River, New Jersey
Glenview, Illinois

Student Edition ISBN: 0-13-050228-6

2 3 4 5 6 7 8 9 10   04 03 02 01 00

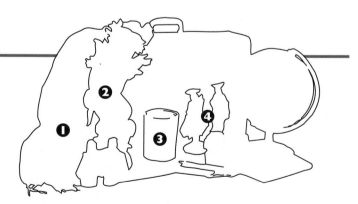

On the Cover

❶ Woven blanket from Mexico

❷ Mexican wood carving of an ancient Mayan snake god

❸ Reproduction of Mayan pottery

❹ Family of dolls from Peru dressed in traditional clothing

Content Consultants for the World Explorer Program

Africa
Barbara Brown
Africa Studies Center
Boston University
Boston, Massachusetts

Ancient World
Maud Gleason
Department of Classics
Stanford University
Stanford, California

East Asia
Leslie Swartz
Harvard University
East Asian Outreach Program at
the Children's Museum
of Boston
Boston, Massachusetts

Latin America
Daniel Mugan
Center for Latin American Studies
University of Florida
Gainesville, Florida

Middle East
Elizabeth Barlow
Center for Middle Eastern and
North African Studies
University of Michigan
Ann Arbor, Michigan

North Africa
Laurence Michalak
Center for Middle East Studies
University of California
Berkeley, California

Religion
Michael Sells
Department of Religion
Haverford College
Haverford, Pennsylvania

**Russia, Eastern Europe,
Central Asia**
Janet Valliant
Center for Russian, Eastern
European, and Central Asian
Studies
Harvard University
Cambridge, Massachusetts

South Asia
Robert Young
South Asia Regional Studies
University of Pennsylvania
Philadelphia, Pennsylvania

Western Europe
Ruth Mitchell-Pitts
Center for West European Studies
University of North Carolina
Chapel Hill, North Carolina

Teacher Advisory Board

Jerome Balin
Lincoln Junior High School
Naperville, Illinois

Elizabeth Barrett
Tates Creek Middle School
Lexington, Kentucky

Linda Boaen
Baird School
Fresno, California

Nikki L. Born
Harllee Middle School
Bradenton, Florida

Barbara Coats Grabowski
Russell Middle School
Omaha, Nebraska

Stephanie Hawkins
Jefferson Middle School
Oklahoma City, Oklahoma

Fred Hitz
Wilson Middle School
Muncie, Indiana

William B. Johnson
La Mesa Junior High School
Canyon Country, California

Kristi Karis
West Ottawa Middle School
Holland, Michigan

Kristen Koch
Discovery Middle School
Orlando, Florida

Peggy McCarthy
Beulah School
Beulah, Colorado

Cindy McCurdy
Hefner Middle School
Oklahoma City, Oklahoma

Deborah J. Miller
Department of Social Studies
Detroit Public Schools
Detroit, Michigan

Lawrence Peglow
Greenway Middle School
Pittsburgh, Pennsylvania

Lyn Shiver
Northwestern Middle School
Alpharetta, Georgia

Mark Stahl
Longfellow Middle
School
Norman, Oklahoma

TABLE OF CONTENTS

LATIN AMERICA

OF SPECIAL INTEREST

A hands-on approach to learning and applying social studies skills

ACTIVITY SHOP

Step-by-step activities for exploring important topics in Latin America

Literature selections by Latin American authors

HEROES

Profiles of people who made a difference in their country

Detailed drawings show how the use of technology makes a country unique

REGIONAL Data Bank

Map and statistics for every nation in Latin America

A view of a country through the eyes of a student artist

READ ACTIVELY

How can I get the most out of my social studies book?

How does my reading relate to my world? Answering questions like these means that you are an active reader, an involved reader. As an active reader, you are in charge of the reading situation!

The following strategies tell how to think and read as an active reader. You don't need to use all of these strategies all the time. Feel free to choose the ones that work best in each reading situation. You might use several at a time, or you might go back and forth among them. They can be used in any order.

BEFORE YOU READ

Give yourself a purpose

The sections in this book begin with a list called "Questions to Explore." These questions focus on key ideas presented in the section. They give you a purpose for reading. You can create your own purpose by asking questions like these: How does the topic relate to your life? How might you use what you learn at school or at home?

Preview

To preview a reading selection, first read its title. Then look at the pictures and read the captions. Also read any headings in the selection. Then ask yourself: What is the reading selection about? What do the pictures and headings tell about the selection?

Reach into your background

What do you already know about the topic of the selection? How can you use what you know to help you understand what you are going to read?

Ask questions

Suppose you are reading about the continent of South America. Some questions you might ask are: Where is South America? What countries are found there? Why are some of the countries large and others small? Asking questions like these can help you gather evidence and gain knowledge.

Predict

As you read, make a prediction about what will happen and why. Or predict how one fact might affect another fact. Suppose you are reading about South America's climate. You might make a prediction about how the climate affects where people live. You can change your mind as you gain new information.

Connect

Connect your reading to your own life. Are the people discussed in the selection like you or someone you know? What would you do in similar situations? Connect your reading to something you have already read. Suppose you have already read about the ancient Greeks. Now you are reading about the ancient Romans. How are they alike? How are they different?

Visualize

What would places, people, and events look like in a movie or a picture? As you read about India, you could visualize the country's heavy rains. What do they look like? How do they sound? As you read about geography, you could visualize a volcanic eruption.

Respond

Talk about what you have read. What did you think? Share your ideas with your classmates.

Assess yourself

What did you find out? Were your predictions on target? Did you find answers to your questions?

Follow up

Show what you know. Use what you have learned to do a project. When you do projects, you continue to learn.

LATIN AMERICA

The ancient peoples of Latin America built great civilizations from the riches of their land. Today, their descendants have mixed with newcomers from around the world to create a modern society with new traditions. Cities of steel and glass rise alongside ancient ruins. From villages in the rain forests, mountains, and countryside, people move to the thriving cities. Every day more families arrive, hoping to make a new life.

Guiding Questions

The readings and activities in this book will help you discover answers to these Guiding Questions.

☞ What are the main physical features of Latin America?

☞ What factors have affected cultures in Latin America?

☞ Why have many Latin Americans been moving to cities in recent years?

☞ What is the relationship of the nations of Latin America with the United States and the world?

☞ How has geography influenced the ways in which Latin Americans make a living?

Project Preview

You can also discover answers to the Guiding Questions by working on projects. Preview the following projects and choose one that you might want to do. For more details, see page 160.

A Latin American Concert Research Latin American music and find some examples on tape to play for your class.

Visions of Latin America Create a diorama and write a short report to show how Latin America's geography affects the way people live.

Latin America in the News Collect articles on Latin America from magazines and newspapers for a bulletin board display.

Explorer's Dictionary Create an illustrated dictionary of important terms translated from Latin American languages.

The woman in the photo above left lives in Jamaica. In the photo above, the colorful clothing of people in Guatemala shows their famous skill with weaving. Students at a school in Lima, Peru, are shown in the photo at left.

EXPLORER'S JOURNAL

A journal can be your personal book of discovery. As you explore Latin America, you can use your journal to keep track of things you learn and do. You can also record your thoughts about your journey. For your first entry, write your thoughts on where in Latin America you would like to go and what you would want to see there.

DISCOVERY ACTIVITIES ABOUT

Latin America

Learning about Latin America means being an explorer and a geographer. No explorer would start out without first checking some facts. Begin by exploring the maps of Latin America on the following pages.

Relative Location

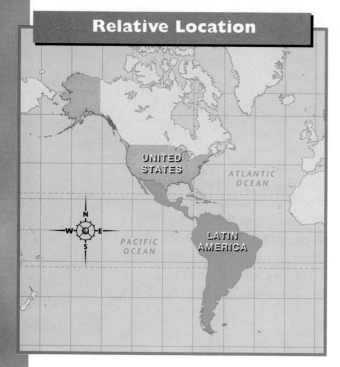

LOCATION

1. Explore Latin America's Location Notice where the United States and Latin America are located relative to the Equator. On the other side of the Equator, seasons come at the opposite time of year. For example, when it's summer here, it's winter there. Think about the season your birthday falls in. In what season would it fall if you lived in Argentina? What if you lived in Panama? How about in Bogotá, the capital city of Colombia? Or in Brasília, the capital of Brazil?

Relative Size

REGIONS

2. Estimate Latin America's Size How long is Latin America's west coast? To get an idea, curve a piece of string along the edge of the continental United States' west coast on the map above. Cut the string the same length as the coast. Now see how many string-lengths fit along the west coast of Latin America. Begin at the edge of the Pacific Ocean where Mexico borders California. Finish at the southern tip of South America. About how many times longer is Latin America's Pacific Coast than that of the United States?

LOCATION

3. Compare the Size of Countries The map below shows the countries that make up Latin America. Which two countries are the biggest in land area? Study the map to make your estimates. Check your answers in the World View section at the back of your textbook.

MOVEMENT

4. Investigate the Languages of Latin America The languages people speak give us clues about their history. Long ago, settlers from other countries took control of Latin America. Where were they from? Here are your clues: Portuguese is the official language of Brazil, and Spanish is spoken in most other Latin American countries.

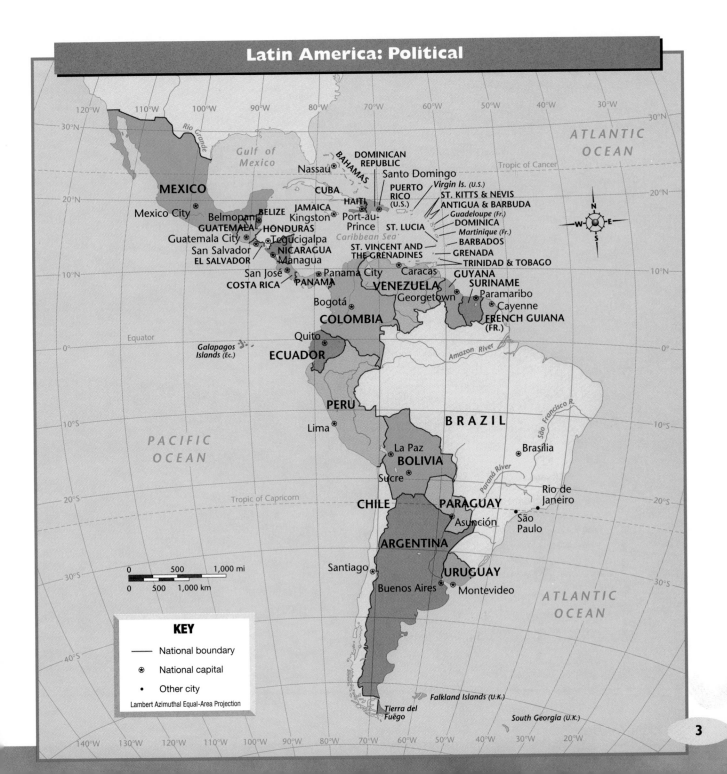

Latin America: Political

KEY

— National boundary

⊛ National capital

• Other city

Lambert Azimuthal Equal-Area Projection

PLACE

5. Examine the Physical Features of Latin America Volcanoes created many of Latin America's dramatic features. Long ago, volcanoes erupting along the west coast of South America formed the Andes Mountains. Volcanoes that exploded under the Caribbean Sea became a chain of islands called the Lesser Antilles. Central America has volcanic mountains, too. Some are still active! Trace the Andes Mountains, the Lesser Antilles, and the mountains in Central America with your finger. Which of these areas has the highest altitude?

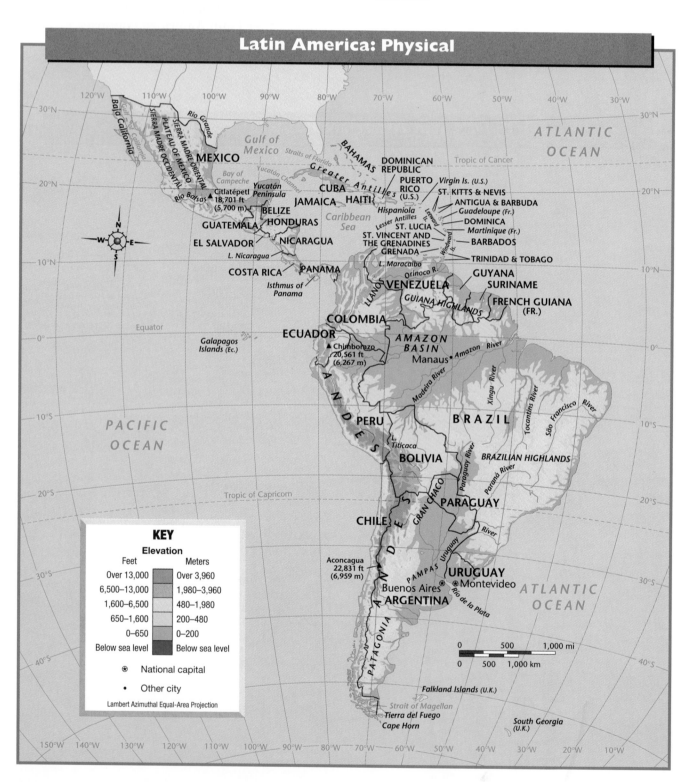

Latin America: Physical

KEY

Elevation

Feet	Meters
Over 13,000	Over 3,960
6,500–13,000	1,980–3,960
1,600–6,500	480–1,980
650–1,600	200–480
0–650	0–200
Below sea level	Below sea level

⊛ National capital

• Other city

Lambert Azimuthal Equal-Area Projection

6. Guide Geo Leo Geo Leo is exploring Latin America by boat, and he's taking you along to navigate. Read the passages below. To answer Geo Leo's questions, use the map below and the map on the opposite page.

A. We board our ship on the south side of the island of Hispaniola. A dense rain forest covers the island's mountain slopes. Which way to the Panama Canal?

B. We are sailing south past one of the Earth's driest deserts. It is in a long, skinny South American country that extends north and south along the continent's west coast. Steep mountains rise to the east. Where are we?

C. From the Falkland Islands, we travel north. For days we sail past desert scrub. Finally, we see tropical rain forest along the coast. What two major cities will we come to next?

D. We continue sailing north, past tropical savanna. We reach more rain forest and sail down a river through a low-lying area. Just ahead the Madeira River joins the one we are traveling on. Which way to the city of Manaus, our final destination?

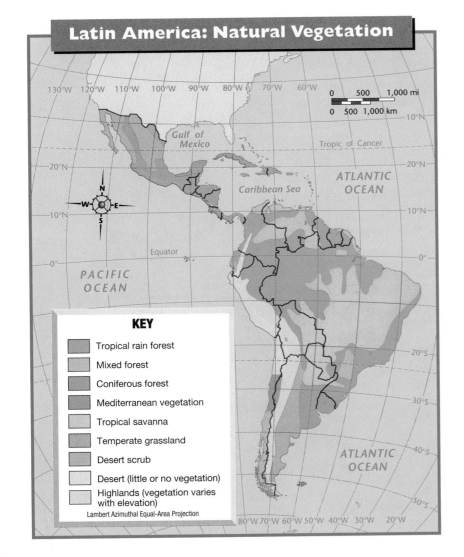

Latin America: Natural Vegetation

KEY

- Tropical rain forest
- Mixed forest
- Coniferous forest
- Mediterranean vegetation
- Tropical savanna
- Temperate grassland
- Desert scrub
- Desert (little or no vegetation)
- Highlands (vegetation varies with elevation)

Lambert Azimuthal Equal-Area Projection

GEO LEO

BONUS

List each body of water you and Geo Leo traveled over.

LOCATION

7. Investigate Latin America's Use of Hydroelectricity Hydroelectricity is electric power that is made by harnessing the power of water. One way to build a hydroelectric power plant is to build a dam across a river. The dam creates a large lake of water. To make electricity, the plant releases water from the lake into the river. As the water moves into the river, it turns a wheel. In some places, hydroelectric plants harness the power of ocean tides. Some of the largest hydroelectric plants are in Latin America. The world's largest is located on the border of Brazil and Paraguay. Look at the map below. What places in Latin America do you think would be good spots to build new hydroelectric power plants?

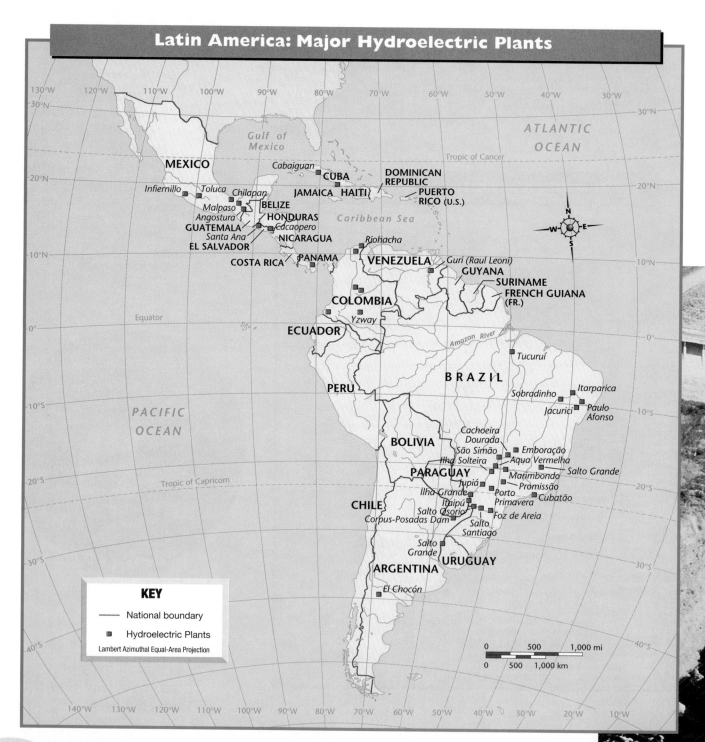

Latin America: Major Hydroelectric Plants

KEY

— National boundary

■ Hydroelectric Plants

Lambert Azimuthal Equal-Area Projection

Biggest Hydroelectric Dams

Name of Dam	Location
1. Itaipú	Brazil/Paraguay
2. Grand Coulee	United States
3. Guri (Raul Leoni)	Venezuela
4. Tucuruíi	Brazil
5. Sayano-Shushensk	Russia
6. Krasnoyarsk	Russia
7. Corpus-Posadas	Argentina/Paraguay
8. LaGrande 2	Canada
9. Churchill Falls	Canada
10. Bratsk	Russia

INTERACTION

8. Explore the Effects of a River Dam Unlike coal and petroleum, water power cannot be used up. It also does not cause air pollution. But building a dam does affect the environment of a river. It creates a large, artificial lake. It also reduces the amount of water that is in the river below the dam. What do you think are some advantages of building a dam across a river? What are some disadvantages?

◀ ▼ What percentage of its energy does Latin America get from hydroelectricity? How does this compare to energy use around the world?

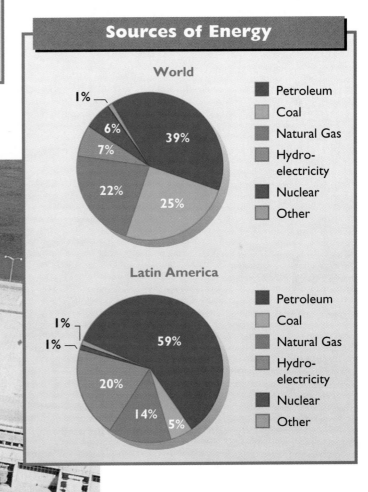

Sources of Energy

World

1% —
6%
7%
22%
25%
39%

- Petroleum
- Coal
- Natural Gas
- Hydro-electricity
- Nuclear
- Other

Latin America

1% —
1% —
59%
20%
14%
5%

- Petroleum
- Coal
- Natural Gas
- Hydro-electricity
- Nuclear
- Other

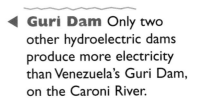

◀ **Guri Dam** Only two other hydroelectric dams produce more electricity than Venezuela's Guri Dam, on the Caroni River.

LATIN AMERICA

Physical Geography

PICTURE ACTIVITIES

These rugged mountains are the Andes (AN deez). They run the length of South America. To help you get to know this part of Latin America, do the following.

Study the picture
What do you think it would be like to live in or near the Andes? Based on what you see in the photograph, where would be the best area to live?

Think about the climate
Have you ever climbed in the mountains? How did the temperature change as you climbed higher? Based on your experience, do you think the climate is the same at the top of the Andes as at the bottom? Where would it be colder? Where would it be warmer?

Land and Water

Reach Into Your Background

No two places in the world are exactly the same. Think about the state in which you live. What features set it apart from other states? List some features that make your state special.

Questions to Explore
1. What are the main geographic regions of Latin America?
2. How do Latin America's geographic features affect the lives of the people?

Key Terms
plateau   pampas
isthmus   tributary
coral

Key Places
Mexico
Central America
Caribbean
South America

igh in the Andes Mountains, planes take off and land at El Alto airport. *El Alto* (ehl AHL toh) is Spanish for "the high one." It is an accurate name, for El Alto is the highest airport in the world. El Alto is the airport for La Paz, Bolivia.

Shortly after leaving the plane, tourists may get mountain sickness. The "thin" air of the Andes contains less oxygen than most people are used to. Oxygen starvation makes visitors' hearts beat faster and leaves them short of breath. Later on in the day, they may get terrible headaches. It takes a few days for visitors' bodies to get used to the mountain air. But the people who live in the Andes do not have these problems. Their bodies are used to the mountain environment.

The Andes mountain range is one of Latin America's major landforms. In this section, you will learn about Latin America's other landforms and about the people who live there.

Where Is Latin America?

Latin America is located in the Western Hemisphere south of the United States. Look at the map in the Activity Atlas. You will see that Latin America includes all the nations from Mexico to the tip of South America. It also includes the islands that dot the Caribbean (ka ruh BEE un) Sea.

Geographic features divide Latin America into three smaller regions. They are (1) Mexico and Central America, (2) the Caribbean, and (3) South America. South America is so large that geographers classify it as a continent. Look at the physical map in the Activity Atlas. Can you identify the geographic features that separate these three areas?

Predict How do you think the physical features of Latin America might be like those of the United States?

Perhaps you are wondering how Latin America got its name. About 500 years ago, Europeans sailed to Latin America. Most came from Spain and Portugal. European colonists brought their own languages and ways of life with them. Today, most Latin Americans speak Spanish, Portuguese, or French. These languages have their roots in the ancient language of Latin. As a result, the region is known as Latin America.

Landforms of Latin America

Imagine mountains that pierce the clouds and grassy plains that never seem to end. Picture wet rain forests and sunbaked deserts. This is Latin America, a region of variety and contrast.

Mexico and Central America   Mexico and Central America stretch 2,500 miles (4,023 km) from the U.S. border to South America. It is a distance that is almost equal to the width of the mainland United States. Mountains dominate this region. These mountains are part of a long system of mountain ranges. This huge system extends from Canada through the United States all the way to the tip of South America.

Between the mountains in Mexico lies Mexico's Central Plateau. A **plateau** (pla TOH) is a large raised area of mostly level land. Mexico's Central Plateau makes up more than half of the country's area. Most of Mexico's people live here. However, the surrounding mountains make it hard for people to travel to and from the Central Plateau. Another major landform in Mexico is the narrow coastal plains.

Central America, located south of Mexico, is an isthmus. An **isthmus** is a narrow strip of land that has water on both sides and joins two larger bodies of land. Find Central America on the map in the Activity Atlas. What two large bodies of land does the isthmus of Central America connect? As in Mexico, narrow plains run along Central America's coasts. Between these coastal plains are rugged, steep mountains. More than a dozen of these mountains are active volcanoes. Volcanic ash has made the soil fertile. As a result, many people tend farms in the region.

The Caribbean Imagine islands made of skeletons. Imagine other islands that are the tops of underwater mountains. The Caribbean is made up of these two types of islands. The smaller islands are made up of the skeletons of tiny sea animals. Over hundreds of years, the skeletons meld together to form a rocklike substance called **coral.**

The larger islands of the Caribbean are the tops of huge underwater mountains. These include Cuba, Jamaica (juh MAY kuh), Hispaniola (his pun YOH luh), and Puerto Rico. Most people on the islands make a living farming.

LINKS TO LANGUAGE ARTS

The Tlaloques According to Aztec religion, a group of rain gods lived on the tops of mountains. They were called the Tlaloques. Tlaloc, the leader of the Tlaloques, was responsible for rain and lightning. The Aztecs were right, in a way—mountains affect rainfall. Clouds cool off and drop rain when they rise over the mountains.

Harvesting Alfalfa in Mexico

In Mexico, farming is an important way of making a living, even in the drier areas of the country. Raising crops requires fertile soil, a source of fresh water, and a long growing season. As in Central America, much of Mexico's fertile soil is the result of volcanic activity.

South America South America contains many types of landforms. Perhaps the most impressive landform is the Andes Mountains. The Andes run some 4,500 miles (7,250 km) along the western coast of South America. In some places, the Andes rise to heights of more than 20,000 feet (6,100 m). That's about the same height as twenty 100-story buildings stacked one on top of another. Except for the Himalaya Mountains in Asia, the Andes are the highest mountains in the world.

The Andes are steep and difficult to cross. But their rich soil has drawn farmers to the region. East of the Andes are rolling highlands. These highlands spread across parts of Brazil, Venezuela (ven uh ZWAY luh), Guyana (gy AN uh), and other South American countries. Farther south are the Pampas (PAHM puz), a large plains area that stretches through Argentina (ar jun TEE nuh) and Uruguay (YOOR uh gway). **Pampas** are flat grassland regions that are very similar to the Great Plains in the United States.

The Pampas and other plains areas, the eastern highlands, and the Andes frame the Amazon River Basin. The Amazon River Basin contains the largest tropical rain forest in the world. This dense forest covers more than a third of the continent.

The Rivers of Latin America

Latin America is famous for its rivers and lakes. They are some of the longest and largest bodies of water in the world. Latin America's waters are important to the people of the region. Rivers serve as natural

Herding Cattle on the Pampas

Grasslands known as the Pampas can also be found in Brazil. These grasslands are perfect for raising cattle. **Critical Thinking** How are these grasslands similar to the Great Plains in the United States?

highways in places where it is hard to build roads. The fish that swim the waters of Latin America provide food. Rushing water from large rivers provides power for electricity.

Amazon: The Ocean River
Latin America's Amazon (AM uh zahn) River is the second-longest river in the world. Only the Nile in Africa is longer. The Amazon flows 4,000 miles (6,437 km) from Peru across Brazil into the Atlantic Ocean.

How large is the Amazon? The Amazon River carries more water than any other river in the world. It contains about 20 percent of all the fresh river water on Earth. The Amazon River gathers power from the more than 1,000 tributaries (TRIB yoo tehr eez) that spill into it. Tributaries are the rivers and streams that flow into a larger river. With its tributaries, the Amazon drains an area of more than two million square miles. No wonder people call the Amazon the "Ocean River."

Other Rivers and Lakes Latin America has many other bodies of water besides the Amazon. The Paraná (pah rah NAH), Paraguay, and Uruguay rivers form the Río de la Plata system. The Río de la Plata separates Argentina and Uruguay. In Venezuela, people travel on the Orinoco River and Lake Maracaibo (mar uh KY boh). Lake Titicaca is the highest lake in the world on which ships can travel. It lies high in the Andes Mountains.

An Amazon Scene

The people who live near the Amazon River in Brazil rely on it for transportation, fish, and water. Families also wash their laundry right at the river bank.

READ ACTIVELY

Visualize How could a ship sail on a lake? What would the lake have to be like?

SECTION 1
REVIEW

1. **Define** (a) plateau, (b) isthmus, (c) coral, (d) pampas, (e) tributary.

2. **Identify** (a) Mexico, (b) Central America, (c) Caribbean, (d) South America.

3. Describe the main landforms of the three regions that make up Latin America.

4. Give one example of how the physical features of Latin America affect the people who live there.

Critical Thinking
5. **Making Comparisons** Explain two ways in which the three regions of Latin America are alike. Explain two differences.

Activity
6. **Writing to Learn** Suppose your family was planning to move to Latin America. If you had your choice, in which of the three regions of Latin America would you live? Explain why.

Climate and Vegetation

Reach Into Your Background

Suppose the temperature outside is 90°F (32°C). Would you feel more comfortable lying on a sandy beach or sitting under a tree in the woods? In what type of climate would you want to vacation someday?

Questions to Explore

1. What kinds of climate and vegetation does Latin America have?
2. In what ways do climate and vegetation affect how Latin Americans live?

Key Terms
El Niño
elevation

Key Places
Andes
Atacama Desert
Patagonia
Amazonian rain forest

Every few years, a warm ocean current flows along the western coast of South America. This warm current drives away fish that thrive in the cold waters of the Pacific Ocean. The current brings other changes to Latin America, too. Instead of dry weather, heavy rains pour down and low-lying regions are flooded. In other places, drought plagues the land and the people.

Just what is this strange ocean current that brings disaster? It is **El Niño** (el NEEN yoh). Because it usually strikes near Christmas time, Latin Americans named the phenomena El Niño, Spanish for "the Christ child." El Niño is one of many factors that affect climate in Latin America.

▼ Mexico's Sonoran Desert shows that even a hot, dry desert can be full of plant life.

Climate: Hot, Cold, and Mild

What's the climate like where you live? Is it hot? Cold? Rainy? If you lived in Latin America, the climate might be any of these. Climate in Latin America can vary greatly even within the same country.

In parts of the Andes, below-zero temperatures would set your teeth chattering. Travel down to the Amazon Basin, and you may be sweating in 80°F (27°C) heat. Don't forget your umbrella: This part of Latin America receives more than 80 inches (203 cm) of rain each year. If you prefer dry weather, visit the Atacama (ah tah KAH mah) Desert in Chile or the Sonoran Desert in Mexico. These are two of the driest places on Earth.

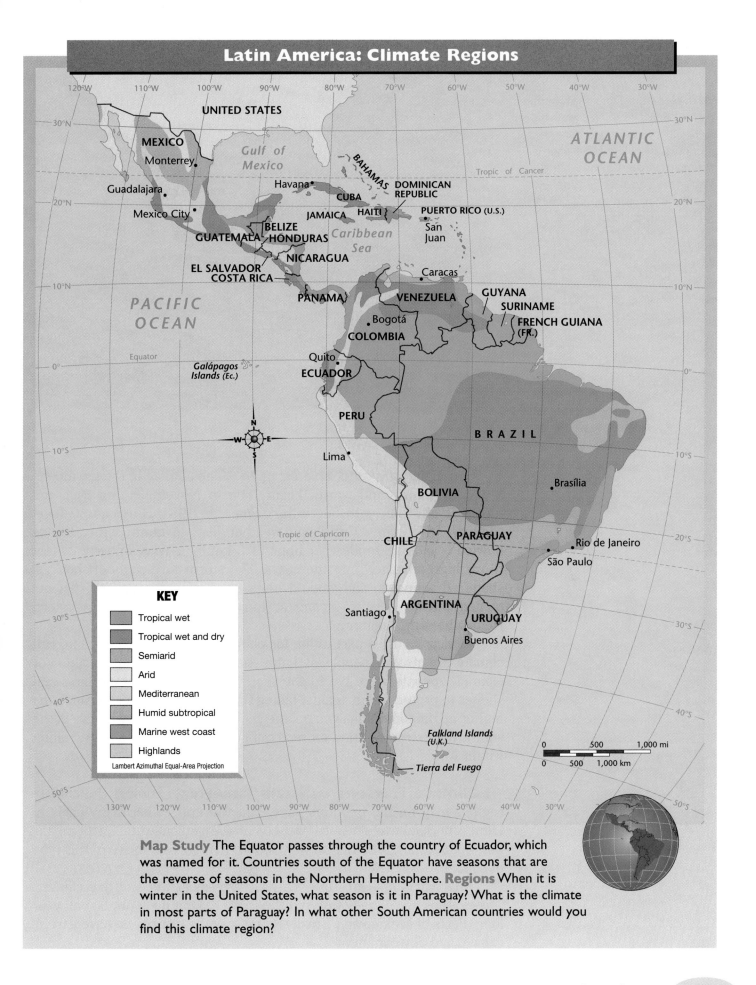

Latin America: Climate Regions

UNITED STATES

MEXICO
Monterrey

Guadalajara

Mexico City

Gulf of
Mexico

Havana

BAHAMAS

CUBA

JAMAICA   HAITI

DOMINICAN
REPUBLIC

PUERTO RICO (U.S.)
San
Juan

BELIZE
GUATEMALA HONDURAS
EL SALVADOR
COSTA RICA

NICARAGUA

Caribbean
Sea

Caracas

PACIFIC
OCEAN

PANAMA

VENEZUELA

GUYANA
SURINAME
FRENCH GUIANA
(FR.)

Bogotá

COLOMBIA

Equator

Galápagos
Islands (Ec.)

Quito
ECUADOR

PERU

N
W—E
S

Lima

B R A Z I L

Brasília

ATLANTIC
OCEAN

Tropic of Cancer

BOLIVIA

Tropic of Capricorn

CHILE

PARAGUAY

Rio de Janeiro
São Paulo

ARGENTINA

Santiago

URUGUAY

Buenos Aires

KEY

	Tropical wet
	Tropical wet and dry
	Semiarid
	Arid
	Mediterranean
	Humid subtropical
	Marine west coast
	Highlands

Lambert Azimuthal Equal-Area Projection

Falkland Islands
(U.K.)

Tierra del Fuego

0   500   1,000 mi

0   500   1,000 km

Map Study The Equator passes through the country of Ecuador, which was named for it. Countries south of the Equator have seasons that are the reverse of seasons in the Northern Hemisphere. **Regions** When it is winter in the United States, what season is it in Paraguay? What is the climate in most parts of Paraguay? In what other South American countries would you find this climate region?

People in the Dominican Republic grow much of their own food, but they also grow sugar cane to export. **Regions** How does the climate in the Caribbean make the area good for farming? How is the climate in the Caribbean dangerous for farms?

The Climate and the People The climate in the Caribbean is usually sunny and warm. From June to November, however, the region is often hit with fierce hurricanes. In 1988, Hurricane Gilbert shattered the sunny Caribbean weather like an atom bomb. Winds howled at over 180 miles per hour (300 km/hr). Waves nearly 20 feet (6 m) high smashed into the coast. The storm tore roofs off houses, shattered windows, and yanked huge trees from the ground. Gilbert turned out to be the strongest hurricane to strike the Western Hemisphere this century.

Hurricanes are a part of life for people living in the Caribbean. But climate affects the people of Latin America in other ways, too. For example, people who live in the mountains need warm clothing and shelter to protect them against falling temperatures. That's because the higher up the mountains you go, the cooler it gets. Those who live in the sunny, warm tropics think more about cooling sea breezes than chilling winter winds.

Climate Regions of Latin America Look at the climate regions map on the previous page. You will notice that many parts of Latin America have a tropical wet climate. A tropical wet climate means hot, humid, rainy weather all year round. Rain forests thrive in this type of climate.

Other parts of Latin America have a tropical wet and dry climate. These areas are equally hot, but the rainy season does not last all year long. Parts of Mexico and Brazil and most of the Caribbean have a tropical wet and dry climate.

Much of Argentina, Uruguay, and Paraguay has a humid subtropical climate, similar to that of parts of the southern United States. People living in this climate usually have hot, wet summers and cool winters. Farmers in these areas can raise such crops as wheat and apples, which need a cold season to grow well. Farther south, the climate turns arid. Farmers raise sheep on the plains of this colder, drier area, called Patagonia (pat uh GOH nee uh).

What Factors Affect Climate? Have you ever hiked in the mountains? If you have, you probably noticed that as you climbed higher the temperature dropped. At some point during your hike, you may have stopped to put on a sweatshirt or jacket.

Elevation, the height of land above sea level, is a key factor in the climate of mountainous Latin America. Look at the diagram below. It shows how elevation affects climate. The higher the elevation, the colder the temperature. Suppose it is a warm 80°F (27°C) at sea level. At 3,000 feet (914 m), the temperature may be 72°F (25°C). Continue up to 6,000 feet (1,829 m), and the temperature may now be only about 65°F (13°C). Above 10,000 feet (3,048 m), the temperature may remain below freezing—too cold for people to live. Temperature also affects what crops people can grow in each region.

Other factors also affect Latin America's climate. Regions close to the Equator are generally warmer than those farther away. Look at the Latin America: Climate Regions map. Find the Equator. Which parts of Latin America are closest to the Equator? Which are farthest away?

Visualize Suppose that you were climbing a mountain. How would the vegetation you see change as you climb higher?

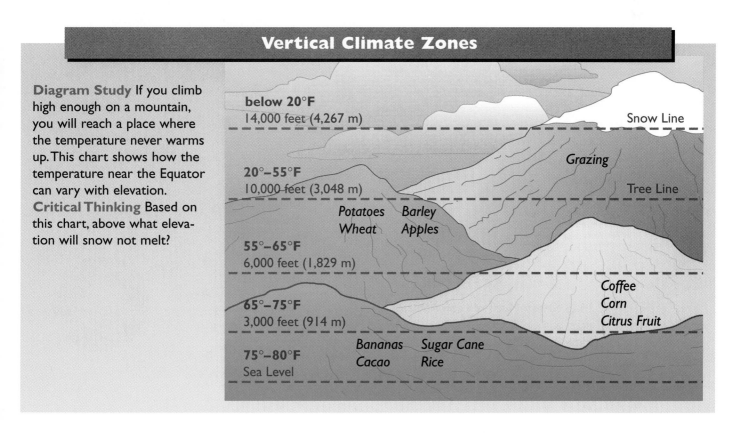

Vertical Climate Zones

Diagram Study If you climb high enough on a mountain, you will reach a place where the temperature never warms up. This chart shows how the temperature near the Equator can vary with elevation. **Critical Thinking** Based on this chart, above what elevation will snow not melt?

below 20°F
14,000 feet (4,267 m)

Snow Line

Grazing

20°–55°F
10,000 feet (3,048 m)

Tree Line

Potatoes   Barley
Wheat   Apples

55°–65°F
6,000 feet (1,829 m)

Coffee
Corn
Citrus Fruit

65°–75°F
3,000 feet (914 m)

75°–80°F
Sea Level

Bananas   Sugar Cane
Cacao   Rice

Latin America: Vegetation Regions

KEY

- Tropical rain forest
- Mixed forest
- Coniferous forest
- Mediterranean vegetation
- Tropical savanna
- Temperate grassland
- Desert scrub
- Desert (little or no vegetation)
- Highlands (vegetation varies with elevation)

Lambert Azimuthal Equal-Area Projection

Map Study Much of Latin America is forested, but some areas are grassland or desert. **Regions** Compare this map with the climate map. How is vegetation affected by climate?

Wind patterns affect the climate too. Winds move cold air from the North and South Poles toward the Equator. They also move warm air from the Equator toward the Poles. In the Caribbean, sea breezes blowing toward shore help to keep temperatures moderate. Winds also affect rainfall in the Caribbean. More rain falls on the sides of islands facing the wind than on sides facing away.

Natural Vegetation and Climate

Imagine a forest so dense and lush that almost no sunlight reaches the ground. Broad green leaves, tangled vines, and thousands of species of trees and plants surround you. The air is hot and heavy with moisture. Welcome to the Amazonian rain forest.

Now, suppose you have traveled to the coast of northern Chile. You're in the Atacama Desert. Winds carry no moisture to this barren land, and there is little sign of life. The Andes shield this parched region from rain. Parts of the desert have never felt a single raindrop.

Latin America's varied climate and physical features make such extremes possible. Look at the natural vegetation map on the previous page. How many different kinds of vegetation does the map show? Note which countries in Latin America have areas of tropical rain forest. Now, find these countries on the climate map. How do the tropical climate and heavy rainfall in these countries contribute to the vegetation that grows there?

Find Uruguay on the vegetation map and on the climate map. Uruguay's climate and vegetation have helped make sheep and cattle raising a key part of the country's economy.

Elevation also affects vegetation. For example, palm trees and fruit trees that grow well in the coastal plains of Mexico and Central America would not survive high in the Andes. To grow at higher elevations, plants must be able to withstand cooler temperatures, chill winds, and irregular rainfall.

READ ACTIVELY

Ask Questions What would you like to know about living in the rain forest?

▲ Tree sloths live in the rain forest trees. They rarely descend from the trees.

SECTION 2 REVIEW

1. **Define** (a) El Niño, (b) elevation.

2. **Identify** (a) Andes, (b) Atacama Desert, (c) Patagonia, (d) Amazonian rain forest.

3. Describe two climates in Latin America. Then explain how climate affects the vegetation that grows in those regions.

4. How do Latin America's climate and vegetation affect how and where the people live?

Critical Thinking

5. **Drawing Conclusions** In what ways would the life of a family living on a Caribbean island be different from a family living high in the Andes?

Activity

6. **Writing to Learn** Latin America has been called a land of extremes. Do you agree or disagree? Write a paragraph or more telling why. Begin with the following sentences: "Many people have called Latin America a land of extremes. I believe that ..." Support your opinion with examples.

SKILLS ACTIVITY

Using Regional Maps to Show Climate

I f you could follow the Earth's weather for many years, no two years would look exactly alike. Think how the weather in your own location varies. Some years are colder, warmer, wetter, or drier than others. The same is true for every place on the planet.

Still, you could notice patterns in the weather. For example, one place may tend to have hot, rainy summers and cold, dry winters. Another place might be hot and dry all year round. The typical weather patterns in a location are called its climate.

Traveling across the Earth, you would find that no two places have exactly the same climate. Even the next town might be a degree cooler than your own. Still, you would find some similarities. Places in a large area that have similar weather make up a climate region.

Get Ready

A region's climate affects how its inhabitants live. Learning to read a climate map can help you understand what life is like in different regions of the world.

Try It Out

Climates in Latin America fall into four general categories: *tropical, dry, mild,* and *highland*. Read about the climates described below. Use the map to answer each question.

A. Find a tropical climate zone. Tropical climates are hot year round. There are two types. Tropical wet zones have rain nearly every day. Tropical wet and dry zones have a wet season and a dry season. Where are tropical wet and

Latin America: Climates

120°W 110°W 100°W 90°W 80°W
0   500   1,000 mi
0 500 1,000 km

UNITED STATES

30°N

C

Gulf of Mexico

Tropic of Cancer

20°N

MEXICO
CUBA   HAITI DOMINICAN
JAMAICA   REPUBLIC
B
BELIZE   PUERTO RICO
HONDURAS Caribbean (U.S.)
GUATEMALA NICARAGUA Sea
EL SALVADOR

10°N
COSTA RICA   VENEZUELA   GUYANA
PANAMA   H   SURINAME
COLOMBIA   FRENCH GUIANA
(FR.)

Galapagos   Equator
Is. (Ec.)   ECUADOR   A

0°

PACIFIC
OCEAN   BRAZIL

10°S
PERU

D   BOLIVIA

KEY

Tropical wet
Tropical wet and dry   CHILE   PARAGUAY   20°S
Semiarid   Tropic of Capricorn
Arid   F
Mediterranean   URUGUAY   30°S
Humid subtropical   E   ARGENTINA
Marine west coast   ATLANTIC
Highlands   G   OCEAN   40°S

Lambert Azimuthal Equal-Area Projection

Falkland Is.
(U.K.)
Tierra del   South Georgia
Fuego   (U.K.)
80°W 70°W 60°W 50°W 40°W 30°W 20°W 10°W

dry zones usually located in relation to tropical wet zones?

B. Find a dry climate. Dry climates have little rain. There are two types. Arid zones may go years without rain. Semiarid zones receive enough rain for short grasses to grow. Where are semiarid zones usually located in relation to arid zones?

C. Find a mild climate. Mild climates are more comfortable than tropical or dry climates. There are three types. Marine climates are wet and have only moderate changes in temperature during the year. Humid subtropical areas are also wet but warmer than marine climates. Mediterranean climates are warm, too, but only rainy in the winter. Where are mild climate regions usually located in relation to large bodies of water?

D. Find a highland climate. Highland climates are found in mountainous regions. In a highland climate, temperatures vary. The higher you climb up a mountain, the colder it gets. Where is South America's highland climate located?

Apply the Skill

A region's climate can affect the kind of homes people build, the jobs they do, and the food they eat. Read the descriptions that follow. Then match each description with a letter on the map.

1. Few trees grow in Mexico's dry central region. Instead of building homes from wood, farmers often use sun-dried brick called adobe. Flat roofs are sometimes made of tile, straw, or sheet metal.

2. In the south of Mexico, more rain falls. The rain would eventually wash away an adobe home. So instead, some farmers build with wooden poles coated with a lime and clay mixture that keeps out the rain. Roofs are slanted so that rain water runs off.

3. Peru's west coast has one of the Earth's driest climates. To raise crops, farmers channel mountain streams to bring water to their fields.

4. Near the base of the Andes Mountains in Colombia, the weather is hot. High in the mountain peaks the climate is cold. In between, the mountain slopes have a mild climate perfect for growing coffee—one of Columbia's leading crops.

5. The Yanomamo are an Indian people living on the border between Brazil and Venezuela. A dense forest grows here. To clear land for crops, the Yanomamo must slash and burn trees. In addition to crops, they eat food found in the forest—anteaters, armadillos, and roasted caterpillars.

Natural Resources

BEFORE YOU READ

Reach Into Your Background

Do you know what natural resources are? They are things found in nature that people can use to meet their needs. For example, trees are a natural resource. List two other natural resources. Describe how people use each one.

Questions to Explore

1. What are Latin America's important natural resources?
2. Why is it important for Latin American nations to have more than one source of income?

Key Terms
hydroelectricity
diversify

Key Places
Jamaica
Venezuela
Brazil
Colombia
Chile

▼ Latin America has about 12 percent of the world's petroleum.

Bolivia has always depended on mineral resources for wealth. At first, silver helped to bring money into Bolivia's treasury. Soon, however, another metal became even more important than silver. That metal was tin.

For many years, Bolivia enjoyed the good times that wealth from tin brought. Then, in the 1920s and 1930s, a world-wide economic crisis hit. Industries stopped buying tin, as well as other natural resources. Bolivia suffered as its main resource failed to bring money into the economy. This economic crisis hit all of Latin America hard. It brought home a problem many Latin American nations have: They rely too much on one resource.

Latin America's Resources

What do the following items have in common? Fish, petroleum, water, silver, and forests. You have probably guessed that all these items are natural resources of Latin America. Latin America's resources are as varied as its physical features and climate.

Mexico and Central America: Riches of Land and Sea

Mexico is a treasure chest of minerals. The country has deposits of silver, gold, copper, coal, iron ore, and just about any other mineral you can name. How many of these mineral resources can you find on the map on the next page? Mexico also has huge amounts of oil and natural gas. In addition, trees cover nearly a quarter of Mexico's land. Wood from these trees is turned into lumber and paper products.

Central America's climate and rich soil are good for farming. The people grow coffee, cotton, sugar cane, and bananas. They also plant cacao trees. Cacao seeds are made into chocolate and cocoa.

Not all of Central America's resources are on land. People catch fish and shellfish in the region's waters. Central Americans use the power of rushing water to produce electricity. This type of power is called **hydro-electricity** (hy droh ee lek TRIS ih tee). Countries build huge dams to harness and control the energy that rushing water produces.

The Caribbean: Sugar, Coffee, and More Caribbean countries also have rich soil and a good climate for farming. Farmers grow sugar cane, coffee, bananas, cacao, citrus fruits, and other crops on the islands.

The Caribbean has other resources as well. For example, Jamaica is one of the world's main producers of bauxite—a mineral used to make aluminum. Cuba and the Dominican Republic have nickel deposits. Trinidad is rich in oil.

Drilling for Oil

Some of Mexico's petroleum reserves can only be reached through offshore drilling, or drilling into the ocean floor. Interaction What special precautions do you think that offshore drillers might have to take to avoid harming the environment?

Latin America: Natural Resources

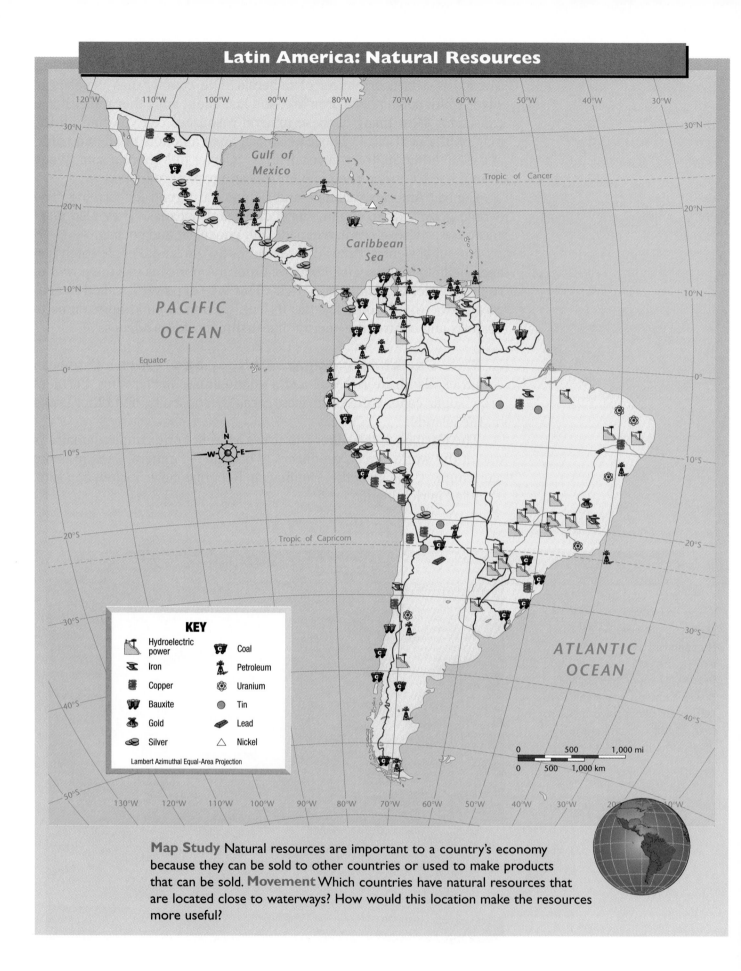

KEY

Hydroelectric power		Coal
Iron		Petroleum
Copper		Uranium
Bauxite		Tin
Gold		Lead
Silver		Nickel

Lambert Azimuthal Equal-Area Projection

Map Study Natural resources are important to a country's economy because they can be sold to other countries or used to make products that can be sold. **Movement** Which countries have natural resources that are located close to waterways? How would this location make the resources more useful?

The hydroelectric power plant at Itaipú Dam is the largest in the world. It harnesses the energy of the Paraná River to provide electric power to Paraguay and Brazil. **Critical Thinking** What detail in this picture is a clue that the dam is used to produce electricity?

South America: A Wealth of Resources Like Mexico, South America is rich in minerals. It contains gold, copper, tin, bauxite, and iron ore. Businesses drill for oil in many South American countries. Much of South America's oil is found in Venezuela.

South America's plants and fish are natural resources, too. Forests cover about half the continent. Trees from these forests provide everything from wood for building to coconuts for eating. People harvest many rain forest plants to make medicines. Tuna, anchovies, and other fish are plentiful in the waters off the Pacific Coast.

Like other parts of Latin America, South America has rich soil. Farmers grow many different crops there. For example, coffee is a key crop in Brazil and Colombia. Wheat is important in Argentina. Many South American economies rely on the production of sugar cane, cotton, and rice.

Natural Resources and Latin America's Economy

Not every country shares in the wealth of Latin America's resources. Some Latin American countries have many resources, while others have few. Some countries do not have the money they need to develop all of their resources. Other countries rely too much on one resource or crop.

ACROSS TIME

Sailors of the Seventh Century South Americans have been trading with the people of Mexico since at least A.D. 600. They sailed north from Ecuador, Colombia, and Peru on rafts. These adventurers traded not only goods, such as tweezers and bells, but also skills and ideas. For example, they taught people of Mexico how to make metal objects such as needles.

Many Latin American economies are based on agriculture. Half of Colombia's exports are coffee, and one third of Honduras' exports are bananas. **Critical Thinking** What problems do you think one-crop economies face?

READ ACTIVELY

Visualize How would the crops in a field look after a hurricane? How would they look after a drought?

Prices, Weather, and Other Factors Depending on one resource or crop can lead to problems. For example, when world copper prices are high, the copper mining industry is very successful. But suppose copper prices drop sharply. Then copper exports are not worth as much. When this happens, the mining industry loses money. Mining workers may lose their jobs. Chile is the leading producer of copper in the world. When prices plunge, Chile's economy suffers.

Many people in Latin America make their living by farming. Some Latin American countries depend on one or two crops, such as coffee, bananas, or sugar. When the price of a crop goes down, exports of that crop bring less money into the country. As a result, workers' wages may drop, and some workers may lose their jobs.

Weather and disease also cause people and businesses to lose money. Hurricanes, droughts, and plant disease can damage crops. Weather sometimes hurts the fishing industry. The warm ocean current El Niño affects the fish that live in South America's coastal waters. Usually, the cold water of the Pacific supports a large number of small water plants on which the fish feed. When El Niño strikes, the warm water kills the plants and the fish die or move to other areas. Peru is among the countries affected by El Niño. Peruvian fishers have suffered great economic losses due to El Niño effects.

Depending on Oil   Oil is one of Latin America's most valuable resources. But it is risky to depend on oil. Oil prices increase and decrease. Sometimes they change suddenly. Mexico, like Venezuela, is a major oil producer. In the mid-1980s, oil companies produced more oil than the world needed. As a result, prices dropped. Mexico earned much less income than it had expected. The same thing happened to Trinidad.

There are other problems as well. In the 1960s, people discovered oil in Ecuador. Soon, oil became the country's main export. But in 1987, earthquakes destroyed Ecuador's major oil pipeline. The country's income was slashed.

Avoiding the Problems of a One-Resource Country
Latin American nations know the risks of depending on one resource or crop. They are trying to diversify their economies. To **diversify** is to add variety. When Latin American nations try to diversify their economies, it means that they are looking for other ways to make money. Many are building factories. Factories make products that can be sold to bring more money into the economy. Factories also provide jobs for people.

Venezuela has been trying to set up more factories and farms. Venezuela is also improving its bauxite and iron mines. Ecuador passed a law to encourage industry. Businesses there built factories to make cloth, electrical appliances, and other products.

Brazil has also been building up its industries. That way Brazil does not have to depend on agriculture. Brazil now exports machinery, steel, and chemicals. Brazil has also encouraged cotton farming. As a result, cotton weaving has become a successful industry.

El Salvador used to depend too heavily on its coffee crop. Now, cotton, sugar, corn, and other crops play an important role in the nation's economy. Trinidad has also encouraged its farmers to raise more kinds of crops. The government realizes that the country depends too much on oil and sugar.

SECTION 3 REVIEW

1. **Define**   (a) hydroelectricity, (b) diversify.

2. **Identify**   (a) Jamaica, (b) Venezuela, (c) Brazil, (d) Colombia, (e) Chile.

3. Describe the important natural resources of Latin America.

4. Why is it important for Latin American nations to diversify their economies?

Critical Thinking

5. **Recognizing Cause and Effect**   Suppose a disease destroyed Colombia's coffee crop. How would this loss affect coffee-plantation workers and their families? How would it affect Colombia's economy?

Activity

6. **Writing to Learn**   Imagine that you are the president of a Latin American country. Your nation depends on bananas for nearly all of its income. What arguments would you use to persuade people to diversify?

Review and Activities

Reviewing Main Ideas

1. List the three main regions of Latin America. Then choose two and describe their features.
2. In what ways do the physical features of Latin America affect the people and their way of life?
3. How does elevation affect climate?
4. (a) Give an example of how climate in one region of Latin America affects the vegetation that grows there.
   (b) How does this affect the way in which people live?
5. How are a country's natural resources tied to its economy?
6. What problems arise when a country depends too heavily on a single source of income? Support your answer with one or two examples.
7. How are the nations of Latin America trying to avoid the problems of relying on a single source of income?

Reviewing Key Terms

Match the definitions in Column I with the key terms in Column II

Column I

1. height of land above sea level
2. plains in Argentina and Uruguay
3. to add variety
4. river or stream that flows into a larger body of water
5. electricity generated by the power of moving water
6. large raised area of mostly level land
7. narrow strip of land that has water on both sides and joins two larger bodies of land

Column II

a. isthmus
b. pampas
c. plateau
d. tributary
e. elevation
f. diversify
g. hydro-electricity

Critical Thinking

1. **Identifying Central Issues** Explain the meaning of this statement, and give examples: "The weather in Latin America is a great friend to the people, but also a terrible enemy."
2. **Drawing Conclusions** "How a country uses its natural resources affects the well-being of its people." Do you agree or disagree with this statement? Explain your answer.

Graphic Organizer

Copy the chart to the right onto a separate sheet of paper. Then fill in the empty boxes to complete the chart. Use the maps in this chapter to help you.

	Physical Features	Climate	Vegetation	Natural Resources
Mexico and Central America				
The Caribbean				
South America				

Map Activity

For each place listed below, write the letter from the map that shows its location.

1. Colombia

2. Brazil

3. Jamaica

4. Mexico

5. Venezuela

Latin America: Place Location

Writing Activity

Writing a Letter
Imagine that you are a visitor to Latin America. You are touring the whole region: Mexico, Central America, the Caribbean, and South America. Write a letter home, describing your trip. Write about such items as these: impressive sights, the weather, interesting facts you've learned, places you liked or didn't like.

Internet Activity

Use a search engine to find *El Salvador — A Country Study.* Then explore the information to write a short report on the geography, climate, economy, or society of El Salvador. If you like, you can add drawings to your report based on the content of the site.

Skills Review

Turn to the Skill Activity.
Review the steps for reading a regional map. Then complete the following: (a) In your own words, describe two factors that vary from climate to climate. (b) What types of climates can be found in Latin America?

How Am I Doing?

Answer these questions to help you check your progress.

1. Can I identify and describe the main regions of Latin America?

2. Do I understand how Latin America's physical features, climate, and vegetation affect the people who live in the region?

3. Can I identify important natural resources of Latin America?

4. Can I explain why Latin American countries want to diversify their economies?

5. What information from this chapter can I use in my book project?

The Surveyor

BY ALMA FLOR ADA

BEFORE YOU READ

Reach Into Your Background

Do people in your family tell you stories about interesting or exciting events that have happened to them? What stories do you remember the best? What do you learn from these stories?

The stories that family members tell each other become part of the family history. Family stories are important because they teach people about their cultural heritage. Alma Flor Ada grew up in Cuba. The following story shows what Ada learned from one of the stories her father used to tell her.

Questions to Explore

1. What can you learn from this story about family life in Cuba?
2. What does this story tell you about how geography affects people's lives in Cuba?

surveyor (sir VAY ur) n.: a person who measures land and geographic features

My father, named Modesto after my grandfather, was a surveyor. Some of the happiest times of my childhood were spent on horseback, on trips where he would allow me to accompany him as he plotted the boundaries of small farms in the Cuban countryside. Sometimes we slept out under the stars, stringing our hammocks between the trees, and drank fresh water from springs. We always stopped for a warm greeting at the simple huts of the neighboring peasants, and my eyes would drink in the lush green forest crowned by the swaying leaves of the palm trees.

Since many surveying jobs called for dividing up land that a family had inherited from a deceased parent or relative, my father's greatest concern was that justice be achieved. It was not enough just to divide the land into equal portions. He also had to ensure that all parties would have access to roads, to water sources, to the most fertile soil. While I was able to join him in some trips, other surveying work involved large areas of land. On these jobs, my father was part of a team, and I would stay home, eagerly awaiting to hear the stories from his trip on his return.

The equipment that surveyors use must be strong and lightweight.

Latin American families tend not to limit their family boundaries to those who are born or have married into it. Any good friend who spends time with the family and shares in its daily experiences is welcomed as a member. The following story from one of my father's surveying trips is not about a member of my blood family, but instead concerns a member of our extended family.

Félix Caballero, a man my father always liked to recruit whenever he needed a team, was rather different from the other surveyors. He was somewhat older, unmarried, and he kept his thoughts to himself. He came to visit our house daily. Once there, he would sit silently in one of the living room's four rocking chairs, listening to the lively conversations all around him. An occasional nod or a single word were his only contribu-

tions to those conversations. My mother and her sisters sometimes made fun of him behind his back. Even though they never said so, I had the impression that they questioned why my father held him in such high regard.

Then one day my father shared this story.

"We had been working on foot in mountainous country for most of the day. Night was approaching. We still had a long way to go to return to where we had left the horses, so we decided to cut across to the other side of the mountain, and soon found ourselves facing a deep gorge. The gorge was spanned by a railroad bridge, long and narrow, built for the sugarcane trains. There were no side rails or walkways, only a set of tracks resting on thick, heavy crossties suspended high in the air.

"We were all upset about having to climb down the steep gorge and up the other side, but

Predict Why do you think that Ada's father admires Félix so much?

recruit (ree KROOT) v.: to enlist or hire to join a group
gorge (gorj) n.: a narrow canyon with steep walls
span (span) v.: to extend across a space

▶ Walking across a railroad bridge is dangerous, because most are just wide enough for a train to pass.

dissuade (dis SWAYD) v.: to persuade not to do something
ominous (OM ih nus) adj.: threatening

the simpler solution, walking across the bridge, seemed too dangerous. What if a cane train should appear? There would be nowhere to go. So we all began the long descent . . . all except for Félix. He decided to risk walking across the railroad bridge. We all tried to dissuade him, but to no avail. Using an old method, he put one ear to the tracks to listen for vibrations. Since he heard none, he decided that no train was approaching. So he began to cross the long bridge, stepping from crosstie to crosstie between the rails, balancing his long red-and-white surveyor's poles on his shoulder.

"He was about halfway across the bridge when we heard the ominous sound of a steam engine. All eyes rose to Félix. Unquestionably he had heard it, too, because he had stopped in the middle of the bridge and was looking back.

"As the train drew closer, and thinking there was no other solution, we all shouted, 'Jump! Jump!', not even sure our voices would carry to where he stood, so high above us. Félix did look down at the rocky riverbed, which, as it was the dry season, held little water. We tried to encourage him with gestures and more shouts, but he had stopped looking down. We could not imagine what he was doing next, squatting down on the tracks, with the engine of the train already visible. And then, we understood. . . .

"Knowing that he could not manage to hold onto the thick wooden crossties, Félix laid his thin but resilient surveyor's poles across the ties, parallel to the rails. Then he let his body slip down between two of the ties, as he held onto the poles. And there he hung, below the bridge, suspended over the gorge but safely out of the train's path.

"The cane train was, as they frequently are, a very long train. To us, it seemed interminable. . . . One of the younger men said he counted two hundred and twenty cars. With the approaching darkness, and the smoke and shadows of the train, it was often difficult to see our friend. We had heard no human sounds, no screams, but could we have heard anything at all, with the racket of the train crossing overhead?

"When the last car began to curve around the mountain, we could just make out Félix's lonely figure still hanging beneath the bridge. We all watched in relief and amazement as he pulled himself up and at last finished walking, slowly and calmly, along the tracks to the other side of the gorge."

After I heard that story, I saw Félix Caballero in a whole new light. He still remained as quiet as ever, prompting a smile from my mother and her sisters as he sat silently in his rocking chair. But in my mind's eye, I saw him crossing that treacherous bridge, stopping to think calmly of what to do to save his life, emerging all covered with soot and smoke but triumphantly alive—a lonely man, hanging under a railroad bridge at dusk, suspended from his surveyor's poles over a rocky gorge.

If there was so much courage, such an ability to calmly confront danger in the quiet, aging man who sat rocking in our living room, what other wonders might lie hidden in every human soul?

resilient (rih ZIL yunt) *adj.:* able to withstand shock and bounce back from changes

treacherous (TRECH ur us) *adj.:* dangerous

READ ACTIVELY

Visualize Visualize the team of surveyors as they watch the train go by. How do you think they looked? How might they have acted?

EXPLORING YOUR READING

Look Back

1. How does this story change the way the author feels about Félix Caballero?

Think It Over

2. Why is surveying land important in Cuba?

3. Why do you think that the author's family accepts Félix Caballero as a member of their extended family?

4. What lesson does the author of this story hope to teach?

Go Beyond

5. What does this story tell you about the character traits that help a person to act in an emergency?

Ideas for Writing: A Short Story

6. Choose a story that has been told to you by a family member or friend. Or, choose a story that you have told others about an event that happened to you. Write the story. Include an introduction and conclusion that explain why the story is important to you.

Shaped by Its History

KEY

Aztec Empire
A.D. 1200s–A.D. 1521

Mayan Empire
A.D. 300–A.D. 900

Incan Empire
A.D. 1400s–A.D. 1535

Lambert Azimuthal Equal-Area Projection

This map shows the location of three civilizations in Latin America that existed before Europeans arrived in the region.

Study the map
(a) What are the names of the civilizations shown on the map?
(b) Which civilization is the oldest?

Consider the geography
Which civilization do you think was the most difficult to defend from invaders? Explain your answer.

Early Civilizations of Middle America

BEFORE YOU READ

Reach Into Your Background

What does the word *pyramid* bring to mind? Write down three things you know about pyramids. Then, compare what you know about pyramids with the pyramids you will read about in this section.

Questions to Explore

1. What were the chief characteristics and accomplishments of Mayan and Aztec civilizations?

2. How have Latin America's early civilizations affected present-day cultures in Latin America?

Key Terms
maize
hieroglyphics

Key Places
Copán
Tikal
Valley of Mexico
Tenochtitlán

F ans cheered as the players brought the ball down the court. Suddenly, the ball flew into the air and sailed through the hoop. Fans and players shouted and screamed. Although this may sound like a championship basketball game, it is actually a moment of a game played over 1,000 years ago. The game was called pok-a-tok.

Pok-a-tok was a game played by the ancient Mayas. Using only their leather-padded hips and elbows, players tried to hit a five-pound (1.9 kg), six-inch (15.2 cm) rubber ball through a stone hoop mounted 30 feet (9.1 m) above the ground.

Mayan Civilization

How do we know about this ancient game? Crumbling ruins of pok-a-tok courts and ancient clay statues of players have been found at sites in Central America and southern Mexico. In these areas, Mayan civilization thrived from about A.D. 300 to A.D. 900. By studying ruins, scientists have learned much about Mayan civilization.

▼ This pok-a-tok court is in Copán, Honduras. How is it similar to a basketball court?

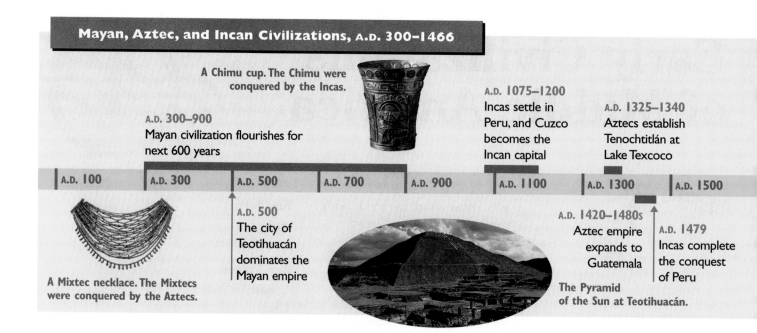

A Chimu cup. The Chimu were conquered by the Incas.

A.D. 300–900
Mayan civilization flourishes for next 600 years

A.D. 1075–1200
Incas settle in Peru, and Cuzco becomes the Incan capital

A.D. 1325–1340
Aztecs establish Tenochtitlán at Lake Texcoco

| A.D. 100 | A.D. 300 | A.D. 500 | A.D. 700 | A.D. 900 | A.D. 1100 | A.D. 1300 | A.D. 1500 |

A.D. 500
The city of Teotihuacán dominates the Mayan empire

A Mixtec necklace. The Mixtecs were conquered by the Aztecs.

A.D. 1420–1480s
Aztec empire expands to Guatemala

A.D. 1479
Incas complete the conquest of Peru

The Pyramid of the Sun at Teotihuacán.

The Mayas built great cities. One such city was Copán (ko PAHN) in the present-day country of Honduras. Another was Tikal (tee KAHL) in present-day Guatemala. Mayan cities were religious centers. A large pyramid-shaped temple stood in the center of the city. The Mayas worshipped their gods there. Farmers worked in fields surrounding the cities. Past the fields lay the dense tropical rain forest.

Mayan Farming and Science The Mayan farmers' most important crop was **maize,** or corn. Maize was the main food of the Mayas. They also grew beans, squash, peppers, avocados, and papayas. Mayan priests studied the stars and planets. They designed an accurate calendar, which they used to decide when to hold religious ceremonies. The Mayan calendar was more accurate than any used in Europe until the 1700s. The Mayas developed a system of writing using signs and symbols called **hieroglyphics** (hy ur oh GLIF iks). They also developed a number system that is similar to the present-day decimal system.

The Great Mystery of the Mayas About A.D. 900, the Mayas suddenly left their cities. No one knows why. Crop failures, war, disease, drought, or famine may have killed many Mayas. Or perhaps people rebelled against the control of the priests and nobles. The Mayas left their cities, but stayed in the region. Millions of Mayas still live in the countries of Mexico, Belize, Guatemala, Honduras, and El Salvador.

Aztec Civilization

Another ancient civilization of Middle America is that of the Aztecs. They arrived in the Valley of Mexico in the 1100s. The Valley of Mexico is in Central Mexico and includes the site of present-day Mexico City.

The Concept of Zero The Mayas created a numbering system that included the idea of zero. Zero is important in math because it is a symbol that shows that there is none of something. For example, to write the number 308, you need a symbol to show that there are no tens. Mathematicians consider the idea of zero to be one of the world's greatest inventions.

The Aztecs wandered about the valley looking for a permanent home until 1325. They finally settled on an island in Lake Texcoco. They changed the swampy lake into a magnificent city, which they called Tenochtitlán (tay nawch tee TLAHN). Tenochtitlán stood on the site of present-day Mexico City.

Tenochtitlán

Tenochtitlán, the Aztec capital, was built in the center of a lake. The Aztecs built floating islands by piling rich earth from the bottom of the lake onto rafts made of wood. After a while, the roots of plants and trees grew down to the lake bottom, anchoring the rafts. Some islands were the size of football fields. What do you think it would be like to live on a lake?

EXPLORING TECHNOLOGY

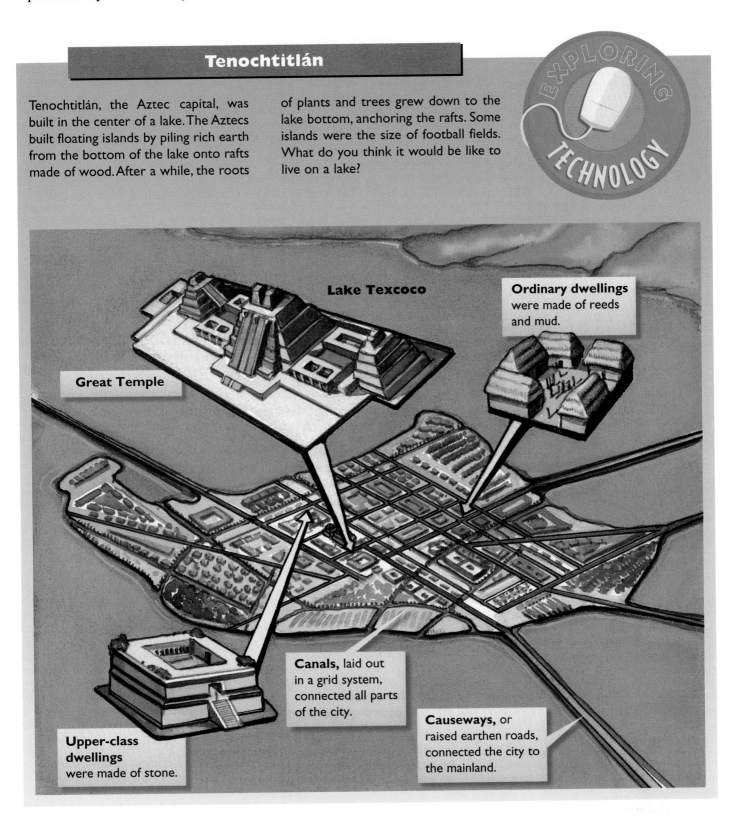

Lake Texcoco

Ordinary dwellings were made of reeds and mud.

Great Temple

Upper-class dwellings were made of stone.

Canals, laid out in a grid system, connected all parts of the city.

Causeways, or raised earthen roads, connected the city to the mainland.

The Aztecs observed the stars and planets carefully. They named them after their gods, like Quetzalcoatl, shown at right. The Aztecs used their knowledge of astronomy to make calendars like the one below.

The Aztecs Expand Their Empire In the 1400s, Aztec warriors began conquering the other people in the region. They forced the people they conquered to pay tribute, or taxes. Tribute could be paid in food, cotton, gold, or slaves. The Aztecs grew rich from the tribute.

The Aztecs had an emperor who ruled over all Aztec lands. The rest of Aztec society had several classes. Nobles and priests helped the emperor. Warriors fought battles. Traders carried goods throughout the empire and beyond. Craftworkers created jewelry, garments, pottery, sculptures, and other goods. Most people, however, were farmers.

Other Aztec Accomplishments Tenochtitlán was a center of trade and learning. Aztec doctors made more than 1,000 medicines from plants. They used the medicines to lower fevers, cure stomachaches, and heal wounds. Like the Mayas, Aztec astronomers predicted eclipses and the movements of planets. Aztec priests kept records using hieroglyphics similar to those used by the Mayas.

SECTION 1 REVIEW

1. **Define** (a) maize, (b) hieroglyphics.

2. **Identify** (a) Copán, (b) Tikal, (c) Valley of Mexico, (d) Tenochtitlán.

3. What were the main features of Mayan civilization?

4. How was Aztec society organized?

Critical Thinking

5. **Distinguishing Fact From Opinion** Tell if the following statements are facts or opinions. Explain why. (a) Mayan calendars were very accurate. (b) Aztec civilization was more advanced than Mayan civilization.

Activity

6. **Writing to Learn** What are some reasons for the decline of Mayan and Aztec civilizations? Does every society decline sooner or later?

The Incas

PEOPLE OF THE SUN

SECTION

2

BEFORE YOU READ

Reach Into Your Background
The United States has roads that run from state to state. These roads are called inter-state highways. Think about some ways that interstate highways are useful. Then, compare what you know about interstate highways with the roads you will read about in this section.

Questions to Explore
1. What was Incan civilization like?

2. How did the Incas interact with and change their environment to increase farmland and farm production?

Key Terms
aqueduct   quipu

Key People and Places
Pachacuti   Cuzco
Topa Inca

The runner sped along the mountain road. He lifted a horn made from a shell to his lips and blew. A second runner appeared and began running beside him. Without stopping, the first runner relayed to the second runner the message he carried. The second runner took off like the wind. He would not stop until he reached the next runner.

The Incas used runners to spread news from one place in their empire to another. Incan messengers carried news at a rate of 250 miles (402 km) a day. Without these runners, controlling the vast empire would have been very difficult.

The Rise of the Incas

This great and powerful empire had small beginnings. In about 1200, the Incas settled in Cuzco (KOOS koh), a village in the Andes that is now a city in the country of Peru. Most Incas were farmers. They grew maize and other crops. Through wars and conquest, the Incas won control of the entire Cuzco valley, one of many valleys that extend from the Andes to the Pacific Ocean.

In 1438, Pachacuti (PAHTCH an koo tee) became ruler of the Incas. The name Pachacuti means "he who shakes the earth." Pachacuti conquered the people who lived near the Pacific Ocean, from Lake Titicaca north to the city of Quito.

▼ The Incas shaped their stones so well that they did not need cement to hold a wall together.

Pachacuti demanded loyalty from the people he conquered. If they proved disloyal, he forced them off their land. He replaced them with people loyal to the Incas.

Pachacuti's son, Topa Inca, expanded the empire. In time, it stretched some 2,500 miles (4,023 km) from what is now Ecuador south along the Pacific coast through Peru, Bolivia, Chile, and Argentina. The 12 million people ruled by the Incas lived mostly in small villages.

Incan Accomplishments

The Incas were excellent farmers, builders, and managers. Their capital, Cuzco, was the center of government, trade, learning, and religion. In the 1500s, one of the first Spaniards to visit Cuzco described it as "large enough and handsome enough to compare to any Spanish city."

The emperor, and the nobles who helped him run the empire, lived in the city near the central plaza. They wore special headbands and earrings that showed their high rank. Most of the farmers and workers outside Cuzco lived in mud huts.

Roads and Aqueducts The Incas built more than 19,000 miles (30,577 km) of roads. The roads went over some of the most mountainous land in the world. The road system helped the Incas to govern their vast empire. Not only did runners use the roads to deliver messages, but Incan armies and trade caravans also used the roads for speedy travel.

Connect How do your family and community depend on roads?

▼Pachacuti built many cities. The most famous one is the "lost city" of Machu Picchu. It lies high in the Andes Mountains, 54 miles (87 km) northwest of Cuzco. **Interaction** Look closely at the picture. How did the Incas adapt their city to the mountains?

The Incas used quipus to record information about births, deaths, trade, and taxes. **Critical Thinking** Think of some other ways to communicate information without using spoken or written words.

The Incas also built canals and aqueducts to carry water to dry areas. An **aqueduct** is a pipe or channel designed to carry water from a distant source. One stone aqueduct carried water from a mountain lake almost 500 miles (805 km) to its destination. The system of canals and aqueducts allowed the Incas to irrigate land that was otherwise too dry to grow crops.

Government and Records The Incas organized their government carefully. The emperor chose nobles to govern each province. Each noble conducted a census to count people so they could be taxed. Local officials collected some of each village's crops as a tax. The villagers also had to work on government building projects. However, the government took care of the poor, the sick, and the elderly.

The Incas did not have a written language. Incan government officials and traders recorded information on knotted strings called **quipus** (KEE poos). Every quipu had a main cord with several colored strings attached to it. Each color represented a different item, and knots of different sizes at certain intervals stood for numbers.

Religion Like the Mayas and the Aztecs, the Incas worshipped many gods. The sun god, Inti, was an important god of the Incas. They believed Inti was their parent. They referred to themselves as "children of the sun." Another important Incan god was Viracocha (vee ra KOCH ah), the creator of all the people of the Andes.

ACROSS TIME

Earthquake-proof Buildings Incan stone walls were so firmly constructed that even violent earthquakes could not knock them down. The walls swayed but did not crumble the way some modern buildings do. Engineers today are learning to make buildings that can resist an earthquake.

The Incas increased the amount of farmland in hilly areas by building terraces into the sides of steep slopes. The terraces helped keep soil from washing down the mountain. These terraces are at Pasaq, an ancient Incan fortress in Peru. **Interaction** Think of some other reasons why farming in the mountains might be hard.

Quechua Descendants of the Incas The Spanish conquered the Incan empire in the 1500s. However, descendants of the Incas still live in present-day Peru, Ecuador, Bolivia, Chile, and Colombia. They speak Quechua (KECH wah), the Incan language.

They use farming methods that are like those of the ancient Incas. The Incan culture also survives in the poncho and in other clothing styles, as well as in cloth woven into brightly colored complex patterns.

SECTION 2 REVIEW

1. **Define** (a) aqueduct, (b) quipu.

2. **Identify** (a) Pachacuti, (b) Topa Inca, (c) Cuzco.

3. Why was a good network of roads important to the Incan empire?

4. Describe a few features of the Incan religion.

Critical Thinking

5. **Drawing Conclusions** Look at the shape of the Incan empire on the map on the opening page of this chapter. In an attack, what features would make the empire difficult to defend? What features would help defend the empire?

Activity

6. **Writing to Learn** Make a list of some of the ways the Incas used land for farming. Do you think the Incas made good use of farmland? Why or why not?

European Conquest

Reach Into Your Background

How do you decide what is right and what is wrong? Think of a time when you were not sure what was the right thing to do. As you read this section, notice how the people made decisions. Think about whether or not you agree with the decisions they made.

Questions to Explore

1. Why did Europeans sail to the Americas?
2. What were the effects of European rule on Native Americans in the region?

Key Terms

Treaty of Tordesillas
treaty
Line of Demarcation
conquistador
mestizo
hacienda
encomienda

Key People

Hernán Cortés
Malinche
Christopher Columbus
Moctezuma
Francisco Pizarro

Hernán Cortés was the Spanish soldier who conquered the Aztecs. He landed in Mexico in 1519 and soon met Malinche (mah LIHN chay). She was the daughter of a Mayan leader. Malinche, whom Cortés called Doña Marina, spoke several languages in addition to Mayan. She quickly learned Spanish. Malinche became Cortés's main translator. She also kept an eye on Aztec spies. Without Malinche, Cortés could not have conquered the Aztecs. Why did European explorers, like Cortés, want to conquer Native Americans? Why did some Native Americans, like Malinche, help the conquerers?

Europeans Arrive in the Americas

In the 1400s, Spain and Portugal searched for new trade routes to Asia. They knew that in Asia they would find expensive goods such as spices and silks. These goods could be traded for a profit.

Columbus Reaches America Christopher Columbus thought he could reach Asia by sailing west across the Atlantic Ocean. Columbus knew the world was round, as did most educated

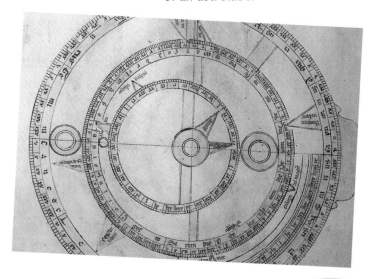

▼ Sailors in the 1400s guided their ships using only the stars, a compass, and an astrolabe. Below is a drawing of an astrolabe.

Map Study Columbus sailed to the Americas in 1492, 1493, 1498, and 1502. His 1502 voyage is shown here. Cortés sailed to the Americas in 1504 and conquered the Aztecs in 1519. Pizarro sailed in 1502 and conquered the Incas in 1533. **Movement** Once they reached the Caribbean, what factors do you think helped the Spanish to find the Aztec and Incan empires so quickly? **Regions** South America has two major language regions: Spanish and Portuguese. How did the Line of Demarcation create these regions?

KEY

→ Christopher Columbus 1502–1504

→ Hernan Cortés 1519–1521

→ Francisco Pizarro 1531

---- Line of Demarcation

Lambert Azimuthal Equal-Area Projection

0   600   1,200 mi
0 600 1,200 km

LINKS TO MATH

Navigating Without Modern Instruments
Explorers like Columbus did not have radar, satellites, and computers to guide their ships. They used the stars as a reference. Sailors imagined a triangle with a straight line from the ship to the horizon, and a line from the horizon to a star. Measuring the angle between the line to the star and the horizon helped them figure out their location.

Europeans. But Columbus believed the distance around the world was shorter than it was. First Columbus asked Portugal to sponsor his voyage. Then he asked Spain. Queen Isabella of Spain finally agreed.

Columbus set sail in early August, 1492. Some 10 weeks later, on October 12, he spotted land. Columbus thought he had reached the East Indies in Asia, so he described the people there as Indians.

Dividing the World Spain and Portugal soon became fierce rivals. Each country tried to stop the other from claiming land in the Americas. In 1494, Spain and Portugal signed the **Treaty of Tordesillas** (tor day SEE yas). A **treaty** is an agreement in writing made between two or more countries. The treaty set an imaginary line from North Pole to South Pole at about 50° longitude, called the **Line of Demarcation.** It gave Spain the right to settle and trade west of the line. Portugal could do the same east of the line. The only part of South America that is east of the line is roughly the eastern half of present-day Brazil. Because of the Treaty of Tordesillas, the language and background of Brazil are Portuguese.

A Clash of Cultures

Spanish explorers heard stories of wealthy kingdoms in the Americas. They hoped to find gold and other treasures. Spanish rulers did not pay for the trips of the explorers. Instead, they gave the **conquistadors** (kon KEES ta dors), or conquerors, the right to hunt for treasure. The conquistadors could also settle in America. In exchange, conquistadors agreed to give Spain one fifth of any treasures they found. If a conquistador failed, he lost his own fortune. If he succeeded, both he and Spain gained fame, wealth, and glory.

Cortés Conquers the Aztecs In 1519, Hernán Cortés sailed to the coast of Mexico in search of treasure. He brought a small army with him. The Aztec ruler Moctezuma (mahk the ZOOM uh) heard that a strange ship was offshore. He sent spies to find out about it. The spies reported back to Moctezuma:

> "We must tell you that we saw a house in the water, out of which came white men, with white hands and faces, and very long, bushy beards, and clothes of every color: white, yellow, red, green, blue, and purple, and on their heads they wore round hats."

The Aztecs demanded heavy tribute from the peoples who lived near them, so these groups disliked the Aztecs. Cortés made agreements with these groups. Then he headed for Tenochtitlán with 500 soldiers and 16 horses. Aztec spies told Moctezuma that the Spanish were coming. The Aztecs had never seen horses before. Moctezuma's spies described the Spanish as "supernatural creatures riding on hornless deer, armed in iron, fearless as gods." Moctezuma thought Cortés might be the god Quetzalcoatl (ket sahl koh AHTL). According to Aztec legend, Quetzalcoatl had promised to return to rule the Aztecs.

With a heavy heart, Moctezuma welcomed Cortés and his soldiers. Cortés tried to convince Moctezuma to surrender to Spain. After several months, Moctezuma agreed. But the peace did not last long. Spanish soldiers killed some Aztecs. Then the Aztecs began to fight against the Spanish. The battle was fierce and bloody. Moctezuma was killed, and Cortés and his army barely escaped.

With the help of the Aztecs' enemies, Cortés surrounded and attacked Tenochtitlán. In 1521, the Aztecs finally surrendered. By then, about 240,000 Aztecs had died and 30,000 of Cortés's allies had been killed. Tenochtitlán and the Aztec empire lay in ruins.

Pizarro Conquers the Incas Francisco Pizarro (fran SIS koh pih ZAR oh), like Cortés, was a Spanish conquistador. He heard stories about the rich Incan kingdom. Pizarro planned to attack the Pacific coast of South America. In 1531, Pizarro set sail with a small force of 180 Spanish soldiers. Pizarro captured and killed the Incan

A Court Welcome

This historical painting shows Moctezuma welcoming Cortés to his court. **Critical Thinking** Based on this painting, what conclusions can you draw about Aztec wealth?

READ ACTIVELY

Connect How would you feel if you saw people riding on a large animal that you had never seen before?

Ask Questions Suppose that you were a doctor living in South America at the time of the Conquest. What questions would you ask to discover why so many Native Americans were dying of European diseases?

emperor. He also killed many other Incan leaders. By 1535, Pizarro had conquered most of the Incan empire, including the capital, Cuzco.

The conquistadors defeated the two most powerful empires in the Americas. It took them only 15 years. How did they do it? The Spanish had guns and cannons that the Native Americans had never seen. They also rode horses. At first, horses terrified Native Americans. The Europeans also carried diseases such as smallpox, measles, and chicken pox. These diseases wiped out entire villages. And, because of local rivalry, some Native Americans like Malinche helped the Spanish conquistadors.

Colonization

By the 1540s, Spain claimed land throughout much of the Americas. Spain's lands stretched from what today is Kansas all the way south to the tip of South America. Brazil was claimed by Portugal.

Spain Organizes Its Empire Spain divided its territory into provinces. Spain also set up a strong government. The two most important provinces were New Spain and Peru. The capital of New Spain was Mexico City. Lima became the capital city of Peru.

Lima's geographic layout was based on the Spanish social classes. The most powerful citizens lived in the center of Lima. They either came from Spain or had Spanish parents. Mestizos, people of mixed Spanish and Native American descent, lived on the outskirts of the city. Many

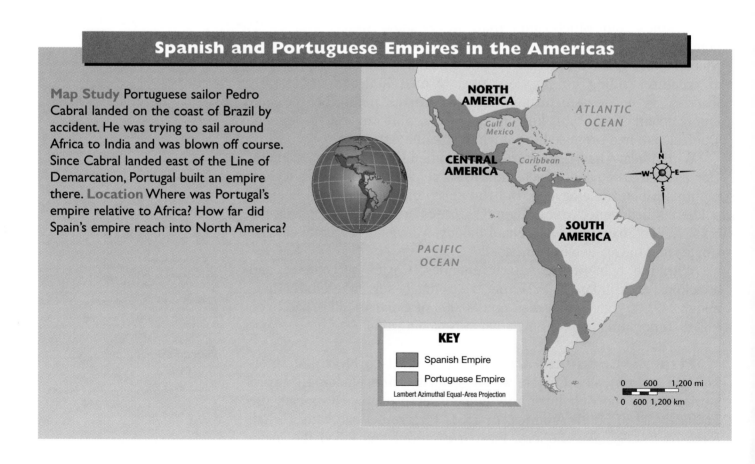

Spanish and Portuguese Empires in the Americas

Map Study Portuguese sailor Pedro Cabral landed on the coast of Brazil by accident. He was trying to sail around Africa to India and was blown off course. Since Cabral landed east of the Line of Demarcation, Portugal built an empire there. **Location** Where was Portugal's empire relative to Africa? How far did Spain's empire reach into North America?

KEY

Spanish Empire

Portuguese Empire

Lambert Azimuthal Equal-Area Projection

0   600   1,200 mi

0   600 1,200 km

mestizos were poor. But some were middle class or quite wealthy. Native Americans were the least powerful class. Most Native Americans continued to live in the countryside. The Spanish forced them to work on haciendas. A hacienda (hah see EN duh) was a plantation owned by Spaniards or the Catholic Church.

The Effect of European Rule Spain gave its settlers encomiendas (en KOH mee en dus), which were rights to demand taxes or labor from Native Americans. Native Americans were allowed to stay on their own land, so the Spanish claimed that encomiendas protected Native Americans. In fact, encomiendas forced Native Americans to work for the settlers. At first, the Native Americans worked only on the haciendas. But when silver was discovered in Mexico and Peru, the Spanish forced Native Americans to also work in the mines. Some died from overwork and malnutrition. Many died from European diseases. In 1519, New Spain had a Native American population of 25 million. Only 3 million survived the first 50 years of Spanish rule. In 1532, 12 million Native Americans lived in Peru. Fifty years later, there were fewer than 2 million.

The Columbian Exchange

Western Hemisphere

Pumpkin
Avocado
Peanut
Beans
  (lima, pole, navy, kidney)
Peppers (bell and chili)
Pineapple
Quinine
Wild rice
Corn
Potato
Tomato

Eastern Hemisphere

Horse
Cattle
Sheep
Chicken
Honeybee
Sugar cane
Wheat, barley, oats
Onion
Lettuce
Peach and pear
Watermelon
Citrus fruit
Banana

Chart Study Goods, as well as people, crossed the Atlantic in the years after the conquest. . Do you think that the Eastern and Western hemispheres benefitted equally from the Columbian Exchange? Why or why not?

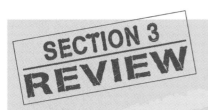

SECTION 3 REVIEW

1. **Define** (a) Treaty of Tordesillas, (b) treaty, (c) Line of Demarcation, (d) conquistador, (e) mestizo, (f) hacienda, (g) encomienda.

2. **Identify** (a) Hernán Cortés, (b) Malinche, (c) Christopher Columbus, (d) Moctezuma, (e) Francisco Pizarro.

3. What was the effect of the Treaty of Tordesillas on the European settlement of the Americas?

4. How did the Spanish conquest affect Native Americans?

Critical Thinking

5. **Recognizing Bias** The Treaty of Tordesillas affected the lives of millions of Native Americans. However, Native Americans were not asked about the treaty. What do you think this says about European attitudes toward Native Americans?

Activity

6. **Writing to Learn** Write two paragraphs: one by a Native American who has just seen a European for the first time and another by a European who has just seen a Native American for the first time.

Using a Time Line

The year is A.D. 2098. Biff Bucko, a star geography student, jumps into his shiny new time machine. He's off on a weekend trip to ancient Mayan civilization.

The centuries whiz by. As our hero approaches the year A.D. 1000, he slows to a stop. "When was Mayan culture at its height?" he wonders. Biff looks to the left and right. "Hmm . . . I think it's this way." Biff should have checked the time line in his glove compartment. If he had, he would have known that Mayan civilization declined after A.D. 900. Instead, he's landed in the 1400s where the Aztecs are busy conquering Middle America. "Oops," thinks Biff as a band of Aztec warriors descends upon him.

Studying the past makes you a kind of time traveler, too. Still, it's always best to know where you're going. Creating a time line can help.

Get Ready

A time line is like a map of the past. It keeps important dates in order so you don't get lost in time. Keep yours handy while you study for a test, research a report, or read for fun.

To make a time line you'll need:
- two sheets of paper
- thirteen paper clips

Try It Out

A. Make a paper ruler. Fold one sheet of paper in half the long way. Now fold it over again. You'll use this paper as a ruler to measure your time line.

B. Mark the divisions of time periods. Attach three paper clips along the top edge of your paper ruler. Slide one to the left corner, one to the right corner, and one to the exact center.

C. Look at dates for your time line. Your time line will cover a span of about 1,200 years. Label the left paper clip on your ruler with the year 300. Label the right paper clip 1500 and the middle one 900.

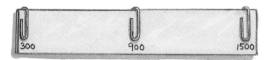

D. Figure out time intervals. Space your other paper clips evenly across the top of the ruler. The space between each will stand for 100 years. Label your clips with the years 400, 500, and so on.

E. Locate the dates on your time line. Turn your other paper so the long side is on top. Draw a straight line across it. Using your ruler, mark the 100-year intervals. Then mark where each of the four time line dates belongs on the line. (Estimate for the dates 1345 and 1438.) Label each mark with its date and event.

Dates for Your Time Line			
300	**900**	**1385**	**1438**
Mayan civilization rises	Mayas leave their cities	Aztecs found the city of Tenochtitlán	Pachacuti founds the Incan Empire

Now choose some other dates in Latin American history that you want to remember. Follow the steps below to create a time line.

① **Design a time line ruler.** First look at the dates you've selected. What time span will your time line cover? For a long span, each paper clip could mark 100 years. For a shorter span, you could mark every 50 years, 10 years, or 1 year. Choose a measurement that makes sense.

② **Find a date to start your ruler.** Take the earliest date you chose for your time line. Round it to a lower number. For example, if you are measuring every 50 years, round the date 1492 down to 1450.

③ **Find a date to end your ruler.** Take your last date. Round it up.

④ **Count the paper clips you'll need.** Say your ruler starts at 1450, ends at 1650, and marks every 50 years. Count: 1450, 1500, 1550, 1600, 1650. That's five clips.

⑤ **Put a clip at each end of the ruler.** Space the others evenly. Label each with its year. Now use the ruler to mark points on your time line. Label each point with its date and event.

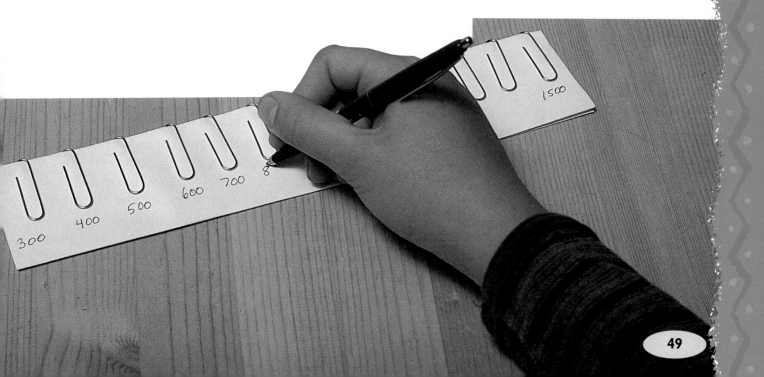

Independence

Reach Into Your Background

What qualities do you think make a hero? What about bravery, or doing the right thing no matter what the personal cost? Jot down at least three qualities that you think a hero should have.

Questions to Explore

1. How did Latin American nations win independence from their European rulers?
2. How did the American and French revolutions influence events in Latin America?

Key Terms
revolution
criollo
caudillo

Key People
Miguel Hidalgo
Agustín de Iturbide
Simón Bolívar
José de San Martín
Dom Pedro

▼ Toussaint L'Ouverture was captured by the French, but his followers won Haiti's independence.

On August 24, 1791, the night sky over Saint-Domingue (san duh MANG) glowed red and gold. The French Caribbean colony was on fire. The slaves were sick of being mistreated by their white masters. They finally had rebelled. Now they were burning every piece of white-owned property they could find. This Night of Fire was the beginning of the first great fight for freedom in Latin America. Toussaint L'Ouverture (too SAN loo vur TOOR), a former slave, led the people of Saint-Domingue in this fight for more than 10 years. Eventually they won. They founded the independent country of Haiti (HAY tee) in 1804.

The flame of liberty lit in Haiti soon spread across Latin America. By 1825, most of the region was independent. Latin Americans would no longer be ruled by Europe.

Independence in Mexico

Haiti's leaders drew encouragement from two famous revolutions. A **revolution** is a political movement in which the people overthrow the government and set up another. During the 1770s and early 1780s, the 13 British colonies in North America fought a war to free themselves from Britain's rule. In 1789, the ordinary people of France staged a violent uprising against their royal rulers. These actions inspired not only the people of Haiti, but also people across Latin America.

Criollos (kree OH yohz) paid particular attention to these events. A **criollo** had Spanish parents, but had been born in Latin America.

Criollos often were the wealthiest and best-educated people in the Spanish colonies. Few criollos had any political power, however. Only people born in Spain could hold government office. Many criollos attended school in Europe. There, they learned about the ideas that inspired revolution in France and the United States. The criollos especially liked the idea that people had the right to govern themselves.

The "Cry of Dolores"   Mexico began its struggle for self-government in 1810. Miguel Hidalgo (mee GEHL ee DAHL goh) led the way. He was a criollo priest in the town of Dolores. With other criollos in Dolores, he planned to begin a revolution.

In September 1810, the Spanish government discovered Hidalgo's plot. But before the authorities could arrest him, Hidalgo took action. He wildly rang the church bells. A huge crowd gathered. "Recover from the hated Spaniards the land stolen from your forefathers," he shouted. "Long live America, and death to the bad government!"

Hidalgo's call for revolution became known as the "Cry of Dolores." It attracted some 80,000 fighters in a matter of weeks. This army consisted mostly of mestizos and Native Americans. They were angry. They wanted revenge against anybody connected with the Spanish government. The rebels won some victories. Their luck, however, soon changed. By the beginning of 1811, they were in full retreat. Hidalgo tried to flee the country. However, government soldiers soon captured him. He was put on trial and convicted of treason. Hidalgo was executed by firing squad in July 1811.

Ask Questions What would you like to know about the attitudes of Mexican criollos toward the revolution?

The Cry of Dolores

Hidalgo made the "Cry of Dolores" on September 16. Mexico celebrates its independence every year on that day. **Critical Thinking** Why do you think that the painter of this mural included so many people in the background behind Hidalgo?

African Independence
Although Africa is closer to Europe than to Latin America, Europeans began to colonize Africa later. Europeans began claiming parts of Africa in the 1880s. Like the people of Latin America, many people in Africa later were inspired by the ideas of self-government and independence. African countries began to achieve independence in the 1950s and 1960s.

Independence Finally Comes The Spanish could execute the revolution's leaders, but they could not kill its spirit. Small rebel groups kept fighting. Then Agustín de Iturbide (ee toor BEE day) joined the rebels. He was a high-ranking officer in the Spanish army. Many people who had opposed the rebellion changed their minds. They had viewed Hidalgo as a dangerous hothead. But Iturbide was different. He was a criollo and an army officer. They could trust Iturbide to protect their interests. They decided to support the rebellion. In 1821, Iturbide declared Mexico independent.

South American Independence

Simón Bolívar (see MOHN boh LEE vahr) was not the first Latin American revolutionary leader. Almost certainly, however, he was the greatest. He was born in the country of Venezuela in 1783. His family was one of the richest and most important families in Latin America. Like most wealthy Latin Americans, he went to school in Spain. There, he met Prince Ferdinand, the heir to the Spanish throne. They decided to play a game similar to present-day badminton. Custom required that Bolívar show respect for the prince by losing. Instead, Bolívar played hard and tried to win. He even knocked the prince's hat off with his racquet! The angry prince demanded an apology. Bolívar refused. He claimed it was an accident. Furious, the prince insisted that they fight a duel. He soon calmed down, however.

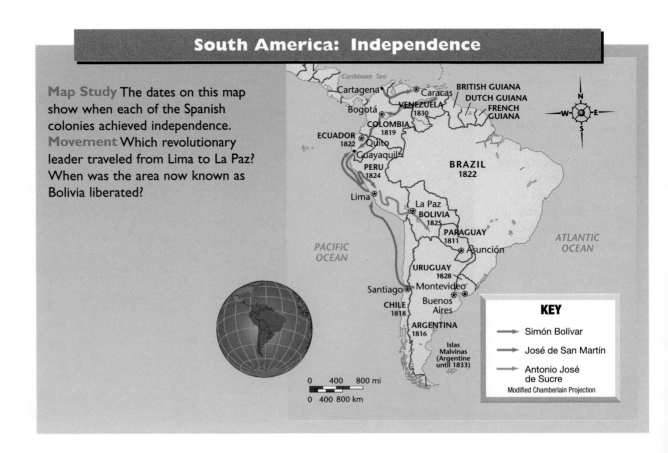

South America: Independence

Map Study The dates on this map show when each of the Spanish colonies achieved independence. **Movement** Which revolutionary leader traveled from Lima to La Paz? When was the area now known as Bolivia liberated?

Caribbean Sea
Cartagena
Caracas
BRITISH GUIANA
DUTCH GUIANA
FRENCH GUIANA
Bogotá
VENEZUELA 1830
COLOMBIA 1819
ECUADOR 1822
Quito
Guayaquil
PERU 1824
BRAZIL 1822
Lima
La Paz
BOLIVIA 1825
PARAGUAY 1811
Asunción
PACIFIC OCEAN
ATLANTIC OCEAN
URUGUAY 1828
Santiago
Montevideo
CHILE 1818
Buenos Aires
ARGENTINA 1816
Islas Malvinas (Argentine until 1833)

0   400   800 mi
0 400 800 km

KEY
→ Simón Bolívar
→ José de San Martín
→ Antonio José de Sucre
Modified Chamberlain Projection

Many years later, these two faced off again. This time, Bolívar knocked Spanish America from under Ferdinand's feet.

Bolívar and San Martín: The Liberators   Bolívar joined the fight for Venezuelan independence in 1804. Six years later he became its leader. Bolívar was completely certain that he would win. His confidence, courage, and daring inspired his soldiers. They enjoyed victory after victory. By 1822, Bolívar's troops had freed a large area from Spanish rule (the future countries of Colombia, Venezuela, Ecuador, and Panama). This newly liberated region formed Gran Colombia. Bolívar became its president. Even though his country was free, Bolívar did not give up the cause of independence. "The Liberator," as he was now known, turned south toward Peru.

José de San Martín (san mahr TEEN), an Argentine, had lived in Spain and served in the Spanish army. When Argentina began its fight for freedom, he quickly offered to help. San Martín took good care of his troops. He shared each hardship they had to suffer. They loved him for it. Many said they would follow San Martín anywhere—even over the snow-capped Andes Mountains. In 1817, his soldiers had to do just that. He led them through high passes in the Andes into Chile. This bold action took the Spanish completely by surprise. In a matter of months, Spain was defeated. San Martín declared Chile's independence. Then he turned his attention to Peru.

Again, San Martín took an unexpected action. This time, he attacked from the sea. The Spanish were not prepared for San Martín's tactics. Spanish defenses quickly collapsed. In July 1821, San Martín pushed inland and seized Lima, the capital of Peru.

▶ Nearly every town or city in South America has a central square with a statue of Bolívar or San Martín. These high school girls are visiting the statue of Bolívar in Meridá, Venezuela.

A year later, San Martín met with Bolívar to discuss the fight for independence. Historians do not know what happened in that meeting. But afterward, San Martín suddenly gave up his command. He left Bolívar to continue the fight alone. This Bolívar did. Eventually, he drove the remaining Spanish forces out of South America altogether. By 1825, only Cuba and Puerto Rico were still ruled by Spain.

Brazil Takes a Different Route to Freedom Portugal's colony, Brazil, became independent without fighting a war. In the early 1800s, French armies invaded Spain and Portugal. Portugal's royal family fled to Brazil for safety. The king returned to Portugal in 1821. However, he left his son, Dom Pedro, to rule the colony. Dom Pedro used more power than the king expected. He declared Brazil independent in 1822. Three years later, Portugal quietly admitted that Brazil was independent.

Challenges of Independence

After winning independence, Latin American leaders faced hard challenges. They had to decide how to govern their nations. Also, after years of fighting, Latin American nations were very poor.

Simón Bolívar dreamed of uniting South America as one country. Gran Colombia was the first step. Bolívar hoped it would become the "United States of South America." In trying to govern Gran Colombia, however, Bolívar found that his dream was impossible. Latin America was a huge area, divided by the Andes and dense rain forests. Also, the leaders of the countries in Gran Columbia wanted little to do with Bolívar. In poor health, he retired from politics.

Even though he did not last long in office, Bolívar set the standard for Latin American leaders. Most were **caudillos** (kow DEE yohs), military officers who ruled very strictly. Bolívar cared about the people he governed. Many other caudillos did not. These others just wanted to stay in power and get rich.

Ask Questions What questions would you ask Simón Bolívar about his dream of a "United States of South America"?

SECTION 4 REVIEW

1. **Define** (a) revolution, (b) criollo, (c) caudillo.
2. **Identify** (a) Miguel Hidalgo, (b) Agustín de Iturbide, (c) Simón Bolívar, (d) José de San Martín, (e) Dom Pedro.

3. What world events influenced the independence movement in Latin America?
4. How was Brazil's path to independence different from that of the rest of South America?

Critical Thinking
5. **Identifying Central Issues** What do you think Simón Bolívar had in mind when he wanted South America to become the "United States of South America"?

Activity
6. **Writing to Learn** Imagine you are a journalist with Bolívar's or San Martín's army. Describe the army's main actions.

Issues in Latin America Today

BEFORE YOU READ

Reach Into Your Background

Most people like the feeling of being able to take care of themselves. What could you do now to prepare for your own independence?

Questions to Explore
1. How are Latin American nations trying to improve their economies?
2. What issues has the move to the cities created in Latin America?

Key Terms
invest
economy
campesino
rural
urban

Key Places
Brazil

Samuel Zemurray came from Russia to the United States in 1892. He worked for his aunt and uncle, who owned a store in Alabama. As part of his job, Zemurray sometimes traveled to the port city of Mobile. He noticed that fruit and vegetable traders there often threw away ripe bananas. They knew the bananas would spoil before reaching stores. Zemurray bought the ripe bananas and delivered them to stores overnight. The quick delivery meant that the fruit was still fit to be sold. Zemurray's business was so successful that he decided to expand. He did this by buying land in the country of Honduras, where bananas were grown. Zemurray soon became a leading banana grower.

▼ Many large-scale farming operations in Latin America are still foreign-owned.

Foreign Investment

In the 1900s, many companies like Zemurray's invested in Latin America. To **invest** means to spend money to earn more money. Some companies owned farms and grew crops such as sugar and bananas. Other foreign companies ran mines. By the mid-1900s, most businesses in Latin America were owned by or did work for foreign companies. As a result, foreign companies became powerful in Latin American economies. A country's **economy** is made up of the ways that goods and services are produced and made available to people. When money from the sale of goods and services comes into or goes out of a country, it affects the country's economy.

Predict What steps do you think Latin American countries took to balance their economies?

Foreign companies made huge profits from their businesses in Latin America. However, these companies did little to help Latin American countries build their economies. Many Latin Americans realized that it was important to improve their economies. They needed to build factories so that they could make their own manufactured goods. They also needed to grow many different kinds of crops and to develop a wide range of resources.

Some Latin American countries soon took steps to carry out these economic building plans. And they proved successful. During the 1960s and early 1970s, the economies of many Latin American countries grew. However, in the early 1980s, oil prices went up. Latin American countries needed oil to run their factories—and they had to pay higher and higher prices for it. At the same time, the prices of Latin American products fell. Latin American countries had to spend more money, but they were making less and less. To make up the difference, they borrowed money from wealthy countries such as the United States. By the 1980s, many Latin American countries had huge foreign debts.

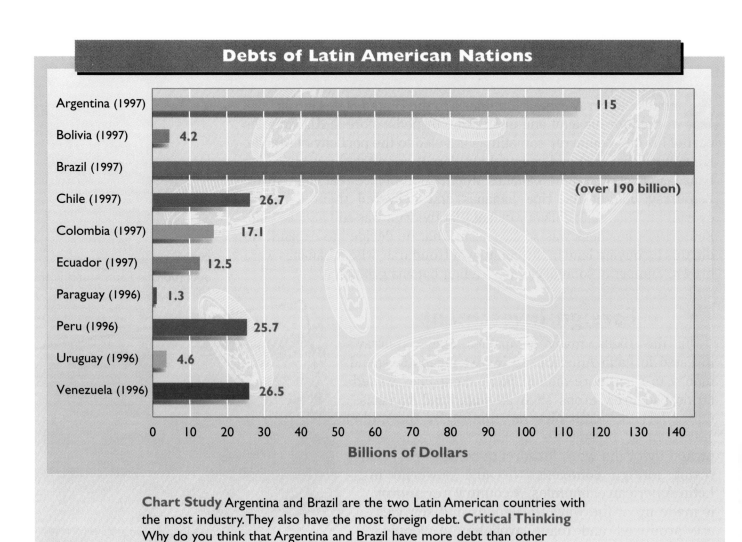

Debts of Latin American Nations

Country	Billions of Dollars
Argentina (1997)	115
Bolivia (1997)	4.2
Brazil (1997)	(over 190 billion)
Chile (1997)	26.7
Colombia (1997)	17.1
Ecuador (1997)	12.5
Paraguay (1996)	1.3
Peru (1996)	25.7
Uruguay (1996)	4.6
Venezuela (1996)	26.5

Billions of Dollars

Chart Study Argentina and Brazil are the two Latin American countries with the most industry. They also have the most foreign debt. Critical Thinking Why do you think that Argentina and Brazil have more debt than other countries?

Facing Economic Challenges

People in Latin American countries have expanded their economies by building more factories and growing different kinds of crops. And they have taken other steps to improve their economies.

Foreign companies still invest in Latin America. But most Latin American countries limit how investments can be made. They want to prevent foreign countries from having too much control over important parts of their economies. Some countries, for instance, have tried to stop foreign companies from acquiring too much land.

Latin American countries have tried to improve their economies by cooperating with one another. For a long time, most Latin American countries did not trade with one another. They did not need to because, for the most part, they all produced the same kinds of goods. Recently, however, some countries have developed new industries. The products these countries make can be traded to other countries in the region. This kind of trade has increased in the last few years. Latin American countries also have formed several organizations that encourage cooperation in the region.

L.I.N.K.S ACROSS THE WORLD

African Economies Many African countries are also trying to improve their economies with less foreign investment. Africans are trying to earn more money by growing more types of cash crops. They are also working to build their own industries and mine their own resources without help from foreign companies.

Land Distribution

The issue of how land is used greatly affects the future of Latin America's economies. Land is one of Latin America's most important resources. Some people and companies own great amounts of land in

Building Televisions on an Assembly Line

In the last 50 years, Latin American countries have begun to produce many more products in factories like this one in Brazil. **Critical Thinking** What skills do you think these factory workers need?

In El Salvador, many farmers do not have modern farming equipment. They use traditional wooden plows and oxen. **Critical Thinking** What would it cost a farmer to own oxen? How would this cost compare to the cost of owning a tractor?

Latin America but most people in the region do not own any land. In Brazil, for example, 45 percent of the land is owned by only 1 percent of the population.

Dividing the Land Much of the farmland in Latin America is owned by a few wealthy families. This land is occupied by haciendas where crops are grown to sell abroad. In contrast, many poor farmers—known as **campesinos** (kahm peh SEE nohs)—own only small tracts of land. They often grow enough only to meet their own needs.

Starting in the 1930s, many Latin American countries tried to help the campesinos by dividing the land more equally. These programs have met with mixed success. In some cases, the land given to the campesinos was of poor quality. No matter how hard they tried, they could not make a living from it. In other cases, the campesinos struggled because they had neither the money to buy seeds and equipment nor the skills necessary for success. Many Latin American countries have begun to see that taking land from one person and giving it to another does not necessarily improve people's lives or the economy.

Using and Protecting the Land Dividing up the land has raised other issues. Brazil gave land to landless peasants by moving them to the Amazonian rain forest. The peasants burned down trees to clear the land for farming. After a few years, however, the soil in the rain forest became unfit for farming.

Many people around the world expressed worries about the clearing of the rain forest. Some believed that this would hurt the environment. Others said that it would change the way of life of the Native Americans who live there. Some people, however, have challenged this view. Economic progress, they say, will come only if Brazil uses all its resources. Brazilian leaders are looking for a balance. They want to find ways to help the economy and the campesinos without destroying the rain forest.

The Move to the City

Many campesinos have decided that making a living from the land is just too difficult. They have left the land and gone to the cities in search of different economic opportunities. This move has resulted in the rapid growth of the populations of large cities. Since the 1950s, many Latin American countries have had a population explosion. The population has increased dramatically in both the **rural,** or countryside, and the **urban,** or city, areas of Latin America. The population of urban areas, however, has gone up the most.

Many Latin Americans who move to the cities are looking for better jobs. They also want to improve the quality of their lives. They hope to find comfortable homes, better medical care, and good schools for their children. However, they do not always realize their hopes. As Latin American countries strive to build their economies, there will be greater opportunities for people to have a better life.

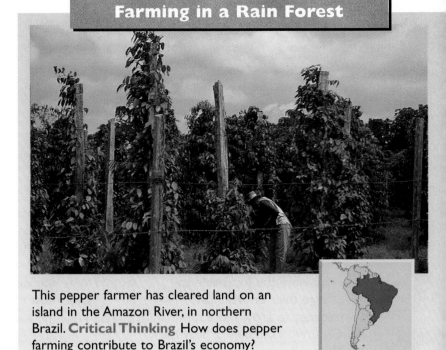

Farming in a Rain Forest

This pepper farmer has cleared land on an island in the Amazon River, in northern Brazil. **Critical Thinking** How does pepper farming contribute to Brazil's economy?

SECTION 5 REVIEW

1. **Define** (a) invest, (b) economy, (c) campesino, (d) rural, (e) urban.

2. **Identify** Brazil.

3. What steps have Latin American countries taken to improve their economies?

4. How have Latin American countries tried to change the landowning system in the region?

Critical Thinking

5. **Recognizing Cause and Effect** How has the increase in population contributed to the growth of cities in Latin America?

Activity

6. **Writing to Learn** You have read that many people oppose Brazil's plans to move poor farmers to the rain forest. Write a paper that explores both the pro and the con sides of the following statement: "A country has the right to use its resources as it sees fit."

Review and Activities

Reviewing Main Ideas

1. Why was an accurate calendar important to Mayan priests?
2. How did the Aztecs expand their empire?
3. How were the Incas able to change their environment in order to grow more food?
4. Give two examples of how the Mayan, Aztec, or Incan empires affect culture in Latin America today.

5. Why was Hernán Cortés able to persuade many Native Americans in the region to fight the Aztecs?
6. (a) Why did Spain gain control over most of Latin America?
   (b) How did Portugal come to control Brazil?

7. What role did the criollos play in the fight for Latin American independence?
8. How did José de San Martín surprise the Spanish in Chile and Peru?
9. How have many Latin American countries been trying to improve their economies in recent years?

Reviewing Key Terms

Use each key term below in a sentence that shows the meaning of the term.

1. maize
2. hieroglyphics
3. aqueduct
4. quipu
5. Line of Demarcation
6. conquistador
7. mestizo
8. hacienda
9. encomienda
10. criollo
11. caudillo
12. invest
13. economy
14. campesino
15. rural
16. urban

Critical Thinking

1. **Recognizing Cause and Effect** What were two causes of the fall of the Aztec and Incan empires? What were two effects on the Native American people of the region?
2. **Making Comparisons** Compare the way in which Mexico gained its independence with the way in which the countries of South America gained theirs.

Graphic Organizer

Copy this tree map onto a separate sheet of paper. Then use the empty boxes to outline Latin American history from Mayan civilization through the Spanish conquest.

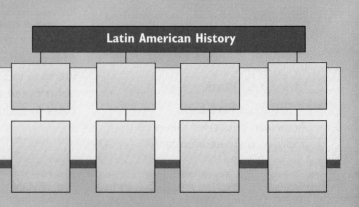

Latin American History

Map Activity

Latin America: Place Location

For each place listed below, write the letter from the map that shows its location.

1. Brazil

2. Guatemala

3. Mexico

4. Chile

5. Peru

6. Andes

7. Mexico City

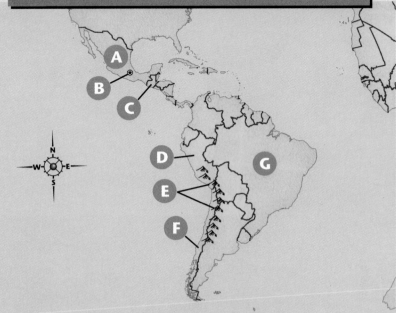

Writing Activity

Writing a Story
The Mayas, Aztecs, and Incas had spoken histories. Information was passed from generation to generation in stories and songs. Suppose that you lived at the time of the Spanish conquest. Write a story or a song that tells about the conquest.

Internet Activity
Use a search engine to find the site **Rabbit in the Moon: Mayan Glyphs and Architecture.** Explore and learn about the ancient Mayan civilization. Then, click on **Your Name in Mayan Glyphs.** Write your name in Mayan hieroglyphics, or play Bul, the on-line Mayan Game of Chance.

Skills Review

Turn to the Skill Activity.

Review the steps for using a time line. Then: (a) Explain in your own words how using a time line can help you to understand history. (b) What kinds of events should you list on a time line?

How Am I Doing?

Answer these questions to help you check your progress.

1. Can I identify and describe characteristics of the Mayan, Aztec, and Incan civilizations?

2. Can I explain how European rule affected Native Americans?

3. Can I explain how Latin American countries achieved independence?

4. Can I explain how foreign investment has affected Latin America?

5. What information from this chapter can I use in my book project?

Cultures of Latin America

PICTURE ACTIVITIES

These people are attending a festival in Peru. Get to know more about the people of Latin America by completing the following.

Link culture and history
Look at the people in this scene. Based on what you know about the history of Latin America, what do you think is the ethnic background of the people in the picture.

Compare regions
The cultures of Latin America are a unique blend of Native American, African, and European influences. How do you think the variety of peoples found in Latin America compares with that in the United States?

The Cultures of Mexico and Central America

Reach Into Your Background

What are your hopes and dreams for the future? Do you hope to work in a particular profession? Do you plan to go to college? Many Mexicans and Central Americans have the same kinds of dreams.

Questions to Explore

1. What is the ethnic heritage of the people of Mexico and Central America?
2. Why have many people in this region been moving from the country to the city?
3. What are the causes of Mexican and Central American immigration to the United States?

Key Terms
diversity
indigenous
injustice
maquiladora
emigrate
immigrant

Key Places
Mexico City

Elvia Alvarado (el VEE ah ahl vah RAH doh) walks the back roads of rural Honduras. She helps poor campesinos make a living. Honduran campesinos are like rural people in all of Central America. Many have little land of their own. It is hard for them to make enough money to support their families.

Alvarado is a mother and grandmother. She works for an organization of campesinos. She helps people get loans to buy seeds and farm machinery. Alvarado also helps them get more land. She works with community groups.

Alvarado's work is not easy. "The communities we work in are hard to get to," she says. "Sometimes I don't eat all day, and in the summertime the streams dry up and there's often no water to drink." Sometimes Alvarado does not get paid. "But I couldn't be happy if my belly was full while my neighbors didn't have a plate of beans and tortillas to put on the table," she says. "My struggle is for a better life for all Hondurans."

Cultural Heritage

Alvarado lives and works in Honduras, in Central America. It is one of seven nations in this area. Together they form a crooked, skinny isthmus. The isthmus links Mexico and South America.

One Region, Many Faces There is much **diversity,** or variety, among the people of Central America. Hondurans, like Alvarado, are mostly mestizo. They have both Spanish and indigenous ancestors. **Indigenous** (in DIJ uh nus) people are descendants of the people who first lived in a region. In Latin America, indigenous people are also called Native Americans or Indians. About half of Guatemala's people are mestizo. The other half are indigenous. Many Costa Ricans are direct descendants of Spaniards. And more than half the people of Belize are of African or mixed African and European descent.

These countries have many languages, too. Guatemala is home to more than 20 languages. Spanish is the language of government and business. But the indigenous people in Guatemala speak their own languages. So do indigenous people in Panama, El Salvador, and Nicaragua. Spanish is the main language in six of the seven countries. People in Belize speak English.

Mexico's Heritage Mexico blends Native American and Spanish influences. Spanish is the first language for most Mexicans, and Mexico is the largest Spanish-speaking country. Some Mexicans speak Native American languages. About 30 percent of the people of Mexico are indigenous, and some Mexicans are mestizos.

The Church Religion is important to the people of Mexico and Central America. In the 1500s and 1600s, Spanish missionaries converted many Native Americans to Christianity. The Roman Catholic Church has been important to this region ever since. Most of the people are Catholic. Native Americans have blended many elements of their religions with Christianity.

Huipiles Huipiles, or Mayan blouses, are works of art as well as clothing. The beautiful designs in a huipile have existed for thousands of years. Diamond-shaped designs stand for the universe. Other designs identify the weaver.

▶ The people of El Salvador are mostly mestizo, and their mixed heritage is reflected in their paintings. **Critical Thinking** What in this painting illustrates the Salvadorans' Spanish heritage?

A Growing Population

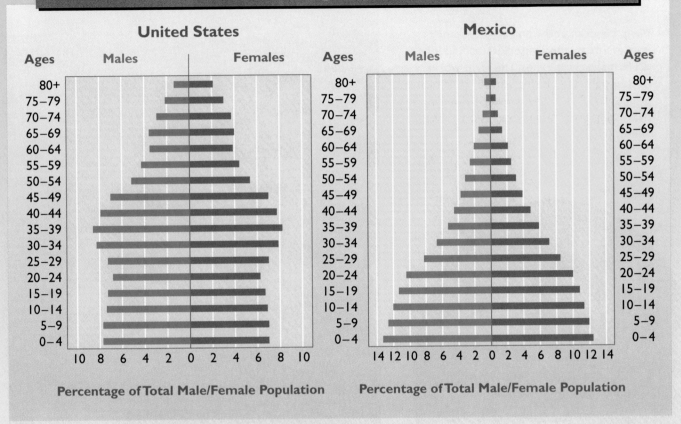

United States

Ages	Males	Females

Mexico

Ages	Males	Females	Ages

Ages: 80+, 75–79, 70–74, 65–69, 60–64, 55–59, 50–54, 45–49, 40–44, 35–39, 30–34, 25–29, 20–24, 15–19, 10–14, 5–9, 0–4

United States scale: 10 8 6 4 2 0 2 4 6 8 10

Percentage of Total Male/Female Population

Mexico scale: 14 12 10 8 6 4 2 0 2 4 6 8 10 12 14

Percentage of Total Male/Female Population

Chart Study Unlike the United States, Mexico is a nation of young people.
Critical Thinking Think about what different skills and needs people have at different ages. What challenges do you think Mexico faces because so many of its people are very young?

Often, the Roman Catholic Church has fought injustice. **Injustice** is the unfair treatment of people. There are many examples of injustice. Injustice occurs when people have their property taken from them unfairly. It also occurs when people are imprisoned without first having a trial. Injustice often happens in countries that have undemocratic governments. Priests and bishops have called for all people to be treated fairly.

Following the Church's lead, many citizens have taken their own steps to end poverty and injustice. People have started their own health clinics, farms, and organizations. Like Elvia Alvarado and her campesino families, they hope that by working together they will be able to create a better way of life.

Looking for Work

The population of Mexico and Central America is growing rapidly. If it continues at the current rate, it will double in 20 to 30 years. Rapid population growth has made it hard for young people in rural areas to

HEROES

A Voice of Protest In the late 1600s, Mexican nun Sor Juana Inez de la Cruz was punished by her bishop for writing a letter defending women's right to learn. Sor Juana was a published poet, but the bishop took away her books and writing materials. However, Sor Juana's essay inspired later generations of women to stand up for their rights.

Many Mexican and Central American immigrants to the United States find jobs on farms, picking crops. The farm workers on the right are picking strawberries near Salinas, California. The worker below is harvesting broccoli in Texas' Rio Grande Valley.

find jobs. Many have left their homes to look for work in the city. Today, most people in Mexico and Central America live in cities.

In Mexico, some people move to towns along the border with the United States. There, they can work in factories owned by American companies. These companies place their factories in Mexico because wages are lower there. Border factories are called **maquiladoras** (ma kee la DOR as).

Life in the City In many cities in the region, there are big contrasts between the lives of the wealthy and the lives of the poor. Wealthy people live in big houses on wide streets. They go to good schools and can afford to pay for medical care. Many of them have a lifestyle similar to that of wealthy people in the United States.

For the poor, however, life in the city can be hard. There is a shortage of housing. It is not easy to find work. Sometimes, the only job available is selling fruit or soda on street corners. It is hard to feed a family

READ ACTIVELY

Ask Questions What questions about maquiladoras would you like answered?

on the wages such work commands. Yet people are willing to live with hardships they find in the city. Cecilia Cruz can explain why. She moved with her husband and their two sons to Mexico City from the southern state of Oaxaca (wah HAH kah). They live in a two-room house made of cinder blocks. It is on the outermost boundary of the city. "We came here for the schools," says Cruz. "There are more choices here. The level of education is much higher." Most newcomers to the city would agree.

Moving to the United States   Most people in Mexico and Central America move somewhere else within their own country if they cannot find work. Some move to cities or border towns. In addition, however, thousands of people emigrate. To **emigrate** means to move out of one country into another. Most leave because they cannot find work at home. Also, rising prices have made living more expensive. Many people emigrate to the United States.

Fermin Carrillo (fair MEEN kah REE yoh) is one worker who did just that. He left his home town of Huaynamota, Mexico. There were no more jobs at home, and his parents needed food and medical care. Carrillo moved to a town in Oregon. Now he works in a fish processing plant. He sends most of the money he earns home to his parents. Carrillo hopes one day to become a U.S. citizen. Other immigrants are different. They want to return home after earning some money to help their families. An **immigrant** is a person who has moved into one country from another.

Many Mexicans and Central Americans, like Fermin Carrillo, have left the region in search of a better life. Many more have followed Elvia Alvarado's example. They have stayed and begun to build a better life for themselves at home.

READ ACTIVELY

Visualize What would a house made of cinder blocks look like? What problems might you notice if you went inside a cinder block house?

SECTION 1 REVIEW

1. **Define**   (a) diversity, (b) indigenous, (c) injustice, (d) maquiladora, (e) emigrate, (f) immigrant.
2. **Identify**   Mexico City.
3. (a) What is the main language and religion of the people of Mexico and Central America? (b) How do the languages and religions of the region reflect its history?
4. What is one reason that rural people in Mexico and Central America are moving to the cities?

Critical Thinking
5. **Recognizing Cause and Effect**   Explain several reasons for Mexican and Central American immigration to the United States.

Activity
6. **Writing to Learn**   Write a journal entry from the point of view of one of the people mentioned in this section. Write about that person's hopes and dreams. How are they like your own? How are they different?

The Cultures of the Caribbean

BEFORE YOU READ

Reach Into Your Background

Have you ever been on an island? Have you ever read a story about someone who lived on an island? What was the island like? What do you remember most about life there?

Questions to Explore

1. How did European, African, and Native American cultures blend to create unique Caribbean cultures?

2. What are the key characteristics of Caribbean cultures?

Key Terms
ethnic group
Carnival

Key Places
Jamaica
Cuba
Hispaniola
Trinidad and Tobago

Dorothy Samuels is a ten-year-old from Jamaica, a tropical island in the Caribbean Sea. She lives in a village near the ocean and goes to a village school. Dorothy is a good student. She hopes one day to go to college in Kingston, Jamaica's capital city. Jamaican laws require that women have as much opportunity to educate themselves as men do. Equality of women is important to Jamaican culture because many Jamaican women are independent farmers and business owners.

Dorothy's family are farmers. They plant yams and other vegetables and fruits. They also plant cocoa beans. Every Saturday, Dorothy's mother and grandmother take their fruits and vegetables to the market to sell. All the traders at the market are women.

▼ Many Jamaican women carry goods on their heads. This practice came to the Caribbean from Africa.

The People of the Caribbean

People in the Caribbean can make a living farming because most Caribbean islands have very fertile soil. These islands stretch over 2,000 miles (3,219 km) from Florida to the northeast coast of South America. As you might expect, a variety of peoples and cultures live within this large area.

The First People of the Caribbean The Caribbean islands are also called the West Indies because when Christopher Columbus arrived there, he thought he had reached the Indies in Asia.

The first people to live in the Caribbean were Native Americans, the Ciboney (SEE boh nay). The Ciboney lived on the islands for thousands of years. In about 300 B.C., they were joined by another indigenous group, the Arawaks (AR ah wahks), who came from South America. In about 1000, the Caribs (KA ribz), another South American group, arrived.

The Caribs gave the region its name. They lived there for more than 400 years before the first Europeans came to the area. Christopher Columbus and other Spaniards enslaved the Native Americans. Almost all of the Caribs, Arawaks, and other groups died of overwork and of diseases the Spanish brought with them. Today, just a few hundred Caribs still live on the island of Dominica.

Other Europeans followed the Spanish. They hoped to make money from the region's wealth of natural resources. Dutch, French, and English colonists began claiming territory in the 1600s. They built large sugar plantations and brought many enslaved Africans to work on them.

READ ACTIVELY

Predict What ethnic groups do you think live in the Caribbean today?

Caribbean Customs

	Jamaica	Puerto Rico	Dominican Republic
Greetings	A handshake; "Good morning/afternoon/evening"; use Mr., Mrs., Miss.	A handshake. Women kiss each other on the cheek.	Shake hands. Greet everyone when you enter a room. Ask about people's families.
Gestures	Show approval of an idea by touching fists. Suck air through your teeth to mean "Give me a break."	Wiggle your nose to mean, "What's going on?" Point with puckered lips.	Point with puckered lips. Clap hands to request your check in a restaurant.
Table Manners	Keep the fork in the left hand. If you buy food from a street cart, eat it on the spot.	Keep both hands above the table. Stay at the table after the meal to relax and chat.	Guests are served first and sometimes separately. They often are given more elaborate food than the hosts.
Clothing	Women wear colorful skirts and matching headdresses. Many people have tailors make their clothes. Jewelry is common.	Casual clothing is worn for everyday occasions. Parties and social events require formal clothing.	Dressing well is considered important. Clothing is always clean and well-pressed. Men have a traditional suit called a chacabana, which is a white shirt over dark trousers.

Chart Study When you visit another culture, knowing the local customs can help you understand what you see. **Critical Thinking** Name some customs that are unique to the United States.

Most of the Caribbean people today are descended from these Africans. Immigrants from China, India, and the Middle East also came to the area to work.

People in the Caribbean Today   Since slavery was legally ended in the Caribbean, its population has grown to about 36 million. Nearly one third of these people live on the region's largest island, Cuba.

Because so many people came to the Caribbean as colonists, slaves, or immigrants, the area has great ethnic variety. An **ethnic group** is a group of people who share race, language, religion, or cultural traditions. The ethnic groups of the Caribbean are Native American, African, European, Asian, and Middle Eastern.

Depending on their island's history, the people of a Caribbean island may speak one of several European languages. Their language may also be a mixture of European and African languages. For example, two countries and two cultures exist on the island of Hispaniola. On the eastern half is one country, the Dominican Republic. Its population is Spanish-speaking and mostly mestizo. West of the Dominican Republic is the country of Haiti. Nearly all of Haiti's people are descended from Africans. They speak French and Creole, which is a blend of French and African languages.

Most West Indians are Christians, but there are also small groups of Hindus, Muslims, and Jews. Some people practice traditional African religions.

A Caribbean Family

Family life is very important to people in the Caribbean. This family, from Montserrat, British West Indies, is made up of parents and their children. Many people in the Caribbean live in family groups that also include grandparents, uncles, aunts, and cousins.

Haiti was one of the first places where the work of folk artists was recognized as real art. Large, colorful murals comment on religious and political themes. Bus drivers gain prestige by painting public buses, called taptaps.

Food, Music, Art, and Fun

Caribbean culture is known for its liveliness. People play music, dance, and tell stories. People also play many sports. Baseball, soccer, and track and field are popular. On some islands, people also play cricket, which is a British game similar to baseball. Dominoes is a popular game throughout the region.

Food   Caribbean food is a mixture from all the cultures of the islands. Caribbean people can enjoy many types of seafood that are not found in U.S. waters. For instance, the people of Barbados love to eat flying fish and sea urchin eggs. Bammy—a bread made from the cassava plant—is still made the way the Arawaks made it. People also cook spicy curries from India, sausages from England, and Chinese dishes. Many tropical fruits grow on the islands. West Indians use the fruit to make many juices and other drinks that are not readily available in the United States.

Music   Caribbean music is famous around the world. Calypso is a form of song that uses humor in its lyrics. You may have heard reggae (REG ay) music. It is from Jamaica. Steel drums are Caribbean musical instruments. They are made from recycled oil drums. A steel drum can be "tuned" so that different parts of it play different notes. Players strike the instruments with rubberized drumsticks. The rubber hitting the drum makes an almost liquid sound.

LINKS TO MUSIC

Soca—Calypso with Soul
In the 1970s, a new form of Caribbean music evolved. It blended calypso with two other styles— funk and ska. Funk is an earthy, blues music. Ska is similar to reggae. The first song to use this music was Lord Shorty's "Soul Calypso." The name of the new musical form comes from the title "Soul Calypso." It is called *soca*.

Many people in Caribbean countries dress in lavish, colorful costumes to celebrate before Lent. **Critical Thinking** What similar celebrations take place in the United States?

Carnival Many islanders observe the Roman Catholic tradition of Lent, which is the period of 40 days before Easter Sunday. People consider Lent to be a very solemn time, so just before Lent they throw a huge party. The party is called **Carnival.**

Different countries celebrate Carnival in different ways. The biggest Carnival takes place in Trinidad and Tobago. People spend all year making costumes and floats. Lent always starts on a Wednesday. At 5 A.M. the Monday before, people go into the streets in their costumes. Calypso bands play. Thousands of fans follow the bands through the streets, dancing and celebrating. At the stroke of midnight Tuesday, the party stops. Lent has begun.

SECTION 2 REVIEW

1. **Define** (a) ethnic group, (b) Carnival.

2. **Identify** (a) Jamaica, (b) Cuba, (c) Hispaniola, (d) Trinidad and Tobago.

3. Who were the first inhabitants of the Caribbean islands?

4. Which traditions does modern Caribbean culture blend?

Critical Thinking

5. **Making Comparisons** What common elements in their histories have shaped the cultures of the various Caribbean islands?

Activity

6. **Writing to Learn** Select one aspect of Caribbean culture (food, music, celebrations, and so on) and jot down what you have learned about it in this section. Then, write ways in which it is similar to and different from your own culture.

The Cultures of South America

BEFORE YOU READ

Reach Into Your Background

Think about the books you read, the music you like to listen to, and the clothes you wear. These things are all part of your culture. How is your culture related to the history of your family and your region? How does the geography in your region affect your culture?

Questions to Explore

1. What major cultural groups live in South America?
2. How has geography created diversity in this region?

Key Terms

subsistence farming
import

Key Places

Andes
Chile
Argentina
Brazil

Between Peru and Bolivia is the deep lake called Lake Titicaca. It lies high in the Andes Mountains. This area is bitterly cold. There are few trees. Native Americans here make their living from totora reeds, a kind of thick, hollow grass that grows on the lakeshore. They use these reeds to make houses, mats, hats, ropes, sails, toys, roofs, and floors. They eat the reeds, feed them to livestock, and brew them into tea. Totora reeds can even be made into medicine. Long ago, some Native American groups built floating islands with totora reeds. They used the islands to hide from the Incas. Today, some Native Americans live on floating islands.

The People of South America

Most South Americans today are descended from Native Americans, Africans, or Europeans. In this way, they are like the people of Mexico and Central America. South America's history is also like that of its neighbors to the north. It was colonized mainly by Spain. Most South Americans speak Spanish and are Catholic. Each nation has its own unique culture, however.

▼ The Native Americans who live on Lake Titicaca use totora reeds to make boats.

Regions Within South America There are four cultural regions in South America. The first region includes Colombia, Venezuela, Guyana, Suriname, and French Guiana, which are in the northern part of South America. They each border the Caribbean Sea. The cultures of these countries are like those of the Caribbean islands.

To the south and west, the culture is very different. Peru, Ecuador, and Bolivia are Andean countries. Many Native Americans live high in the Andes. In Bolivia, there are more indigenous people than mestizos. The Quechua and Aymara (eye muh RAH) people each speak their own languages.

The third cultural region consists of Chile, Argentina, and Uruguay. The long, thin country of Chile has mountains, beaches, deserts, forests, and polar regions. Although its geography is diverse, its people are not. Most people in Chile are mestizos. The big cities of Argentina and Uruguay, however, are very diverse. Many different ethnic groups live there. Another culture exists on Argentina's Pampas, or plains. On the Pampas, gauchos (GOW chohz), or cowhands, herd cattle.

Brazil is South America's largest country. Brazil was a colony of Portugal. Its people speak Portuguese. However, Brazil is culturally diverse. Many Native Americans live in Brazil. So do people of African and European descent. Some Brazilians are of mixed descent. Many people have moved to Brazil from other countries. Brazil's largest city, São Paulo (sow PAW loh), is home to more Japanese than any other place in the world except Japan!

Connect How are the Pampas of Argentina like the plains of the United States?

Herding Llamas in Peru

Some of the indigenous people of the Andes raise llamas, a relative of the camel. Interaction How do you think the people of the Andes use llamas?

A Peruvian Scene

Yhaninc Puelles Enriquez
age 12
Cuzco, Peru

The scene shown by this student artist is similar to the photograph on the previous page. **Critical Thinking** How are the scenes in the art and the photograph alike and different?

Art and Literature in South America South America has produced many famous artists, novelists, filmmakers, and poets. Chilean poets Pablo Neruda (PAH bloh nay ROO duh) and Gabriela Mistral (gah bree AY lah mees TRAHL) both were awarded the Nobel Prize for their work. Neruda wrote about everyday objects, including rain, tomatoes, and socks. Mistral wrote for and about children. Colombian Gabriel García Márquez (gah bree EL gar SEE uh MAR kays) and Chilean Isabel Allende (EES uh bel ah YEN day) both are famous for writing novels telling about several generations of life in one family. García Márquez was awarded the Nobel Prize.

Country and City Life

South America contains cities with millions of people, but it also has vast areas with hardly any people at all. Many people still live in the countryside. Others are leaving farms and moving to cities.

Farming in South America Outside of Chile, Argentina, and Uruguay, most rural people with land of their own do **subsistence farming.** That means they grow only enough food for their families to eat. They only have small plots of land. Farmers plant corn, beans, potatoes, and rice.

Gabriela Mistral Chilean poet Gabriela Mistral was awarded the Nobel Prize for Literature in 1945. But Mistral considered herself to be more a teacher than a writer. Mistral taught school in rural Chile in the early 1900s, but she was frustrated by the low quality of the textbooks that were available. In response, Mistral began to write poetry and prose for children.

Very large farms grow crops to export to other countries. The main export crops of South America are coffee, sugar, cocoa, and bananas. Export farming uses so much land for cash crops that South America has to import food to eat. To **import** means to buy from another country.

Brasília

Brasília is a planned city. Some people think it looks like a bow and arrow. Others think it looks like a jet plane. Government offices and shopping areas are located in the middle of the city, where the two "wings" meet. The wings contain superblocks, or residential neighborhoods. Each includes 10 to 16 apartment buildings, a school, and shops. What would you like about living in a completely new city? What would you dislike?

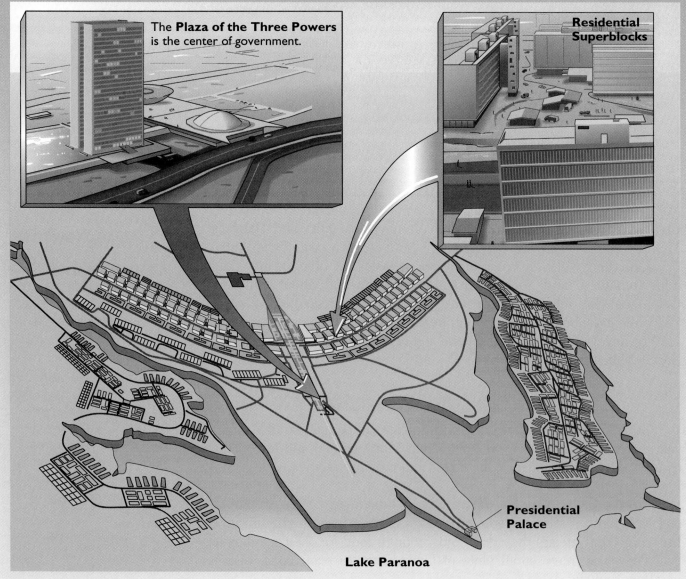

The **Plaza of the Three Powers** is the center of government.

Residential Superblocks

Presidential Palace

Lake Paranoa

The population of South America is booming. Latin America is the fastest-growing region in the world. Like Mexicans and Central Americans, South Americans cannot find enough jobs in rural areas. Every day, thousands of rural South Americans move to the cities looking for work.

South America's Cities The cities of South America illustrate the region's mix of cultures. Many major cities—Lima, Peru, and Buenos Aires, Argentina, for example—were built by Spanish colonists more than 400 years ago. Some of the buildings in these older cities follow Native American designs. In contrast, modern office blocks and apartment buildings of concrete, steel, and glass tower above the downtown areas. One or two cities were built quite recently. Brasília, the Brazilian capital, was constructed in the 1950s. It was a completely planned city, designed to draw people to the country's interior.

By contrast, one of the unplanned things about many South American cities is the slums. They are called *favelas* (fuh VEH luz) in Brazil and *barrios* (BAR ee ohs) in Venezuela. More and more people have migrated into the cities in recent years. Usually they have ended up in poor neighborhoods. City governments try to provide electricity and running water to everyone. But people move into cities so quickly that it is hard for city governments to keep up.

The Role of Women In some ways, women do not yet play a role equal to that of men in South America. Women in South America are more likely than men to be poor. They also do not attend school for as many years as men do.

More and more women in South America today are fighting to make a living for themselves and their children. They are demanding equal rights. Women are struggling for the rights to go to school, to get into different types of jobs, to have good health care, and to have a voice in government. Some women are getting bank loans to start small businesses. These businesses are sometimes based on traditional skills such as sewing, weaving, or preparing food.

HEROES

Working Together From 1976 to 1983, Argentina had a military government. The government took thousands of people prisoner. Many were never seen again. The mothers and grandmothers of the "disappeared" marched in protest every day for six years in Buenos Aires. Their actions forced the government to explain what happened to the missing people.

SECTION 3 REVIEW

1. **Define** (a) subsistence farming, (b) import.
2. **Identify** (a) Andes, (b) Chile, (c) Argentina, (d) Brazil.
3. What pressures does rapid population growth place on the countries of South America?
4. Name two ways in which the geography of South America has shaped how people live.

Critical Thinking

5. **Recognizing Cause and Effect** What is one cause of rapid population growth in the cities? What is one effect?

Activity

6. **Writing to Learn** Choose one region of South America you'd like to visit, and write a paragraph explaining why.

SKILLS ACTIVITY

Distinguishing Facts From Opinions

Kate was nervous, but excited. This was her first trip out of the United States. For two weeks, she had seen more fantastic things in Mexico than she could have dreamed of: beautiful countryside, ancient ruins . . . the list was endless. Now, she was about to start a new adventure.

Today, she would travel from Mexico City to Paplanta, a small town near the coast to the east. A fellow traveler had discouraged her. "The train trip is very long," she had said.

> The train trip is very long and boring!

> The train ride to Paplanta is three hours long.

"And boring. There's nothing to look at out the windows. The town is not interesting, either. You should skip that trip altogether."

"Hmmm," Kate thought as she pulled out her guidebook and train schedule. The guidebook said that the ruins of an old Spanish mission were located at Paplanta. The El Tajin ruins were also there. On Sundays, the town hosted an open-air market. The train schedule said it was only a three-hour train ride away, through mountainous country. "A long trip? Nothing to look at? Ha!" More determined than ever, Kate headed to the train station.

Get Ready

Kate decided to go to Paplanta because she relied on facts instead of opinions. Facts are statements that can be proved true. Opinions are beliefs. That the train ride was three hours long is a fact. The traveler's statement that the train ride "is very long" is an opinion. Distinguishing facts from opinions, as Kate found out, is a valuable skill.

Distinguishing facts from opinions is something you will need to do almost every day of your life. You will do it as you watch television, read books and magazines, and—like Kate—as you reach your own decisions.

How can you distinguish, or tell the difference between, facts and opinions? It's as simple as A-B-C:

A. Facts can be proved true.

B. Opinions cannot be proved true.

C. Opinions are often indicated by words and phrases like "I think," "I believe," "should," and "ought to," and by adjectives like "beautiful" or "ugly."

Ladinos make up about 50 percent of the population of Guatemala.

F

Guatemala is the most beautiful country in Latin America.

O

Try It Out

Learn to distinguish facts from opinions by playing a simple game. All you need are some note cards, a couple of pens, and a partner.

A. Deal the cards. Deal ten note cards to your partner and ten to yourself. Each of you should then write one fact or one opinion about Latin America on each of your note cards. You can get the facts from your textbook. The opinions should be your own beliefs. On the back of each note card, write an F if you wrote a fact and an O if you wrote an opinion. Don't let your partner see these!

B. Shuffle the cards. Shuffle your cards, and give them to your partner. Challenge him or her to identify each sentence as a fact or an opinion. Award one point for each correct answer. Give a bonus point if your partner can explain how the statement could be proved true if it is a fact or how your partner knew it was an opinion. Total your partner's score, and write it down.

C. Switch cards. Now try your hand at your partner's note cards. Compare scores. Which of you won? The winner should help the loser learn more about distinguishing fact from opinion.

Apply the Skill

Now distinguish facts from opinions in a real case.

1 **Read for understanding.** Read the paragraph in the box below once or twice, until you are sure you understand its meaning.

2 **Read for facts and opinions.** Now reread *one sentence at a time*. For each sentence, apply the A-B-C method of distinguishing facts from opinions. Ask yourself: A) Is this a fact that *can* be proved true? B) Is this an opinion that *cannot* be proved true? C) Are there words in the sentence that identify it as an opinion? Which sentences are facts and which are opinions? How could you prove the facts true? How do you know the other sentences express opinions?

Urbanization takes place when people move from rural areas to urban areas. I believe that urbanization in Mexico is a bad thing. First, the cities are already too crowded. There are thousands of homeless people in urban areas. Lots of people can't find jobs. Second, the city streets were not designed for so many cars. Traffic jams are a huge headache. Finally, the water and electric systems do not have the capacity to serve more people. I think the time has come for the government to try to stop urbanization.

Review and Activities

Reviewing Main Ideas

1. **(a)** What are maquiladoras?
   (b) Why are they important to the economy of Mexico?
2. To which country are some Mexicans and Central Americans emigrating to find jobs?

3. **(a)** Who were the first people on the Caribbean islands?
   (b) What happened to those people?
4. What are some of the musical styles that began in the Caribbean?

5. How do some of the people of the Andes make a living?
6. **(a)** How is the country of Chile geographically diverse?
   (b) How is Brazil culturally diverse?

Reviewing Key Terms

Decide whether each statement is true or false. If it is true, write "true." If it is false, change the underlined term to make the statement true.

1. Border factories are called <u>mestizos.</u>
2. <u>Indigenous</u> people are descendants of a region's first inhabitants.
3. To <u>emigrate</u> is to move from one's home country to another country.
4. Many Mexicans become <u>pampas</u> in the United States because they cannot find jobs in their home countries.

5. Ethnic <u>diversity</u> refers to people with a variety of cultures, customs, religions, or languages.
6. <u>Imports</u> occur when a government does not respect people's human rights.
7. To <u>immigrate</u> means to buy from another country.

Critical Thinking

1. **Making Comparisons** Consider these three regions: Mexico and Central America; the Caribbean; South America. What do the cultures of these regions have in common? How are they different?
2. **Recognizing Cause and Effect** What is the main reason that many Latin Americans move from one region or one country to another?

Graphic Organizer

Copy the chart to the right onto a separate sheet of paper. Then fill in the empty boxes to complete the chart.

	Mexico and Central America	The Caribbean	South America
Languages			
Religions			
Ethnic Background			
Special Features			

Map Activity

For each place listed below, write the letter from the map that shows its location.

1. Andes
2. Argentina
3. Brazil
4. Honduras
5. Jamaica
6. Mexico City
7. Trinidad and Tobago

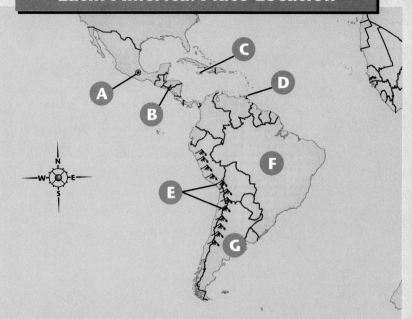

Latin America: Place Location

Writing Activity

Writing a Magazine Article

In this chapter, you've taken a guided tour of the cultures of Latin America. Write an article for a travel magazine describing the "high points" of your tour. As you write, consider how historical events and geography influenced the region's culture.

Internet Activity

Use a search engine to find the site **Mexico OnLine Mexican Art and Culture Directory.** Explore several links to learn about various aspects of Mexican culture. Make a travel brochure highlighting some of your favorite findings, create a portfolio of Mexican culture, or give a class presentation on the aspect that interested you the most.

Skills Review

Turn to the Skill Activity.

Review the steps for distinguishing facts from opinions. Then, write a brief paragraph about the cultures of Latin America that includes both facts and opinions.

How Am I Doing?

Answer these questions to help you check your progress.

1. Can I explain how the cultures in a region reflect its history?

2. Can I explain how most people make a living in the countryside?

3. Can I identify the reasons why many people in Latin America are moving from rural to urban areas?

4. What information from this chapter can I use in my book project?

Exploring Mexico and Central America

MAP ACTIVITIES

Look at the map above. Notice that the shape of Mexico and Central America is like a funnel, wide at the top and narrowing to a point. To learn more about this region, complete the following activities.

Study the map
How many countries are there in Central America? What bodies of water do they border?

Consider the geography
Mexico is a large country, while the countries of Central America are small. How do you think geography helped divide Central America into small countries?

Mexico

ONE FAMILY'S MOVE TO THE CITY

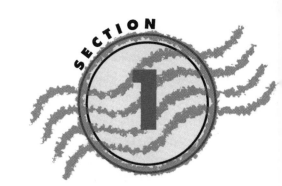

SECTION 1

BEFORE YOU READ

Reach Into Your Background

Have you ever moved from one house to another or from one city to another? Did you have to change schools? Think about what the move was like and make a few notes about how you felt at the time.

Questions to Explore

1. Why have many Mexicans been moving from the countryside to the city?

2. What challenges do Mexicans from the country face when they build new lives in the city?

Key Terms
squatter
plaza
migrant farmworker

Key Places
Mexico City

R amiro Avila (rah MEE roh ah VEE lah) is one of seven children. He grew up in the state of Guanajuato (gwah nuh HWAH toh), in central Mexico. In his small village, Ramiro knew everyone and everyone knew him.

Ramiro's family were campesinos who owned no land. Even as a young child, Ramiro had to work to help support the family. He and his father had jobs as farm laborers. They worked on someone else's farm. They made less than a dollar a day.

The Move to Mexico City

Ramiro's village is located in the southern part of the Mexican Plateau. This area has Mexico's best farmland. It also is home to more than half of the country's people. Not surprisingly, it is the location of Mexico's largest city— Mexico City. Find Mexico City on the map on the previous page.

When Ramiro was 13, his parents decided to move the family to Mexico City. They hoped to find better work. The city was far away and their lives would be completely different. But moving offered them a chance to make a decent living.

Mexico's Population

Chart Study What pattern of population movement does this chart show?

	Total Population	Urban (%)	Rural (%)
1995	93,986,000	71.0	29.0
2000*	102,912,000	77.7	22.3
2010†	120,115,000	81.6	18.4

* Estimated population
† Projected population

Country Profile: Mexico

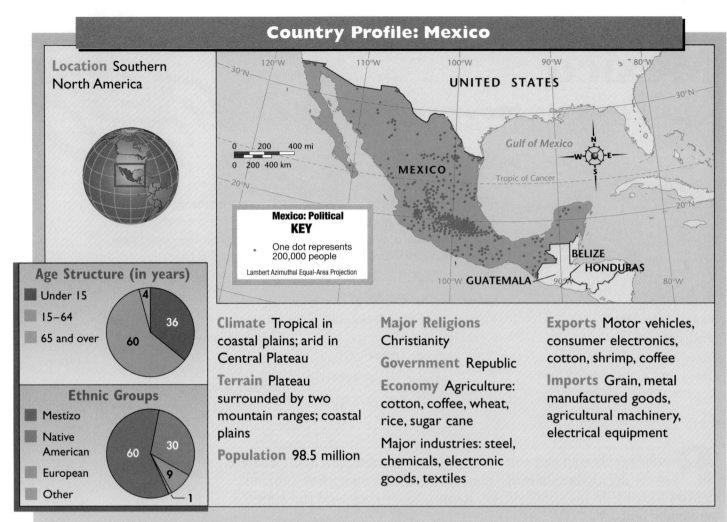

Location Southern North America

Age Structure (in years)
- ■ Under 15
- ■ 15–64
- ■ 65 and over

(pie chart: 4, 36, 60)

Ethnic Groups
- ■ Mestizo
- ■ Native American
- ■ European
- ■ Other

(pie chart: 60, 30, 9, 1)

Mexico: Political KEY
- One dot represents 200,000 people

Lambert Azimuthal Equal-Area Projection

Climate Tropical in coastal plains; arid in Central Plateau

Terrain Plateau surrounded by two mountain ranges; coastal plains

Population 98.5 million

Major Religions Christianity

Government Republic

Economy Agriculture: cotton, coffee, wheat, rice, sugar cane

Major industries: steel, chemicals, electronic goods, textiles

Exports Motor vehicles, consumer electronics, cotton, shrimp, coffee

Imports Grain, metal manufactured goods, agricultural machinery, electrical equipment

Map Study The map above shows Mexico's population distribution. Some parts of Mexico are sparsely populated, while others are very crowded.

Location Where do most of Mexico's people live? Why do you think that they live in that area and not elsewhere?

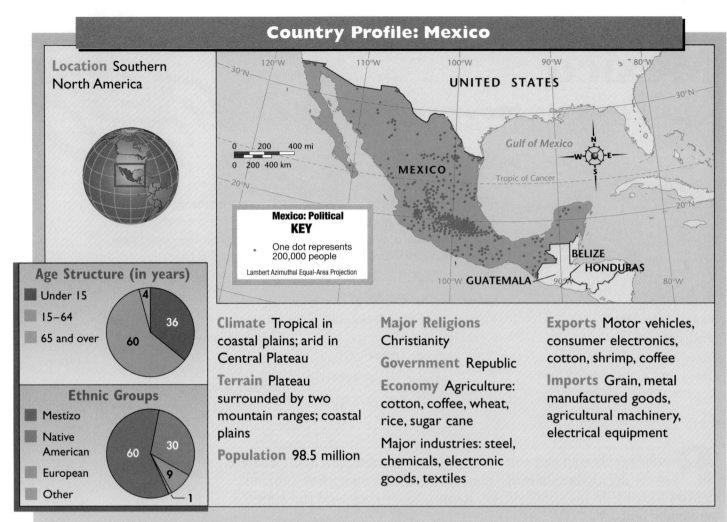

Ask Questions What would you like to know about campesinos who move to the city from the countryside?

Housing in the City Like thousands of other campesino families coming to the city, Ramiro's family did not have much money. When they arrived in Mexico City, they could not afford a house. They went to live in Colonia Zapata, which is one of many neighborhoods where poor people become **squatters.** That means they settle on someone else's land without permission. Many small houses of squatters cling to the sides of a steep hill in the Colonia. The older houses near the bottom of the hill are built of concrete. However, most people cannot afford to make sturdy houses when they first arrive. Therefore, many of the newer houses higher up the hill are constructed of scrap metal.

Ramiro's family made a rough, one-room house of rock. Ramiro felt that his new house was ugly. He and his family hoped that soon they would be able to buy land from the government. Then they could build a real house with a garden and a patio.

Work and School   Ramiro went to school in Mexico City, but he also worked as a cook in a tiny restaurant. He started work at 7 A.M. and worked until 2 P.M., preparing scrambled eggs and sausage. For these seven hours of work he earned about $3. His mother and some of his brothers and sisters worked, too. Ramiro went to a school that held night classes, attending classes until 9:30 at night.

Ramiro's father could not get a job in Mexico City. He decided to go to Texas in the United States. He found work as a farm laborer there. He sent money home every month. The move to Mexico City brought a lot of responsibilities for Ramiro. It became his job to look after his younger brothers and sisters while his father was gone. Ramiro's life was very different from how it had been in his village.

Life in Rural Mexico

Before Ramiro's family moved, they lived in a village where life has changed little over the years. Every village has a church and a market. At the center of most villages is a public square called a **plaza.** Farm families grow their own food. If they have extra food, they sell it at the market. Rural people buy nearly everything they need—clothing, food, toys, housewares—at the market rather than in stores.

Markets of Rural Mexico

This photograph shows a market in Oaxaca, Mexico. People in rural Mexico buy many of their groceries and housewares from markets like these. **Critical Thinking** What details in this photograph show similarities between rural markets and urban supermarkets? What details show differences?

Farm Work   Most farm families in Mexico and Central America are poor. Many campesinos work their own small farms. They often plow the land and harvest their crops by hand because they cannot afford expensive equipment. **Migrant farmworkers** do not own land. Like Ramiro and his father, they work on large farms owned by rich landowners. Migrants travel from one area to another, picking the crops that are in season.

Lack of Jobs   Mexico's population has risen dramatically over the last 20 years. The country's population is growing at a rate of more than two percent each year—one of the highest rates in the world. There is not enough farm work for so many people. A large family cannot support itself on a small farm. And there are not enough jobs for all the migrant workers. Many people move to the cities because they cannot find work in the countryside.

About 70 percent of Mexico's people now live in cities and large towns. Many of them live in Mexico City. If you count the people in all the outlying areas, Mexico City has over 23 million people. Only Tokyo, Japan, has more people than Mexico City.

Mexico City: A Megacity

Mexico City is huge. Its population sprawls over a large area. It is a megacity, an urban center where many of Mexico's people live. Unlike most big cities, Mexico City does not have many skyscrapers and major streets. Two- and three-story buildings still form its downtown. Only a

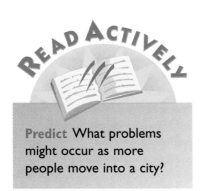

Predict What problems might occur as more people move into a city?

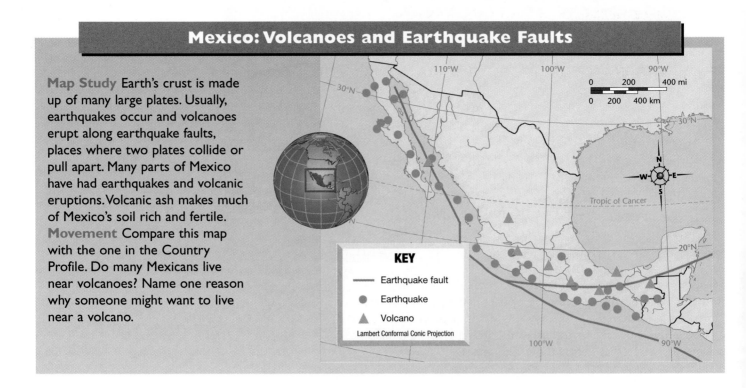

Mexico: Volcanoes and Earthquake Faults

Map Study Earth's crust is made up of many large plates. Usually, earthquakes occur and volcanoes erupt along earthquake faults, places where two plates collide or pull apart. Many parts of Mexico have had earthquakes and volcanic eruptions. Volcanic ash makes much of Mexico's soil rich and fertile. **Movement** Compare this map with the one in the Country Profile. Do many Mexicans live near volcanoes? Name one reason why someone might want to live near a volcano.

KEY

— Earthquake fault

● Earthquake

▲ Volcano

Lambert Conformal Conic Projection

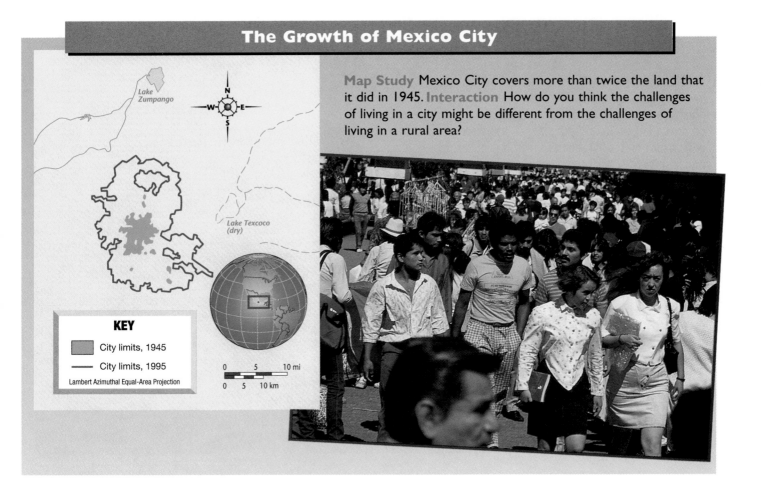

The Growth of Mexico City

Lake Zumpango

Lake Texcoco (dry)

KEY

City limits, 1945

City limits, 1995

Lambert Azimuthal Equal-Area Projection

0   5   10 mi
0   5   10 km

Map Study Mexico City covers more than twice the land that it did in 1945. **Interaction** How do you think the challenges of living in a city might be different from the challenges of living in a rural area?

few streets are wide enough for the city's traffic. The subway, the underground railroad system, carries thousands of people each day.

Small neighborhoods of very wealthy people are tucked away from the rest. But most of Mexico City's residents are not wealthy. They live in all areas of the city. The poorest, like Ramiro and his family, live on the outskirts. Some must travel several hours a day to get to their jobs and back.

Pollution and Geography   Because the cities have grown so large, Mexico's capital and other large cities in the region are facing problems of pollution and traffic jams. Four million cars and trucks jam Mexico City's narrow streets. They compete with taxis, trolleys, and buses. Mexico City's location traps pollution close to the city. The city spreads across a bowl-shaped valley. The mountains surrounding the valley stop winds from carrying away factory smoke, automobile exhaust fumes, and other pollution. The pollution creates smog. It hangs over the city like a black cloud.

Making a Living   Large cities offer many ways to make a living. Factories and offices employ millions of people. Thousands more sell goods from stalls in the street. Ramiro's sister, Carmela, is a street vendor. She sells juice at a stand in the bus station near their neighborhood.

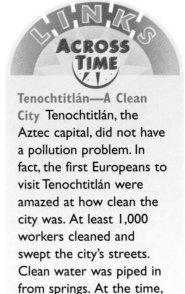

LINKS
ACROSS TIME

Tenochtitlán—A Clean City Tenochtitlán, the Aztec capital, did not have a pollution problem. In fact, the first Europeans to visit Tenochtitlán were amazed at how clean the city was. At least 1,000 workers cleaned and swept the city's streets. Clean water was piped in from springs. At the time, European cities did not have fresh, clean water.

LATIN AMERICA   **87**

Even on a sunny day, buildings a few blocks away appear dim and blurry in Mexico City because of smog. **Interaction** Why do you think Mexico City has so much smog? How do you think the smog affects the way people in Mexico City live?

Every morning, she gets up at 5:30 to make juice from oranges and carrots. People on their way to work buy her juice for their long trip into the city.

Mexico City is not the only city that is growing. All of Mexico's major cities are becoming more crowded. City life is not easy for most Mexicans. Hard work and hope are what keep people going.

SECTION 1 REVIEW

1. **Define** (a) squatter, (b) plaza, (c) migrant farmworker.

2. **Identify** Mexico City.

3. What is the main reason that rural people from all over Mexico have been moving to the cities?

4. What difficulties do rural people face when they move to Mexico City?

Critical Thinking

5. **Expressing Problems Clearly** How do the lives of rural Mexicans improve when they move to the city? How do their lives continue to be difficult?

Activity

6. **Writing to Learn** Write an entry in your journal comparing and contrasting Ramiro's life with your own. How are your lives different? What similarities do you notice?

Guatemala

DESCENDANTS OF AN ANCIENT PEOPLE

BEFORE YOU READ

Reach Into Your Background

Have you ever felt that you had an important opinion about something, but no one was listening to it? What are some ways that people can voice their opinions?

Questions to Explore

1. How are the indigenous people of Guatemala a unique culture?

2. What are the main issues that indigenous people face?

3. What kinds of changes have been taking place in Guatemala recently?

Key Terms
ladino
ethnic group
political movement
strike

Key Places
Guatemala

Juanita Batzibal (wahn EE tah baht zee BAHL) had a childhood "like all Indian girls, at the side of my mother, making tortillas and learning to weave and embroider." Juanita is Guatemalan, and was born in the town of Patzun (paht ZOON). She is also Cachickel (kahkt chee KAHL), which is one of many Mayan groups in Guatemala. The mountains of Juanita's homeland are beautiful. But Juanita's family was poor. Though her family raised corn on a tiny plot of land, they could not earn enough money to survive. Juanita had to weave throughout her childhood to bring in extra money. She hoped to go to school one day. She remembered, "my big dream was to study economics or literature...."

The Struggle for Land

Juanita's childhood home was in the mountains of Guatemala. This southern neighbor of Mexico is "first" in Central America in many categories. For example, it has the largest population among Central American countries. To learn more about Guatemala, study the Country Profile on the next page.

▼ Most Mayas who live in the highlands of Guatemala have only small plots of land to farm.

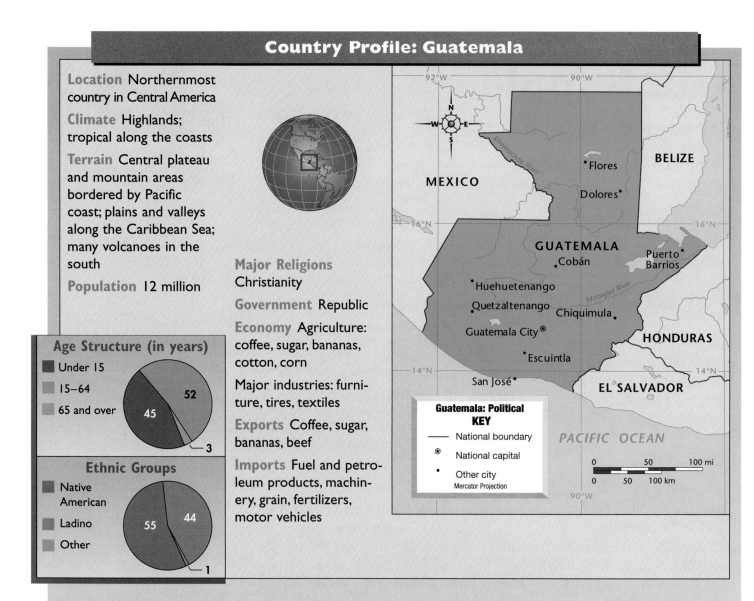

Location Northernmost country in Central America

Climate Highlands; tropical along the coasts

Terrain Central plateau and mountain areas bordered by Pacific coast; plains and valleys along the Caribbean Sea; many volcanoes in the south

Population 12 million

Major Religions Christianity

Government Republic

Economy Agriculture: coffee, sugar, bananas, cotton, corn

Major industries: furniture, tires, textiles

Exports Coffee, sugar, bananas, beef

Imports Fuel and petroleum products, machinery, grain, fertilizers, motor vehicles

Age Structure (in years)

- Under 15
- 15–64
- 65 and over

52
45
3

Ethnic Groups

- Native American
- Ladino
- Other

55
44
1

MEXICO

Flores
Dolores

BELIZE

GUATEMALA
Cobán

Puerto Barrios

Huehuetenango
Quetzaltenango
Chiquimula

Guatemala City ⊛

Escuintla

HONDURAS

San José

EL SALVADOR

Guatemala: Political
KEY
— National boundary
⊛ National capital
• Other city
Mercator Projection

PACIFIC OCEAN

0   50   100 mi
0   50   100 km

Map Study This map shows the country of Guatemala. **Location** What four countries border Guatemala? **Chart Study** The chart on the bottom left shows the percentages of ethnic groups in Guatemala. Most Mayas live in rural communities, speak a Mayan language, and follow Mayan customs. Ladinos speak Spanish, have adopted Spanish customs, and often live in towns or cities. **Critical Thinking** Which ethnic group do you think has been more involved in Guatemala's government? Why?

Most Mayas lived in the mountains because it was the only land available to Native Americans. Most land in Guatemala belongs to a few rich families. The rich landowners of Guatemala are **ladinos** (luh DEE nohs), mestizos who are descended from Native Americans and Spaniards. Native Americans who follow European ways are also considered to be ladinos.

Though families like Juanita's worked hard to make their land produce crops, they often failed. The soil of the Guatemalan highlands is not very good, and soil erosion is a serious problem there. The Mayas have had many challenges to overcome.

Losing Their Homes During most of Juanita's childhood, there was a civil war going on in Guatemala. The Mayas were caught in the middle. Indigenous people do not always think of themselves as citizens of the country in which they live. A Mayan woman is more likely to think of herself as a Maya than as a Guatemalan.

Also, most Native Americans in Guatemala cannot read or write. Most Mayas have not filed any papers with the government showing that they own land. The Mayas often have no way to prove that their land belongs to them. Mayan people worked hard for many years to grow crops. But then the civil war and landowners caught up with them.

In hundreds of villages throughout Guatemala, soldiers came to challenge the Mayas. Sometimes the landowners sent them to claim the Mayas' land for themselves. Other times, they just wanted to exert control over the Mayas by taking away their land and possessions from them.

Mayan survivors from these villages have similar stories to tell. Most of them lost all of their belongings and were forced out of their villages. Many Mayas had to move to other countries to live. Juanita, for example, had to start her life over again in Costa Rica.

ACROSS THE WORLD

The Sami The Sami live in the far north of Norway, Sweden, Finland, and Russia. The governments of these countries consider the Sami their citizens. Most Sami, however, look upon themselves as part of a separate nation. In recent years, the Sami have won some degree of self-government. The Sami of Norway, for example, have their own elected assembly.

A Guatemalan Market

Mayas in rural Guatemala do much of their shopping at open-air markets like this one. **Movement** What types of goods are being traded or sold at this market?

Mayan communities each have their own hand-woven style of clothing. **Critical Thinking** What skills do you think are needed to weave cloth into a certain pattern?

Overcoming Obstacles Justina Tzoc travels through rural Guatemala, teaching Quiché Maya women about their rights and teaching them to read. Her work is dangerous, because she sometimes travels through areas that are torn by civil war. But Tzoc is determined to help every woman she can reach.

A 500-Year-Old Struggle Juanita's story is a common one. The indigenous people of Guatemala have fought against injustice for 500 years. They started when the Spanish first arrived.

The Spanish conquered Native Americans by force. Many were killed. Others died of hunger or the hardships of slavery. Still others died from European diseases. In many Latin American countries, there are few indigenous people left.

But in Guatemala, Native Americans are the majority of the population. They form 23 ethnic groups. An **ethnic group** is a group of people who share the same language, ancestors, culture, or religion. The indigenous groups of Guatemala are related to each other. However, each group is different. Each has its own language and customs. Juanita is Cachickel Maya; the largest group is the Quiché Maya.

The Peace Process in Guatemala

Juanita Batzibal now teaches classes on Mayan culture in Costa Rica, and also conducts international seminars. Her goal is for Mayas inside Guatemala to learn about and be proud of their unique culture and traditions. In her words, "we want to write with our own hands and speak with our own mouths what we feel."

Other Mayas have started **political movements**, which are large groups of people who work together to defend their rights or to change the leaders in power. One such movement, called Nukuj Akpop (noh KOOHJ ahk POHP), is striving to fight poverty and bring human rights to Mayas. Their Founding Declaration states, "Our cries, pain, and woe from the last several hundred years have begun to end, and now we can begin to listen to our own voices."

Some Mayan political movements seek to defend campesino rights. People involved in these movements help villages plan ways to protect themselves. They teach people the history of their land and how to read. They also help organize meetings, protests, and **strikes**, or work stoppages. Above all, they are determined to defend Native American land rights.

All of these efforts have brought about change in Guatemala. For the first time, Mayas have gained a voice in their own government. For example, Guatemala's government appointed 21 Mayan priests to advise officials about Mayan culture. New Mayan organizations are being formed every day. In addition, Mayan languages are being used in books, newspapers, and radio programs.

In 1996, a number of agreements were signed in Guatemala, paving the way for peace. Among these was a promise that indigenous communities would be rebuilt. However, the agreements are only one step toward real peace. It is up to the people of Guatemala—both ladino and Mayan—to make sure that equality and justice are carried out. As one Guatemalan points out, "The war was difficult. But I think the next phase, the building of the peace, will be even harder."

Ask Questions What questions would you like to ask a member of a Mayan political organization about his or her activities?

SECTION 2 REVIEW

1. **Define** (a) ladino, (b) ethnic group, (c) political movement, (d) strike.

2. **Identify** Guatemala.

3. How does Juanita Batzibal describe her childhood?

4. How do most indigenous people in Guatemala make a living? What difficulties do they face?

Critical Thinking

5. **Identifying Cause and Effect** Explain the main reason that Guatemala's indigenous people and other farmers have formed a political movement.

Activity

6. **Writing to Learn** Write a short essay explaining what you would have done if you were a Mayan villager during the civil war. Then, explain what you would do if you were the president of Guatemala.

Previewing a Reading Selection

Sean asked his mom if he could go for a bike ride before it got dark. His mom said, "Sure, if you finish your homework first." Sean didn't have much homework. "If I can finish it in an hour," Sean thought to himself, "I'll have a whole hour for a killer mountain bike adventure."

He settled down to study. His assignment was to answer ten questions about the Panama Canal using two books he had checked out from the school library. He read the first question: "What are three obstacles workers faced when building the Panama Canal?" He picked up the first book and began reading on page 1. Five pages and 10 minutes later he didn't have his answer. He tried the other book. Ten pages and 20 minutes later he still hadn't found what he was looking for. "Half an hour gone and not one question answered!" he thought, disgustedly. "No bike ride tonight!"

Sean missed out on his bike ride because he forgot to apply an important skill: previewing. Previewing means looking over a book or chapter before you read it or try to find information in it. Previewing is a valuable study skill that will help you read more efficiently.

Get Ready

How do you preview? You might be surprised to learn that this is one skill you already know! If you've ever seen a preview for a movie, you've "previewed" that movie. You have a gen-

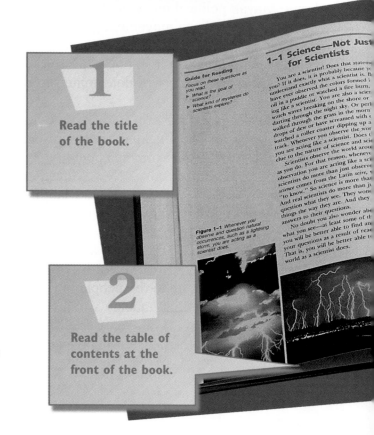

1 Read the title of the book.

2 Read the table of contents at the front of the book.

eral idea what the movie is about. If you've ever looked over a menu, you've "previewed" your meal. You have a general idea of what the food will be like.

Of course, previewing a reading selection is a little different from previewing a movie or meal. Previewing means looking over something you are about to read in a general way to become familiar with it. The idea is to get a "sense" of the material. To get a sense of what a book is about, you can use five things: the title, the table of contents, the illustrations, the index, and sample paragraphs. To do this with a chapter, you can use titles, subtitles, illustrations, and captions.

3 Study the illustrations throughout the book. They include pictures, charts, diagrams, and maps.

4 Thumb through the book, reading short passages.

5 Scan the index at the back of the book.

Try It Out

You can practice previewing a book in a fun and easy way by playing a "What Does It Tell Us?" game with a group of six students. Choose your group members, and choose a book. Then sit down and preview it together. Your group will follow the script to the right. After each person reads his or her part to the group, the other group members should work together to answer the question. Group Member 6 is the group secretary, who writes the answers down.

Group Member 1: "The title indicates the main subject of the book. Many books have a subtitle that gives even more information. What does the title of our book tell us?"

Group Member 2: "The table of contents is like a menu at a restaurant. It tells us what general topics are available in the book. What does the table of contents tell us?"

Group Member 3: "The illustrations in a book provide clues to the subjects discussed in the book. What do the illustrations tell us about the book?"

Group Member 4: "The index lists the specific topics in a book and the pages where they are discussed. What does the index tell us about the content of our book?"

Group Member 5: "By thumbing through a book and reading a few paragraphs here and there, you can get an idea of how a book is written. You can see if there are special headings in the book. What does a little reading tell us about our book?"

When you've completed this process, use the secretary's notes to find specific information in the book. If you are going to read the whole book, this process can help you get the most out of your reading.

Apply the Skill

Now that you know how to preview, practice by previewing Chapter 4. What do the titles and subtitles tell you about the chapter? How about the illustrations and captions? Take notes as you preview the chapter. Then, use your notes to write a short description of the chapter. Finally, as you read through the chapter, see how it matches your description.

Panama

WHERE TWO OCEANS MEET

BEFORE YOU READ

Reach Into Your Background

Have you ever agreed to a deal or given away something and then wondered if you made the best choice? Think about how you felt. Write down some ways you might try to undo the deal.

Questions to Explore

1. What geographic and political factors made Panama a good site for a canal?
2. How was the Panama Canal built?
3. How did Panama gain control of the Panama Canal?

Key Term
lock

Key Places
Panama Canal
Canal Zone

The Panama Canal is the shortcut of the Western Hemisphere. It's the only way to get from the Pacific Ocean to the Atlantic by ship without going all the way around South America. That's a savings of 7,800 miles (12,553 km).

But be prepared to wait. Traffic jams can leave you bobbing in the ocean for up to 20 hours. Then the trip through the 40-mile (64.4-km) canal takes another eight hours. That's about walking speed. Then there is the toll: as much as $34,000.

Going Through the Canal

Cruising through the Pacific Ocean, a tanker approaches the city of Balboa, in the country of Panama. It is heading for the Panama Canal. The ship is loaded with petroleum. Other ships sailing toward the canal carry lumber, metal ores, and other cargo. Ships pass through the Panama Canal 24 hours a day, 365 days a year. The canal is crowded. The tanker must get in line.

The tanker enters the canal at sea level. But parts of the canal go through mountains and are not at sea level. The tanker will need to be raised and lowered several times as it travels toward the Atlantic Ocean.

Miraflores Lock   The ship sails north to Miraflores (mee ruh FLOR uhs) Lock. A **lock** is a section of waterway in which ships are raised or lowered by adjusting the water level. The tanker passes through a set of gates into a lock chamber. The water in the chamber is still at sea level. Then, more water comes pouring into the chamber

Country Profile: Panama

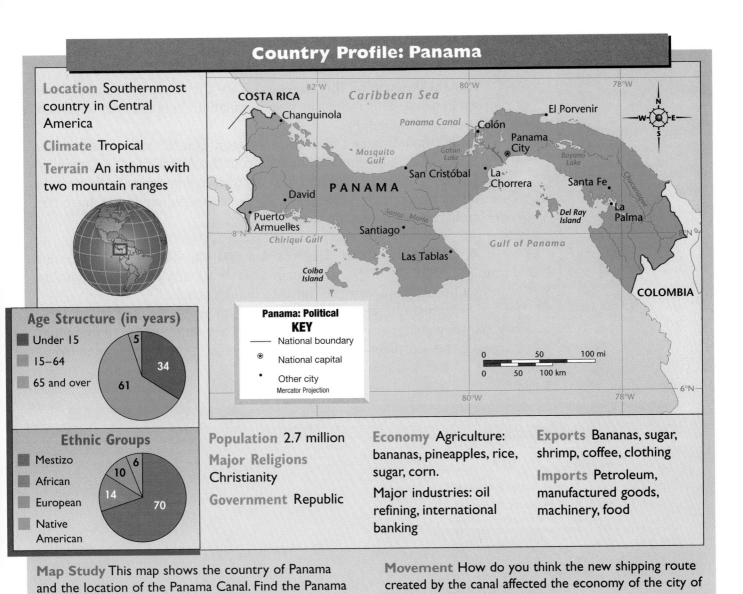

Location Southernmost country in Central America

Climate Tropical

Terrain An isthmus with two mountain ranges

Age Structure (in years)
- Under 15 — 5
- 15–64 — 61
- 65 and over — 34

Ethnic Groups
- Mestizo — 70
- African — 14
- European — 10
- Native American — 6

Panama: Political
KEY
— National boundary
⊛ National capital
• Other city
Mercator Projection

Population 2.7 million

Major Religions Christianity

Government Republic

Economy Agriculture: bananas, pineapples, rice, sugar, corn.

Major industries: oil refining, international banking

Exports Bananas, sugar, shrimp, coffee, clothing

Imports Petroleum, manufactured goods, machinery, food

Map Study This map shows the country of Panama and the location of the Panama Canal. Find the Panama Canal on the map.

Movement How do you think the new shipping route created by the canal affected the economy of the city of Colón? Explain your answer.

through valves. The tanker rises like a toy boat in a bathtub filling with water. When the water rises high enough, the ship passes through a second set of gates and enters a small lake. It proceeds to the next lock, and the water level is raised again.

Galliard Cut During the voyage, the tanker will pass through two more sets of locks. It will zigzag through the eight-mile (13-km) Galliard (GAL yurd) Cut. The Galliard Cut was blasted through the hard rock of Panama's mountains. The tanker will sail through a huge artificial lake and past an island that is home to a wild game preserve. Finally, eight hours after entering the canal, the tanker exits at Limón (lih MOHN) Bay in the city of Colón (kuh LOHN). It has traveled only 40 miles (64 km), but it is now in the Atlantic Ocean.

The Idea for a Canal Takes Hold

Look at the map on this page and trace the route the canal follows across Panama. This waterway has dominated life in Panama for much of the twentieth century.

Sailors had dreamed of a canal through Central America since the 1500s. A canal could shorten the trip from the Atlantic to the Pacific by thousands of miles. It would cut the cost of shipping goods by thousands of dollars for each ship. But not until the 1900s did engineers have the technology to make such a canal.

A Struggle Over Rights to Build The first real attempt came in 1881. At that time, Panama was part of Colombia. Colombia gave a French company the rights to build a canal.

Digging through Panama posed several problems for the builders. First, they struggled with mud slides as they dug. Second, a mountain range, the Cordillera de San Blas (kord ul YEHR uh day san blas),

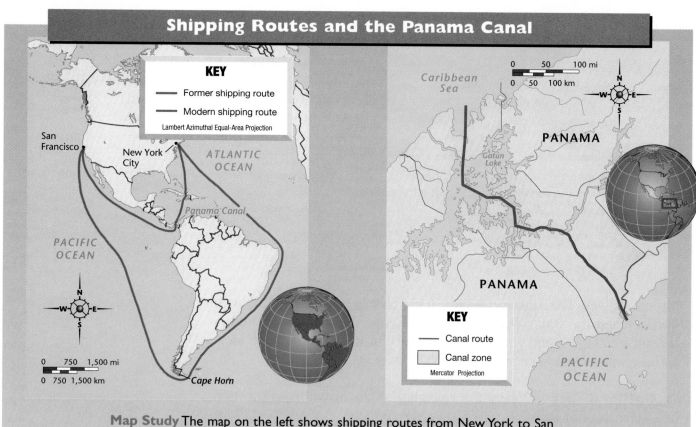

Map Study The map on the left shows shipping routes from New York to San Francisco before and after construction of the Panama Canal. The map on the right is a close up of the Panama Canal route. Before the Panama Canal was built, ships had to travel more than 13,000 miles (20,900 km) around South America. After the Canal was built, ships only had to travel 5,200 miles (8,370 km). **Movement** Why do you think that Panama and the United States both wanted to control the Canal Zone?

Panama's Tropical Rain Forest

Panama's Barro Colorado rain forest is inside the Canal Zone. **Critical Thinking** This photograph shows a trail through the rain forest. Where is it? Based on this photograph, think of some difficulties that might have faced the Panama Canal workers.

blocked the way. Disease was also a problem. Much of Panama is covered with dense tropical forest. Tropical diseases such as malaria and yellow fever killed many workers. After several years of digging and blasting, the French company went bankrupt. Work on the canal stopped.

In 1902, the United States government bought what was left of the French company. Then, the United States began talks with Colombia about getting the rights to continue building a canal.

Colombia refused to grant the United States rights to build the canal. The businesspeople of Panama were disappointed. They knew that a canal would bring business to Panama. They wanted the canal to be built as soon as possible. Also, many Panamanians wanted to be free of Colombia's rule. They saw the canal as a chance to win independence.

In November 1903, the United States helped Panama revolt against Colombia. Two weeks after Panama declared its independence, the United States received the rights needed to build the canal.

LINKS ACROSS THE WORLD

Not Made in Panama You would assume the "Panama hat," a hand-woven straw hat, is made in Panama. However, you would be wrong—the hats were originally made in Ecuador. They were named for Panama because it was a shipping center for hats in the 1800s. Ecuadorans still make the Panama hat. But today, many hats are made even farther from Panama—in Asia.

Like Digging Through Sand

The cut through Panama's soft earth hills was the hardest part of the canal to build. Earth still slides into the canal there today. **Movement** Based on the picture on the left, how were workers and supplies moved to and from the canal?

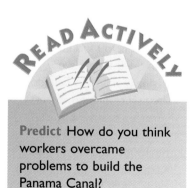

Predict How do you think workers overcame problems to build the Panama Canal?

Building the Canal The builders of the canal faced numerous problems. They had to scoop out and remove mountains of earth and rock. The hills were made of soft earth. Whenever the diggers carved out a hole, more earth would slide into its place. The project called for a dam to be built to form a lake. There were locks to design and build.

While the work was difficult and slow, by far the biggest problem facing the project was disease. Some 25,000 workers had died of malaria and yellow fever while the French worked on the canal. Scientists did not know what caused these diseases, so they could do little to prevent them.

In the early 1900s, doctors discovered that malaria and yellow fever were both carried by mosquitoes. The mosquitoes bred in swamps and also in people's drinking water. In 1904, the Panama Canal Company hired a doctor and a large crew to deal with the mosquito problem. It took one year, 1,000 tons (907 metric tons) of timber, 200 tons (181 metric tons) of wire mesh, and 4,500 workers to do the job. Workers burned sulfur in every house to kill mosquitoes. They covered every water vessel with mesh so mosquitoes could not get in. They filled in swampy breeding grounds with dirt. Without this effort, the Panama Canal probably could not have been built.

Modern medicine and machinery were important to the project. So was good planning. Still, it took eight years and the sweat of 45,000 workers, mostly Caribbean islanders, to make the waterway. The Panama Canal remains one of the greatest engineering feats of modern times.

Control of the Canal

When the United States gained rights to build a canal, it signed a treaty with Panama. The treaty gave the United States the right to build the Panama Canal, and to control it forever.

The Canal Zone The United States also controlled an area called the Canal Zone. The Canal Zone included the land on either side of the canal, the ports, the port cities, and the railroad. The treaty allowed the United States to run the Zone according to its laws, and gave the United States the right to invade Panama to protect the canal.

Many Panamanians felt this was too high a price to pay for the privilege of having the canal in their country. The canal gave the United States a great deal of power in Panama. The United States built 14 military bases in the Canal Zone and stationed thousands of soldiers there.

For years, Panama talked with the United States about regaining control of the canal. In the 1960s and 1970s, many Panamanians grew angry. They rioted to protest U.S. control.

A Change of Ownership In 1978, after years of talks, U.S. President Jimmy Carter signed two new treaties with Panama's government. The Panama Canal Neutrality Treaty and the Panama Canal Treaty gave Panama more control over the canal. In 1999, Panama finally gained full control of the Panama Canal.

READ ACTIVELY

Ask Questions What would you like to know about life near the Canal Zone?

SECTION 3 REVIEW

1. **Define** lock.

2. **Identify** (a) Panama Canal, (b) Canal Zone.

3. How did a canal come to be built in Panama?

4. What difficulties did the builders of the canal face?

5. How did the United States gain control of rights to build the canal?

6. Two sets of treaties have determined the control of the Panama Canal, the original treaty of 1903 and two in 1978. Describe the terms of these treaties.

Critical Thinking

7. **Identifying Central Issues** It has been very important to Panamanians to regain control of the canal. Explain why, in both political and economic terms.

Activity

8. **Writing to Learn** Imagine that you are a newspaper editor in 1900. Decide whether you think Panama or Nicaragua is a better choice for the location of the canal, and write a short editorial defending your position.

Review and Activities

Reviewing Main Ideas

1. Describe the movement of Mexicans from one area to another—rural to rural, rural to urban. Why do many people make these moves?
2. What problems has Mexico City experienced as a result of its rapid population growth?

3. How are the indigenous cultures of Guatemala distinct from the ladino culture?
4. What are the main challenges that indigenous Guatemalans face?
5. How did the United States gain the rights to build a canal in Panama?

6. **(a)** Why was the canal important to the United States and Panama?

   (b) How did control of the canal recently change?

Reviewing Key Terms

Match the definitions in Column I with the key terms in Column II.

Column I

1. a landless person who travels from one area to another working other people's land
2. a section of a waterway in which ships are raised or lowered by adjusting the water level
3. a person who settles on someone else's land without permission
4. a work stoppage
5. a public square
6. people who share race, language, religion, and cultural traditions

Column II

a. squatter

b. plaza

c. migrant farmworker

d. ethnic group

e. strike

f. lock

Critical Thinking

1. **Identifying Central Issues** What are the main demands that Mayas have made of the government and landowners? How has the government responded?
2. **Drawing Conclusions** Over the years, the United States has exercised a great deal of economic and political influence in Central America. How does the history of the Panama Canal demonstrate U.S. influence in the region? What do you think the changes that took place over the control of the canal say about U.S. influence in the region today?

Graphic Organizer

Copy the tree map onto a piece of paper. In the first set of boxes, note the three kinds of population movement. In the second set, note details about these movements.

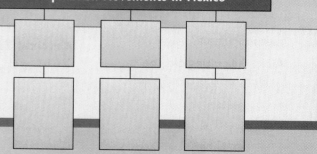

Population Movements in Mexico

Map Activity

For each place listed below, write the letter from the map that shows its location.

1. Guatemala
2. Colón, Panama
3. Panama
4. Mexico City

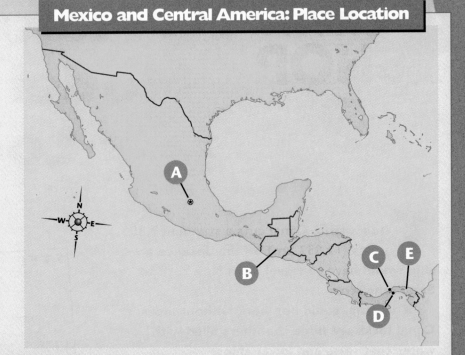

Mexico and Central America: Place Location

Writing Activity

Writing News Stories
Imagine you are a writer for a radio news program. Write brief news stories on population movements in Mexico, the work of political movements, and the history of the Panama Canal. Be sure that each of your stories can be read in two to three minutes.

Internet Activity

Use a search engine to find the site **Ancient Guatemala.** Read **Our Mayan Legacy.** Then, click on **Guatemalan Home Page.** Click on the links **Modern Guatemala** and **Our People.** Make a chart comparing the architecture, language, people, and culture of ancient and modern Guatemala.

Skills Review

Turn to the Skill Activity.
Review the steps for previewing. Then use these steps to preview Chapter 5. Based on your preview, write a brief paragraph describing what you expect to read in the chapter.

How Am I Doing?

Answer these questions to help you check your progress.

1. Can I explain why a Mexican family might decide to leave the countryside for the city?
2. Do I understand the major challenges that face the indigenous peoples of Guatemala?
3. Can I describe the building of the Panama Canal and its impact on the Panamanian people?
4. What information from this chapter can I use in my book project?

Making a Model Canal Lock

The Panama Canal cuts a stunning 7,800 miles (12,553 km) off the distance a ship would have to travel from New York to San Francisco.

The canal could not work without locks. Canal locks are huge chambers filled with water that raise and lower ships.

The Panama Canal needs locks because the sea level at the Atlantic and the Pacific entrances to the canal is not the same. Also, the path of the canal is not level—it goes up one slope to the continental divide and down the other.

STEP ONE
gates
wax
tape

STEP TWO
cork
paper clip

Purpose

The best way to understand how canal locks work is to build a model of one. As you complete this activity, you will understand how a real ship travels through a real canal.

Materials

- two half-gallon cardboard juice or milk cartons
- modelling wax
- scissors
- duct tape
- a ballpoint pen
- a cork
- a paper clip
- a pitcher of water

Procedure

STEP ONE

Construct a model canal and lock. Follow the illustrations. Cut the cartons in half lengthwise. Line up three of the four halves lengthwise and connect them on the outside with duct tape. Then carefully cut out the walls of cardboard that separate the boxes and divide your canal. Line three edges of each cut-out wall with modelling wax. Then replace the walls. Use

STEP THREE

both gates in

cork

STEP FOUR

first gate is out

cork

both gates in

cork

cork

second gate is out

both gates in

cork

enough wax to make a watertight seal. These are the gates in the canal lock.

STEP TWO

Use the pen, cork, and paper clip to make a model ship. Look at the picture for an example. Stick the paper clip into the bottom of the ship to make it float upright.

STEP THREE

Fill your canal with water. Fill one end and the middle of the carton with water about one inch deep. Fill the other end with water almost to the top. Float your boat in the end of the canal with the lower water level.

STEP FOUR

Operate the canal lock to raise your ship to the higher water level. Remove the gate that separates your ship from the middle chamber. Sail your ship into the middle chamber and close the gate behind it by carefully replacing it. To raise your ship to the next level, slowly pour water into the middle chamber until the water level matches the level in the last chamber. Remove the second gate, sail your ship into the last chamber, and replace the gate. You have successfully navigated a canal!

Observations

❶ How did you raise your ship from one level to a higher level?

❷ Why does the canal lock need gates to work?

ANALYSIS AND CONCLUSION

1. How do you think the water level is raised in a real lock?

2. Repeat the activity in reverse. How will you lower your ship?

Exploring the Caribbean

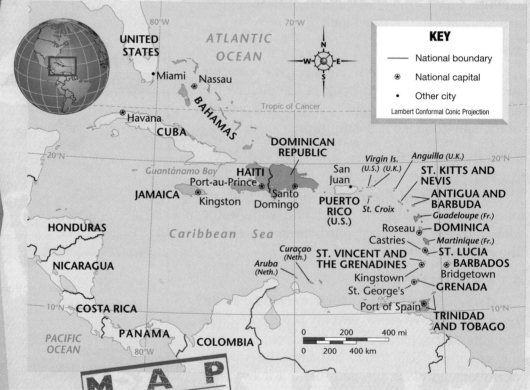

M A P
ACTIVITIES

The islands of the Caribbean
stretch about 1,500 miles
(2,414 km) across blue-green
waters. Each island has its own
traditions and cultures. To learn
more about the Caribbean,
complete the following activities.

Understanding geography
How do you think the sea may
have affected the economies of the
Caribbean islands?

Study the map
Before the Europeans arrived in
the region, how do you think the
sea may have served as both a
highway and a barrier to contact
with other people?

Cuba

CLINGING TO COMMUNISM

Reach Into Your Background

Suppose that you had to move tomorrow and you could pack exactly one suitcase. You could never come back for the things you left behind. What would you pack?

Questions to Explore

1. What is life in Cuba like today?
2. What ties do Cuban Americans have to Cuba?

Key Terms

dictator
communist
exile
illiterate

Key People and Places

Fidel Castro
Fulgencio Batista
Miami

Twelve-year-old Venesa Alonso (vuh NEH suh uh LAHN zoh) lives in Miami, Florida. Her home is just a few miles away from the ocean. Venesa hardly ever goes to the beach, however. The blue waves and roaring surf remind her of her trip from Cuba to the United States. The memory still gives her nightmares.

Venesa and her family left Cuba in the summer of 1994. They built a rickety raft and carried it to the ocean. They were among the 35,000 Cubans who took to the sea that summer. They sailed on anything that would float—rubber tires, old boats, and home-made rafts. One hope kept them going. It was the thought of making it to the United States. They planned to apply to enter the United States as immigrants.

Venesa's family and thousands of others left Cuba for two main reasons. The first reason was that Cuba's economy was in bad shape. People often did not have enough food to eat. Clothing, medicine, and other basic necessities were hard to get. A desire for freedom was the second reason why many people left. Cuba's leader, Fidel Castro (fee DEL KAS troh), does not allow Cubans to speak out against government policies they disagree with.

▼ Cubans trying to reach the United States in 1995 took to the sea in boats like this one.

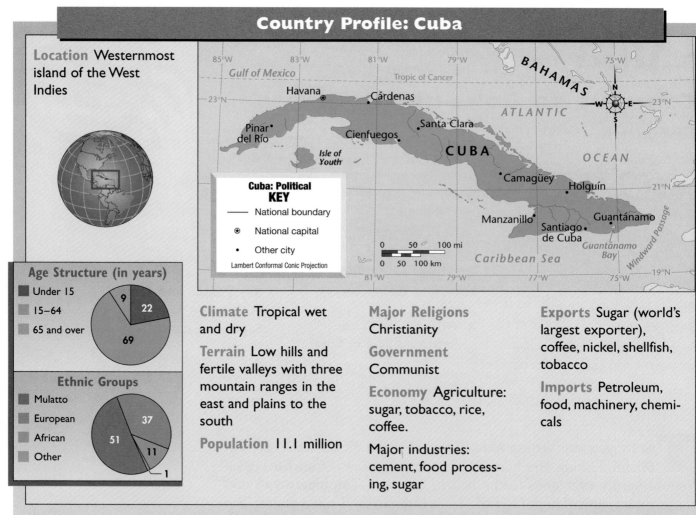

Location Westernmost island of the West Indies

Age Structure (in years)
- Under 15
- 15–64
- 65 and over

9
22
69

Ethnic Groups
- Mulatto
- European
- African
- Other

37
51
11
1

Cuba: Political KEY
- National boundary
- ⊛ National capital
- • Other city

Lambert Conformal Conic Projection

0   50   100 mi
0   50 100 km

Climate Tropical wet and dry

Terrain Low hills and fertile valleys with three mountain ranges in the east and plains to the south

Population 11.1 million

Major Religions Christianity

Government Communist

Economy Agriculture: sugar, tobacco, rice, coffee.

Major industries: cement, food processing, sugar

Exports Sugar (world's largest exporter), coffee, nickel, shellfish, tobacco

Imports Petroleum, food, machinery, chemicals

Map Study Hundreds of thousands of Cubans have left Cuba in recent years. Many Cubans traveled on small boats and on rafts made of plywood and inner tubes. They were trying to cross 90 miles (145 km) of ocean to reach Florida. **Location** What is the capital of Cuba? Where are Cuba's capital and most of its major cities located?

Cuba's History

Cuba is a small country. It is about the size of the state of Pennsylvania. Cuba's farmland is fertile, and Cuba is the third largest sugar producer in the world. Look at the political map in the Activity Atlas in the front of your book. Cuba is located between the two entrances to the Gulf of Mexico. It also has excellent harbors. This makes it a good place to trade with the United States and other parts of the Caribbean. But Cuba's relationship with the United States and many of its neighbors has not been friendly since the 1960s.

Cuban Independence Cuba's government and economy were not always like they are now. Cuba was a Spanish colony. In 1898, the United States defeated Spain in the Spanish-American War, and Cuba won its independence. In the years that followed, Cuba became the richest country in the Caribbean. Sugar planters made money

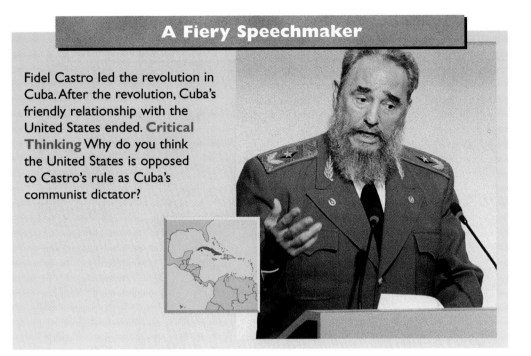

A Fiery Speechmaker

Fidel Castro led the revolution in Cuba. After the revolution, Cuba's friendly relationship with the United States ended. **Critical Thinking** Why do you think the United States is opposed to Castro's rule as Cuba's communist dictator?

READ ACTIVELY

Ask Questions If you could interview Fidel Castro, what questions would you ask him?

selling to people in the United States. Hotels were built, and tourists came to Cuba to enjoy its beautiful beaches and great climate. Many Cubans became businesspeople, teachers, doctors, and lawyers.

Not all Cubans shared the country's wealth, however. Most farm and factory workers earned low wages. Cuba also had many harsh leaders who ruled as dictators. A **dictator** is a ruler who has complete power. In the 1950s, Fulgencio Batista (fool HEN see yoh bah TEE stah) was Cuba's leader. During his rule, some people formed rebel groups to remove Batista and change the country.

Communism in Cuba   A young lawyer named Fidel Castro led one of these small rebel groups. He tried three times to overthrow the government during the 1950s. By his third attempt, he had gained many supporters. Finally, Batista gave up and left the country in 1959.

When Batista left, Fidel Castro took control of Cuba. He still holds power today. Castro's government is **communist.** In a communist country, the government owns all large businesses and most of the country's land. Under Castro, the Cuban government took over private businesses and land. Further, Castro said that newspapers and books could print only information supporting his government. Anyone who disagreed with government policy was put in jail. Huge numbers of Cubans fled the island. Many settled in Miami, Florida.

Cuba became a communist country in the early 1960s. At the same time, it became friendly with the Soviet Union. The Soviet Union was then the most powerful communist nation in the world. It sent money and supplies to Cuba. The United States and the Soviet Union, however, were not friendly. As a result, Cuba's relationship with the United States became tense. Relations grew worse when the United States openly welcomed the people who fled from Cuba.

CITIZEN HEROES

To Be a Leader When José Martí grew up in Cuba in the 1800s, it was still a colony of Spain. At age 16, he started a newspaper dedicated to Cuban independence. Martí later became famous for his poems and essays. In 1895, he led the revolution that eventually liberated Cuba. By the time independence was achieved, however, Martí had died in a battle with the Spanish.

There is a large Cuban American community in Miami, Florida. These men are playing dominoes in a Miami park. Behind them is a mural showing the presidents of many countries in the Western Hemisphere.

Cubans Leaving Cuba

Lydia Martin left Cuba in 1970. She was only six years old. Her mother had grown tired of the limits on freedom and lack of opportunity in communist Cuba. She wanted to take Lydia to the United States with her. Lydia's father begged her to stay.

"For years [my mother] had been anxious to leave Cuba . . . to take me to a place where I could learn about freedom. Her exit papers had finally arrived, but my father wouldn't let me go. . . . There was no talking sense into a man who feared losing his little girl forever. . . . While my mother was away at the church, I called him.

"I'm leaving with my mother," I told him with all the bravery a six-year-old could muster. . . .

"Have you stopped to think you may never see me again?" my father asked. . . . "

Cuban Exiles Many Cuban exiles tell stories like Lydia's. An **exile** is a person who leaves his or her homeland for another country because of political problems. From the 1960s onwards, large numbers of people left Cuba. Many families were torn apart.

Dreams of Returning to Cuba Some Cubans never got over the loss of their home. In the 1970s, relations between the United States and Cuba grew worse. Even if she wanted to, Lydia Martin could not write to her father. The government might punish him if he got a letter from the United States. Still, Lydia hoped to reunite with him one day. Lydia's mother now spoke of Cuba with longing. She said that in Cuba, the sky was bluer, the sand whiter, and the palm trees greener.

In 1991, the government of the Soviet Union collapsed and could no longer help Cuba. Food, medicine, tools, and other necessities became more scarce. Lydia began worrying about her father and her other relatives. In 1995, she flew back to the island for the first time. Visitors from the United States are not always welcome in Cuba, especially if they once fled the island. Lydia was nervous.

Cuba: Today and Tomorrow

When Lydia stood on the beach in Cuba, she thought of her mother. Her mother had been right. The sky did seem bluer here, the sand whiter, and the palm trees greener.

Lydia had heard about the food shortages in Cuba, but she had not known how bad they were. Her father's new family sometimes had little more than rice to eat. When Lydia unpacked the shoes, soap, powdered milk, and underwear she had brought, her father and his new family took them with joy. They cooked her a delicious meal of lobster and rice on her first night. They had been saving money for it for months.

LINKS ACROSS THE WORLD

Livan Hernandez At 21 years old, Livan Hernandez was close to becoming a star pitcher in the Cuban Baseball League. He left Cuba for a chance to make millions of dollars pitching for a major league team in the United States. If that decision sounds easy, consider that Hernandez left behind everyone who is dear to him in Cuba. Hernandez hopes his family can one day enjoy the same freedom he has found.

◄ After Lydia Martin (left) departed from Cuba, she did not see or talk to her father (right) again for 25 years.

A Cuban High School

At many of Cuba's rural schools, students spend four hours in the classroom and four hours doing manual labor. **Critical Thinking** How is this school similar to yours? How is it different?

One thing that Cubans do not need to save money for is education. In the 1960s and 1970s, Castro overhauled Cuba's schools. At the time, many Cubans were **illiterate,** or unable to read and write. Castro sent students and teachers into the countryside to teach. Soon, more Cubans could read and write than ever before. Today, about 95 percent of Cubans can read and write.

Schools in Cuba may have helped many Cubans to learn how to read. However, they teach only communist ideas. But because Cuba is close to the United States, Cubans can tune in to American radio stations. Cuban teenagers listen to popular American dance music. They wear jeans from the United States whenever they can get them. Castro has allowed some businesses to be privately owned. The tourist industry is growing.

No one knows what Cuba's future will bring. Many think the time is near when those who left Cuba will be able to return home to visit or live there in freedom.

SECTION 1 REVIEW

1. **Define** (a) dictator, (b) communist, (c) exile, (d) illiterate.

2. **Identify** (a) Fidel Castro, (b) Fulgencio Batista, (c) Miami.

3. How did the collapse of the Soviet Union affect Cuba's economy?

4. What problems did communism bring to Cuba?

Critical Thinking

5. **Drawing Conclusions** Do you think that Cubans born in the United States feel as strongly about Cuba as their Cuban-born parents do? Why or why not?

Activity

6. **Writing to Learn** Work with a partner. One of you will write a letter to a relative in Cuba from the point of view of a Cuban exile in the United States. The other will write a response from the point of view of a Cuban who has never left Cuba.

Haiti

THE ROAD TO DEMOCRACY

BEFORE YOU READ

Reach Into Your Background

Is there something in your life that you have had to try many times to achieve? What strate-gies did you use to try to get what you wanted? Did they work? Why or why not?

Questions to Explore

1. How did Haiti's struggle for democracy affect people's lives?

2. How does the history of Haiti affect the culture of its people?

Key Terms

Creole
dialect

Key People and Places

Jean-Bertrand Aristide
Toussaint L'Ouverture
François Duvalier
Jean-Claude Duvalier
Port-au-Prince

▼ After his exile, Haitian President Jean-Bertrand Aristide returned to Haiti amid cheers of support.

The plane dipped toward Port-au-Prince (port oh PRINS), the capital of Haiti. It flew over a spreading slum. The slum was a neighborhood of crumbling cardboard huts with tin roofs. In the streets, people were jammed into a solid mass. All heads turned up toward the sky.

As if in one voice, a cheer of joy rose from the crowd. In the plane, Haiti's president, Jean-Bertrand Aristide (zhan behr TRAHND uh ris TEED), was returning to his country after a three-year exile. He had been elected by the people, but Haiti's military had forced him to leave. Then, a group of generals had taken over the country. The United States and other nations had pressured the military to give power back to Aristide. Many hoped that Aristide's return would also bring back democracy.

Haiti's Struggle for Democracy

Aristide was the first president to be elected democratically in many years. This does not mean that most Haitians did not want democracy. Their country was born out of a desperate struggle for freedom. Haiti is the only nation in the Americas formed from a successful revolt of enslaved Africans.

113

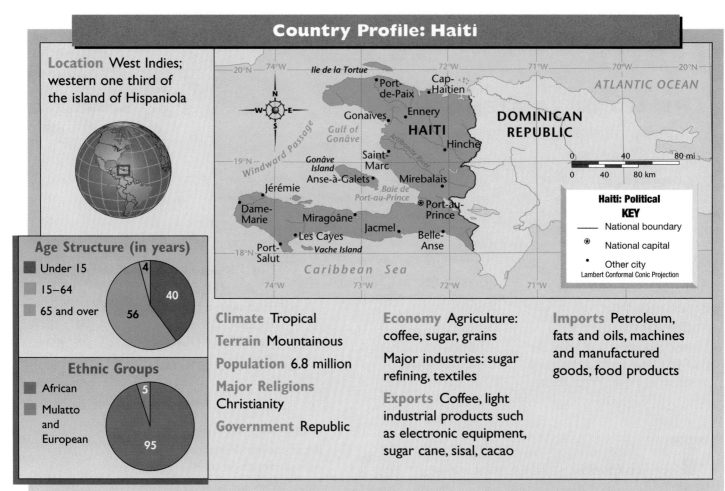

Country Profile: Haiti

Location West Indies; western one third of the island of Hispaniola

Age Structure (in years)
- Under 15
- 15–64
- 65 and over

4
40
56

Ethnic Groups
- African
- Mulatto and European

5
95

Climate Tropical

Terrain Mountainous

Population 6.8 million

Major Religions Christianity

Government Republic

Economy Agriculture: coffee, sugar, grains

Major industries: sugar refining, textiles

Exports Coffee, light industrial products such as electronic equipment, sugar cane, sisal, cacao

Imports Petroleum, fats and oils, machines and manufactured goods, food products

Haiti: Political KEY
— National boundary
⊛ National capital
• Other city
Lambert Conformal Conic Projection

Map and Chart Study This map shows the country of Haiti. Haiti is on the island of Hispaniola. **Region** What other country is on the island? Find the city of Cap-Haïtien. This is near the spot where Columbus landed in 1492. **Location** On what side of the island is Cap-Haïtien? In 1492, the Arawaks lived on Hispaniola. Look at the chart of ethnic groups. Do the Arawaks, a Native American group, still live in Haiti? What group makes up the largest part of the population?

The Birth of Haiti   As you can see on the Country Profile above, Haiti lies on the western third of the island of Hispaniola. Haiti was once a colony of France. Europeans brought enslaved Africans to Haiti to work on sugar cane and coffee plantations. In the 1790s, slave revolts began. A Haitian leader named Toussaint L'Ouverture helped banish slavery from Haiti in 1801. He also offered Haitians a new way of life, based on the idea that all people could live as equals.

Troubled Years In the years that followed, Toussaint L'Ouverture's goal of freedom and equality was never fully realized. Most of Haiti's presidents became dictators once they got into power. One of the worst was François Duvalier (frahn SWAH doo VAHL yay), who took power in 1957. Because Duvalier had been a country doctor, Haitians called him "Papa Doc."

Papa Doc died in 1971. He was followed by his son, Jean-Claude Duvalier (zhan KLAHD doo VAHL yay), or "Baby Doc." Both Papa Doc and Baby Doc were cruel leaders. They stole government funds and used violence to keep power. During their rule, Haiti became the poorest country in the Western Hemisphere.

In 1986, rebels forced Baby Doc to leave the country. Many Haitians thought a period of freedom and prosperity was about to begin. But this was not to be. Haiti was ruled by one military leader after another. And most Haitians still made a living trying to farm small plots of land.

READ ACTIVELY

Connect How do most people in the United States make a living?

Life on a Farm When farmer Pierre Joseph stands at the top of his land, he can see the calm waters of the Caribbean. When he looks down, he sees the dry, cracked earth of his one acre.

About two thirds of the people in Haiti make their living by farming. The land has been overused. Most trees have been cut. Rains wash the topsoil into the sea. Joseph is thin because he rarely gets enough to eat. "The land just doesn't yield enough," he says. He points to the few rows of corn and beans that he can grow on his one acre.

Farmers like Pierre Joseph can barely make a living, but many feel they are rich in other ways. Haitian culture blends African, French, and West Indian tradition. The blend of traditions gives Haiti a Creole culture. **Creole** is a word referring to people of mixed ancestry.

Creole also refers to the dialect spoken in Haiti. A **dialect** is the different version of a language that is spoken in a particular region. The Creole dialect is based on both French and African languages.

Papa Doc and Baby Doc

François (left) and Jean-Claude Duvalier (right) often used violence to rule Haiti. The country also became much poorer during their rule. By the time Baby Doc was forced from power, the average Haitian earned only about $300 a year.

Life in the City Haiti's capital, Port-au-Prince, is a blend not only of cultures, but also of rich and poor. The wealthy live in spacious wooden houses on the hills overlooking the city. There is a small middle class of doctors, lawyers, teachers, and owners of small businesses, that also live fairly well. Many poor people from the country live in tiny homes of crumbling concrete.

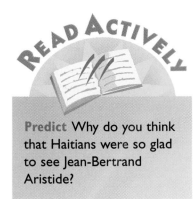

Predict Why do you think that Haitians were so glad to see Jean-Bertrand Aristide?

Hopes for the Future

In December 1990, Jean-Bertrand Aristide was elected president. Haitians held high hopes for the future. Aristide was a Catholic priest who had long defended the rights of the poor. He took office in February 1991.

A Military Takeover Aristide served as president for seven months. Then Haiti's military forced him to leave the country. The military also attacked his supporters. "We have been in hiding since police shot up our house in October," an Aristide supporter told reporters in 1991. "We got away because people warned us they were coming."

The year after the election, thousands of Aristide supporters fled the capital. They feared for their lives. They squeezed into trucks by the dozen and went to hide in the hills. Others tore their homes apart to make rafts. Then they took to the sea. Many headed for the United States. Some were sent back.

Cange Walthe
age 12
Haiti

This student drawing of rural Haiti contrasts with the urban scene on the next page. **Critical Thinking** What clues does this student provide to show that this village is in a rural area? What clues show that the village is in a place that has a tropical climate?

A Rural Village in Haiti

Haiti's people danced in the streets of Port-au-Prince when they heard that Aristide was returning to the country. They hoped that peace would return to Haiti along with Aristide.

Hundreds of children also left Haiti on rafts. Fifteen-year-old Fresenel Pierre (frehz uh NEL pea EHR) was one. He had an older brother waiting for him in Miami, where there is a large Haitian community. The children Fresenel sailed with were the children of Aristide supporters. Many were coming to the United States with no one to take them in.

Good Times and Bad   In 1994, Aristide came back to Haiti, restoring democratic government. Haitians rejoiced, believing that peace and progress would follow. Instead, by 1998, quarreling between Haiti's parliament and its new president, René Préval, had nearly shut down the government. A powerful hurricane struck Haiti that same year, leaving more than 150,000 homeless and destroying precious crops. As a result, Haiti remains the poorest nation in the region, and its people continue to face an uncertain future.

SECTION 2
REVIEW

1. **Define**   (a) Creole,
   (b) dialect.

2. **Identify**   (a) Jean-Bertrand Aristide, (b) Toussaint L'Ouverture, (c) François Duvalier, (d) Jean-Claude Duvalier, (e) Port-au-Prince.

3. How did Haiti win its independence?

4. What obstacles to making a living do farmers like Pierre Joseph face?

Critical Thinking

5. **Making Comparisons** Give an example of how Haitian culture blends African and European traditions.

Activity

6. **Writing to Learn**   Write a diary entry from the point of view of Pierre Joseph about how economic and political conditions in Haiti affect his life.

Locating Information

M arisol felt like a sailor lost at sea.

She was surrounded by an ocean of information. Shelves overflowing with books towered above her. Beyond the bookshelves, more shelves loomed, filled with magazines. Past the magazines were computer terminals. Enough information to fill millions of pages could be accessed through them. Although she was in her community library, Marisol felt just as lost as if she were adrift in a lifeboat.

Marisol had gone to the library to find information about Toussaint L'Ouverture. Marisol had read in her textbook how L'Ouverture had led the Haitian people to freedom more than 200 years ago. Marisol's assignment was to write a one-page biography, or life story, about L'Ouverture. One question loomed in her mind: Where should she begin?

Get Ready

Locating information is an essential skill. Throughout your school career, you will need to locate information to complete homework assignments and class projects. As an adult, you will need to locate information to help you decide many things such as where to live, what job to do, and how to do it.

The first rule about locating information is *Don't panic!* Marisol felt lost in the library. But libraries and other sources of information are carefully designed to make your search for information as easy as possible. Just like a sailor at sea, it's a matter of choosing your destination, planning your route, and finally sailing to the one little island where the information you need is located.

Try It Out

Locating the information you need can be an exciting adventure. When you locate the information you've been searching for, you will feel the satisfaction and excitement of an explorer who finds the right island. Work with a partner to plan a voyage out into the Sea of Information:

A. Choose your destination. Your destination is the information you need. You and your partner should pick one now, and write it down. It might look like this: *"Destination: Information about how many Cubans live in the United States."*

B. Determine the best way to get there. Just as there are many ways to travel, there are many ways to locate information. Five important routes to information are listed in the box to the right. Discuss each source of information with your partner. Choose the source most likely to have the information you seek.

C. Prepare for your journey. You're about to depart, so pack your bags! You'll need a notebook and a pencil to jot down information. You might need a few coins for the copy machine.

D. Use signposts. Just as signposts can help you find your way on a real journey, different "signposts" can help you on your journey to find information. Read about these "signposts" in the box.

Five Important Routes To Information

Libraries Most of the world's information is stored in libraries. *Signposts:* the card catalog and librarians.

Books There are books about nearly every subject. *Signposts:* book titles and tables of contents.

Periodicals Magazines and newspapers can provide up-to-date information on a huge range of topics. *Signposts:* magazine indexes and newspaper indexes found in libraries.

The Internet The Internet is a worldwide network of computers containing information. *Signposts:* special electronic search indexes on the Internet.

People By interviewing experts, you can learn what they know about their specialties. *Signposts:* the telephone directory to locate appropriate people to interview.

Apply the Skill

Now that you've made an information-seeking journey with a partner, it's time to do it alone. Choose one of the following destinations:

- Destination: Information that identifies the chief agricultural product grown in Cuba.

- Destination: Information that identifies the President of Haiti.

- Destination: Information that identifies three historic sites you could visit in Puerto Rico.

Once you have reached your destination by locating the information, draw a map to show how you found it.

Puerto Rico

CULTURAL IDENTITY OF A PEOPLE

BEFORE YOU READ

Reach Into Your Background

Do you ever feel that you have "two selves"? One that acts a certain way with some people? And another that comes out when you are with other people? Are both of them the real you?

Questions to Explore

1. What factors influenced Puerto Rican culture?

2. What is Puerto Rico's relationship with the United States?

Key Terms
citizen
commonwealth
constitution

Key Places
San Juan
Condado

Puerto Rican Esmeralda Santiago (ez mur EL duh sant ee AHG oh) can never forget the first time she saw the movie *West Side Story.* She was living in New York. It was 1961 and she was 13 years old. The movie was about Puerto Ricans living in New York, but most of the actors who played them were English-speaking whites. To her, they just didn't seem like Puerto Rican people.

Seeing the movie was a turning point in Esmeralda's life. She knew the movie was not about her. But she did not know what the film should have been like. Realizing this made her feel confused.

▼ Esmeralda Santiago moved from Puerto Rico to New York City when she was 13 years old.

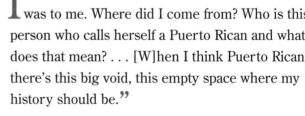

" I had no sense of Puerto Rican culture or what it was to me. Where did I come from? Who is this person who calls herself a Puerto Rican and what does that mean? . . . [W]hen I think Puerto Rican, there's this big void, this empty space where my history should be. "

Puerto Rican and American

Even though Esmeralda felt confused about who she was, she remembered her early days in Puerto Rico vividly. When Esmeralda's mother brought her to New York City, everything changed.

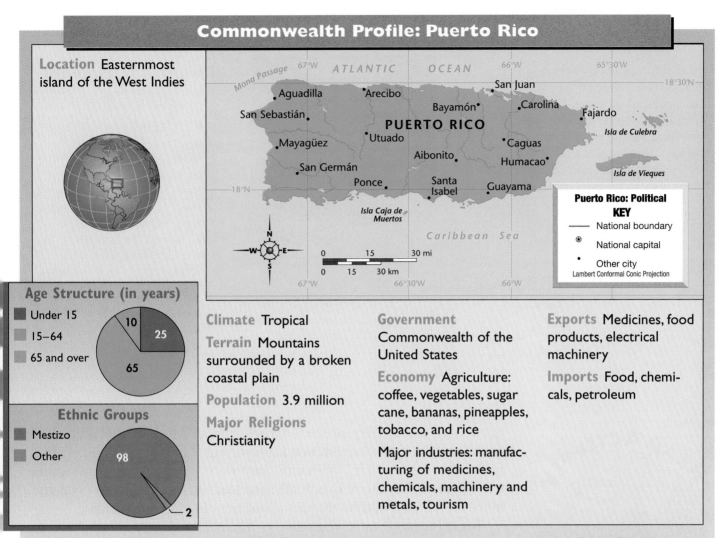

Location Easternmost island of the West Indies

Age Structure (in years)
- Under 15
- 15–64
- 65 and over

10
25
65

Ethnic Groups
- Mestizo
- Other

98
2

Puerto Rico: Political KEY
— National boundary
⊛ National capital
• Other city
Lambert Conformal Conic Projection

Climate Tropical

Terrain Mountains surrounded by a broken coastal plain

Population 3.9 million

Major Religions Christianity

Government Commonwealth of the United States

Economy Agriculture: coffee, vegetables, sugar cane, bananas, pineapples, tobacco, and rice

Major industries: manufacturing of medicines, chemicals, machinery and metals, tourism

Exports Medicines, food products, electrical machinery

Imports Food, chemicals, petroleum

Map and Chart Study This map shows Puerto Rico. **Location** Read the description of Puerto Rico's terrain. Where are Puerto Rico's mountains located? How do you know? **Movement** How do you think most exports are shipped out of Puerto Rico? **Critical Thinking** Look at the chart that shows age structure. Would you say that Puerto Rico's population is old, young, or evenly balanced? Why?

It was not that Esmeralda was completely separated from her people. Puerto Ricans are U.S. citizens. **Citizens** are individuals with certain rights and responsibilities under a particular government. However, Puerto Ricans cannot vote in U. S. presidential elections. They do not pay U.S. taxes. And they have only a non-voting representative in the U.S. Congress. Puerto Rico is a commonwealth of the United States. A **commonwealth** is a place that has its own government but also has strong ties to another country. Esmeralda had the right to return to Puerto Rico whenever she chose.

Esmeralda found life on the mainland strange and confusing. One problem was that to succeed in school, she had to improve her English. Esmeralda was also confused by her new group of friends. She found that Puerto Ricans living on the mainland were different from her friends on the island of Puerto Rico. Instead of the salsa and merengue

Chart Study Many Puerto Ricans have moved to the mainland United States. **Critical Thinking** Which region of the mainland has the most Puerto Ricans? What do you think draws Puerto Ricans to a particular area?

Population	
Total	2,728,000
Northeast	1,872,000
Midwest	258,000
South	406,000
West	192,000

Distribution by Region

9.4%
7.0%
14.9%
68.6%

- Northeast
- Midwest
- South
- West

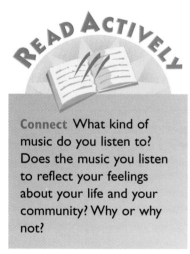

READ ACTIVELY

Connect What kind of music do you listen to? Does the music you listen to reflect your feelings about your life and your community? Why or why not?

music she loved, they preferred rock music. Most of the time they spoke neither pure Spanish nor English, but a mixture of the two that they called "Spanglish." Although they were Puerto Rican, Esmeralda felt different from them. Eventually, she learned their ways. She became more like them and thought less about her old life on the island.

Most Puerto Ricans who move to the mainland keep connections to Puerto Rico. As people travel back and forth between the mainland and Puerto Rico, they bring customs and products with them. If you visited Puerto Rico, you would see many influences from the U.S. mainland. You would also see that in Puerto Rico, there is a strong cultural connection to the Caribbean. Most people are a mix of Spanish and African ancestry. Some Puerto Ricans like to look even further back into their history by calling themselves "Boricuas" (bohr ee KOO uhs). The name comes from the Boriqueno (bohr ee KAY noh), an indigenous farming people who lived on the island before the Spanish arrived.

More Than the Four Walls

The land of Puerto Rico is a memory no Puerto Rican forgets. Some, like Esmeralda Santiago, never go back to it. But others return, longing for the familiar ways they left behind. Julia de Jesus Chaparro (HOO lee a day HAY soos sha PAHR ro) moved back to a small mountain village in Puerto Rico after more than 14 years in Boston. She is fond of saying that where she lives now there are "more than the four walls of the city." To prove what she means, she takes visitors to her back porch. Outside it, one can see a row of steep mountains. Peeking between them is the bright blue of the Caribbean Sea. The mountain slopes steeply down from her back porch, but she has managed to clear some land. Her garden of mangoes, coconuts, grapefruit, and lemons thrives in the sun. Behind a nearby tree, a hen and six chickens are pecking in the dirt.

On other parts of the island, farmers ride horses through fields of tall sugar cane. Higher in the hills, Puerto Rican cowhands, called *jíbaros* (HEE bahr ohs), hunt, fish, and raise chickens, pigs, and cattle. To the southwest, where the land gets lower, fishing villages dot the coast.

Puerto Rico is an island of cities as well as countryside. Puerto Rican cities show influences of Spanish, Caribbean, and U.S. mainland cultures. About 70 percent of Puerto Ricans live in cities. Many city people work in factories. Others work in the hotels and restaurants that draw many tourists. Puerto Rico's capital, San Juan (san HWAHN), has a large waterfront area known as the Condado (kohn DAH do). It is packed with luxury hotels. Not far away, modern skyscrapers pierce the brilliant sky. In the old section of San Juan, Spanish-style buildings are everywhere. A 450-year-old Catholic church built by the Spanish has been carefully restored. Not far from it sit ancient houses graced with iron balconies in lacy Spanish style.

READ ACTIVELY

Visualize What might you see if you looked out the back door of an apartment in the city? What might you see if you looked out the back door of a house in the countryside?

A Commonwealth in Question

In 1951, Puerto Ricans voted to adopt their own constitution. A **constitution** is a statement of a country's basic laws and values. This gave Puerto Rico its own group of lawmakers. But it was still connected

New York City's Spanish Harlem

Puerto Ricans are the largest ethnic group in New York City's Lower East Side, and they make up about 12 percent of the city's total population.

to the United States. Puerto Rico is bound by many United States laws. Puerto Ricans have many questions about this. Is it good for Puerto Rico? Should Puerto Rico become independent? Or should it become a state of the United States?

What Direction to Take? Puerto Ricans have many disagreements over the answers to these questions. Many feel that having "one foot" in Puerto Rico and "one foot" in the United States can lead to problems. Others point out how the relationship with the United States has helped Puerto Rico. U.S. businesses on the island have raised the standard of living. Each year, the U.S. government sends millions of dollars to the island to help people in need.

Some people still feel that Puerto Rico has a disadvantage because people there cannot vote in U.S. elections. They say Puerto Rico should try to become a state. But if it does, it will become the poorest state in the union. Puerto Ricans earn more money than people in other Caribbean countries. However, they earn less than people on the U.S. mainland. Also, if Puerto Rico becomes a state, Puerto Ricans will have

Connect Would people in your area want to become part of another state? Why or why not?

San Juan: Old and New

San Juan, Puerto Rico's oldest city, is famous for historic forts and the wrought iron balconies of its oldest neighborhoods. But San Juan is also a vacation spot for tourists, with modern hotels lining its sandy beaches.

▶ These women are celebrating Puerto Rico's Spanish heritage. Puerto Ricans celebrate many holidays with traditional music and dancing.

to pay U.S. taxes. This could lower the earnings of many who have little to spare. For these reasons, in 1993 and again in 1998, Puerto Ricans voted not to become the 51st state of the United States.

The Question of Independence   Some people who voted against statehood have even bigger dreams for the country. They want Puerto Rico to become a separate nation. If not, they fear that Puerto Ricans will become confused about their identity, just as Esmeralda Santiago became confused about hers. They stress Puerto Rico's connection to other Caribbean nations. They want to make sure that Puerto Ricans always identify with the Spanish language and Spanish culture. But for now, Puerto Rico will keep its links to the mainland. Many Puerto Ricans hope that their relationship with the United States will lead to a profitable and peaceful future.

SECTION 3 REVIEW

1. **Define**   (a) citizen, (b) commonwealth, (c) constitution.

2. **Identify**   (a) San Juan, (b) Condado.

3. What is the political connection between Puerto Rico and the United States?

4. Compare life in the mainland United States with life in Puerto Rico.

Critical Thinking
5. **Identifying Central Issues**   What are the three options Puerto Ricans consider in terms of their relationship with the United States? What are the benefits and drawbacks of each?

Activity
6. **Writing to Learn**   Try to put yourself in Esmeralda Santiago's place. Write a paragraph telling what it was like to move to New York from Puerto Rico.

Review and Activities

Reviewing Main Ideas

1. What happened to Cuba when the communist regime in the Soviet Union fell?
2. What changes did Lydia Martin notice when she visited Cuba in 1995?
3. How is Haiti's history unique?
4. What were two results of Jean-Bertrand Aristide's forced exile from Haiti?
5. How do the cultures of Spain and the United States influence Puerto Rico? Give one example of how each has influenced Puerto Rico.
6. How have frequent trips to the U.S. mainland affected some Puerto Rican families?

Reviewing Key Terms

Use each key term below in a sentence that shows the meaning of the term.

1. communist
2. dictator
3. exile
4. illiterate
5. Creole
6. dialect
7. commonwealth
8. citizen
9. constitution

Critical Thinking

1. **Making Comparisons** Both Cubans and Puerto Ricans have settled in the United States. How has the experience been similar for both? How has it been different?
2. **Drawing Conclusions** How do you think Toussaint L'Ouverture's fight for independence inspires Haitians to fight for democracy?

Graphic Organizer

Copy the chart to the right onto a piece of paper, then fill in the empty boxes to complete the chart.

	Cuba	Haiti	Puerto Rico
Form of government			
United States Influence			

Map Activity

For each place listed below, write the letter from the map that shows its location.

1. Port-au-Prince
2. San Juan
3. Havana
4. Miami
5. Gulf of Mexico
6. Guantánamo Bay
7. Dominican Republic

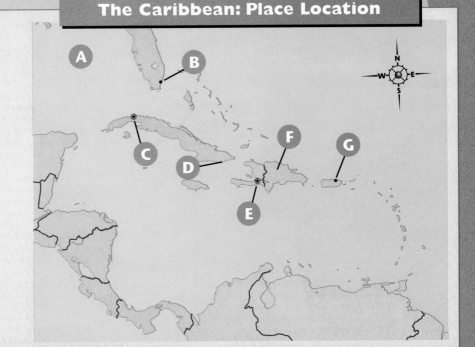

The Caribbean: Place Location

Writing Activity

Writing a Poem
Write a poem describing the culture in your region. Does your region have a blend of cultures, like Haiti? Why or why not? How does the culture in your region affect the way you feel about yourself?

Internet Activity
Use a search engine to find the site **Nueva Vista: Latino/Puerto Rican Issues, Views and Links.** Click on **Viewpoint.** Then, click on **The 51st State: the State of Confusion** and read one person's view on Puerto Rico's status as a U.S. commonwealth. Use this information to debate the issue with your classmates.

Skills Review

Turn to the Skill Activity.

Review the steps for locating information. Then write a one page biography of Fidel Castro. Make a list of four routes you could take to find information.

How Am I Doing?

Answer these questions to help you check your progress.

1. Do I understand why many Cubans have emigrated to the United States?
2. Can I explain how Haiti's people have struggled for democracy?
3. Do I understand Puerto Rico's relationship with the United States?
4. Can I describe what factors have affected culture in the Caribbean islands?
5. What information from this chapter can I use in my book project?

Exploring South America

KEY

— National boundary

⊛ National capital

• Other city

Lambert Azimuthal Equal Area Projection

MAP ACTIVITIES

South America is more than two times as large as the mainland United States. Because it is so large, its geography and cultures are diverse. To learn more about South America, complete the following activities.

Understanding geography
Much of South America is located south of the Equator. If you were to start at the Equator and travel south, how do you think the climate would change? Why?

Study the map
How do you think the Andes Mountains may have affected political boundaries in South America?

Brazil

RESOURCES OF THE RAIN FOREST

Reach Into Your Background

In this section, you will learn about the rain forests in Brazil.

List three things you already know or can guess about the rain forests.

Questions to Explore

1. Why are the rain forests in Brazil a global issue?
2. How does what happens to the rain forests affect Brazil's economy?

Key Terms

canopy
photosynthesis

Key People and Places

Rio de Janeiro
Salvador
Yanomamo
Brasília

Deep in the rain forest in Brazil, the light barely penetrates. At the top of the trees, the leaves form a dense mass called a **canopy**. Sun and rain beat down upon the canopy. But on the ground, the air feels almost chilly. The only sounds are the calls of birds, monkeys, and insects.

▼ The canopy of Brazil's rain forest parts only where rivers slice through it.

Brazil and Its Rain Forests

Brazil, the largest country in South America, is nearly as large as the United States. It is also one of the richest countries in the world in land and resources. Until recently, its immense rain forests remained undisturbed. Only the few Native American groups that had lived in them for centuries ever explored them.

Brazil's Geography Brazil's rain forests take up about one half of the country. Look at the map in the Country Profile. In the southeast, the forests give way to a large plateau divided by mountain ranges and river valleys. The plateau reaches Brazil's long coast. Many harbors lie along the coast. Large cities, such as Rio de Janeiro (ree oh day zhuh NER oh), grew up around harbors. Most of Brazil's people live near the coast, far from the rain forests.

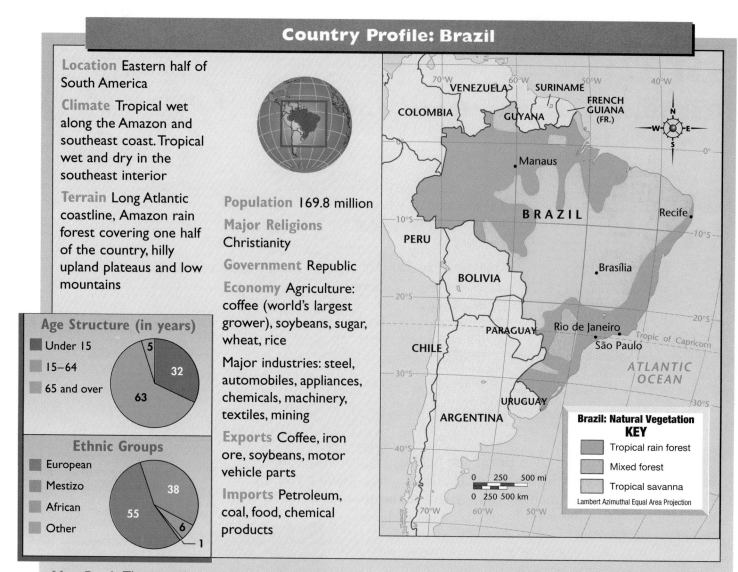

Country Profile: Brazil

Location Eastern half of South America

Climate Tropical wet along the Amazon and southeast coast. Tropical wet and dry in the southeast interior

Terrain Long Atlantic coastline, Amazon rain forest covering one half of the country, hilly upland plateaus and low mountains

Population 169.8 million

Major Religions Christianity

Government Republic

Economy Agriculture: coffee (world's largest grower), soybeans, sugar, wheat, rice

Major industries: steel, automobiles, appliances, chemicals, machinery, textiles, mining

Exports Coffee, iron ore, soybeans, motor vehicle parts

Imports Petroleum, coal, food, chemical products

Age Structure (in years)

- Under 15
- 15–64
- 65 and over

5, 32, 63

Ethnic Groups

- European
- Mestizo
- African
- Other

38, 55, 6, 1

Brazil: Natural Vegetation KEY
- Tropical rain forest
- Mixed forest
- Tropical savanna

Lambert Azimuthal Equal Area Projection

Map Study This map shows the vegetation regions of Brazil. Brazil contains over 1 million square miles (2,589,900 sq km) of rain forest. Northern Brazil contains part of the largest rain forest in the world, the Amazonian rain forest. Alaska could fit inside Brazil's Amazonian rain forest twice. Texas could fit inside it five times. **Location** What four Brazilian cities are located in the rain forest?

The People of Brazil

The Native Americans living in the rain forest were some of the first people to live in Brazil. Today, most Brazilians are a mix of Native American, African, and European heritages.

Many parts of African culture still flourish in Brazil. The most African of Brazilian cities, Salvador, lies on the coastal plains. Visitors are surprised by how much Salvador is like a town in Africa. Most of the people who live here descend from the millions of Africans brought to Brazil as slaves.

Working on Farms and in Factories Many Africans in Brazil were forced to work the coffee plantations. Brazil used their labor to become the world's largest coffee grower. When the slaves were freed in the late 1800s, they became paid but cheap labor.

Coffee prices dropped in the first few years of the 1900s. Brazilians realized that they could not depend on one or two crops to survive. In the 1930s, the government discouraged coffee production and tried to diversify the economy by building more factories. Today, Brazil produces many goods, including iron and steel, cars, and electrical equipment. Since 1960, about 30 million people have left farms and plantations to get jobs in these new industries. They moved into the cities.

A Brazilian City   Brazilian cities are home to the rich and the very poor. Rio de Janeiro is a good example of these contrasts. It lies on the coast, surrounded by huge mountains that dip to the sea. If you climbed to the top of one, you could see the whole city. To the south, you would see expensive hotels and shops for tourists. In the downtown area, you would see old palaces and government buildings.

But to the north, you would see clusters of small houses where factory workers live. Below this neighborhood is an even poorer one, crowded with homes that have no electricity or running water. About a quarter of Rio's 12 million people live in these neighborhoods known as *favelas* (fuh VEH lus). However, most of Rio's people live in well-built houses with electricity and running water.

Connect How is the history of Africans in Brazil like the history of Africans brought to the United States?

Brazil's African Heritage

In Salvador, Brazil, people cook food similar to the food eaten in West Africa. Food in both places is seasoned with coconut milk, pepper, and palm oil, and cooked in earthenware pots. The women of Salvador wear lacy dresses and turbans, like many of the women of West Africa.

Using the Rain Forest's Resources

Visualize What do you think you would see if you climbed to the top of a tree in the rain forest?

On a sunny January in 1994, two boys who lived in the rain forest scrambled up the trees. The boys were Yanomamos. The Yanomamo are a Native American group that lives in the rain forests. The boys pointed to a plane soaring close to the treetops. The plane dipped down and landed on a dirt strip. "Foreign visitors!" the boys called excitedly.

Brazil's New Capital: Brasília The visitors were from Brasília (bruh ZIL yuh), the capital city of Brazil. Brasília is closer to the rain forest than the coastal cities are. On the vast interior plain where Brasília now stands, there used to be nothing but a savanna called the Cerrado (suh RAH doh). The Cerrado was a region 10 times larger than the state of Kansas. The government thought that moving the capital there would attract some people from the coastal areas.

The government wanted to develop Brazil's interior region using the resources of the rain forest. The rain forests are important to Brazil's economy because people cut timber, mine for gold, and farm there. Now, the government hoped to develop industry using the resources of the rain forest.

Worldwide Impact of the Rain Forest The rain forest where the Yanomamo live is very important to life all around the Earth. Scientists estimate that rain forests produce about one third of the world's oxygen. Green plants and trees produce their own food using

▼São Paulo is the largest city in Brazil. It contains more than 20,000 factories, which provide jobs for 600,000 workers.

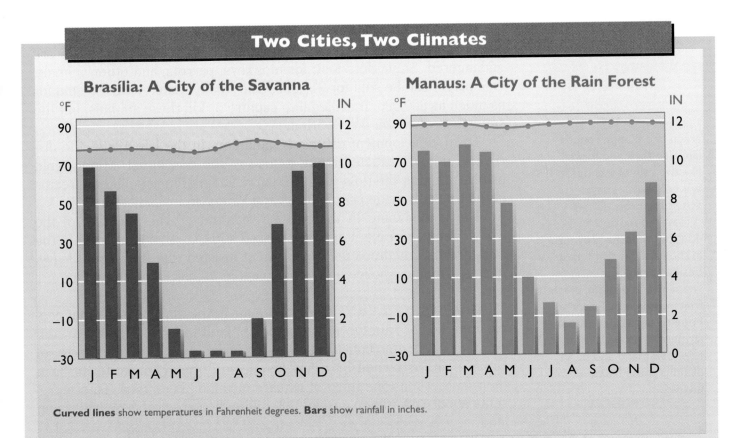

Brasília: A City of the Savanna

Manaus: A City of the Rain Forest

Curved lines show temperatures in Fahrenheit degrees. **Bars** show rainfall in inches.

Chart Study A climate graph shows rainfall and temperature in the same space. The bars show rainfall, while the curved lines show temperature. **Critical Thinking** How are the seasons in Brasília and Manaus different from each other?

water, carbon dioxide, and sunlight. This process is called **photosynthesis** (foht oh SIN thuh sis). In the process of photosynthesis, oxygen is given off. All people and animals need oxygen to breathe.

The rain forest also holds about one fifth of the world's fresh water. Many scientists think that when people come to the rain forest, they may upset the delicate balance of nature.

Protecting the Rain Forest Brazil's government is taking care to use the rain forest's resources without upsetting this balance. The government has started using satellites to keep an eye on the rain forest. That way, the government can respond fast to protect the rain forest from the following dangers.

First, if too much timber is cut down, there will not be enough trees to absorb the carbon dioxide in the atmosphere. The carbon dioxide layer may trap heat near the Earth, changing the world's climate. When part of the forest is destroyed, the animals and plants that live there may not survive. When plant life is destroyed, less oxygen is produced.

A Voice of Protest Friar Hector Turrini moved from Italy to Brazil more than 45 years ago. At that time, there were so few roads that Turrini had to learn to fly a plane to get around his parish. He dedicated himself to protecting the Native Americans and rubber tappers who depend on the rain forest. Now Turrini is working to protect the rain forest.

Amazon Fruit What is green and bumpy, round like a softball, and looks like the sole of a shoe? It is a conde (KON day). Scientists in Brazil have discovered more than 40 types of fruits growing in the Amazon rain forest. Besides being high in vitamins and protein, these fruits taste good. Scientists hope to persuade Amazon farmers to stop clearing rain forest land and begin planting these fruits instead.

Second, there is the problem of smuggling. Each year, Brazil loses about 12 million animals to smugglers. Many of these animals are endangered. Smugglers look for monkeys, parrots, and other animals. One parrot can be sold for $10,000. One woolly monkey can be sold for as much as $50,000. It is illegal to capture or kill these animals, but the smugglers often get away with it.

Third, development can cause pollution. In the late 1980s, the discovery of gold attracted many miners to the rain forest. Mining gold involves mixing the gold with mercury. The mercury polluted streams in the forest. It made people in several Yanomamo villages sick.

The gold mining in the rain forest attracted the attention of the world. The government of Brazil passed strict laws about mining in the rain forest. Sometimes the government insisted that the miners leave. At times, military police had to be called in to make sure they did.

Giving Land to the Poor   One of the main reasons that people come to the rain forest is the lack of land to farm. This may seem strange when one considers Brazil's large size. However, most of Brazil's land is owned by a few people who may choose not to farm their land. About one third of Brazil's farmland is unused. This represents about 300 million acres (122 million hectares) of crop and ranch land.

In 1995, Brazil's president gave some of this unused land to poor farmers. The goal is to resettle more than 3,600 poor families who want a new place to live and who want to return to farming. The process is a slow one. However, life for some resettled Brazilians is improving.

People are starting small farms just north of Rio de Janeiro. The farms help people make a living for themselves. On a balmy July day in 1995, farmer Joe Brum showed a reporter his farm. Brum had received the 17-acre plot from the government. Now his tin-roofed house was shaded by the coconut and banana trees he had planted. He had a couple of pigs and had earned enough money to buy a satellite dish and a television.

Brum's eyes gleamed as he pointed to the rows of vegetables. "What I have here," he explained to the reporter, "I made myself."

SECTION 1 REVIEW

1. **Define**   (a) canopy, (b) photosynthesis.

2. **Identify**   (a) Rio de Janeiro, (b) Salvador, (c) Yanomamo, (d) Brasília.

3. Why are Brazil's rain forests important to the whole world?

4. In what ways does Brazil depend on its rain forest?

Critical Thinking

5. **Expressing Problems Clearly**   Some people want Brazil to stop using rain forests completely. Is this reasonable? What do you think it would do to Brazil's economy?

Activity

6. **Writing a Journal Entry** Use what you know about the rain forest to write a journal entry about a visit to it.

Peru

LIFE IN THE ALTIPLANO

BEFORE YOU READ

Reach Into Your Background

Did you choose your clothing according to the weather report this morning? The decision you made was affected by climate. Think of other ways that climate affects your life.

Questions to Explore

1. How has geography affected the lifestyle of Native Americans of the altiplano?
2. How do people on the altiplano survive?

Key Terms

altiplano
sierra
montaña
tundra

Key People and Places

Lake Titicaca
Uros
Quechua
Cuzco

When people on Tribuna, an island in Lake Titicaca, play soccer, they must be careful. That's because the island is made of straw. The ground is uneven, and when they walk on it they can feel the water shifting below. "It seems crazy to play soccer on water," says Luis Colo, who lives on Tribuna. "We don't jump on each other after a goal, or we'd probably fall through the field."

Tribuna is one of about 70 islands made by the Uros (oor OHSS). The Uros have adapted to the geography of Lake Titicaca. The Uros make their islands out of totora reeds. They join the floating roots of totora reeds together and then lay cut reeds on top. This process creates an island that is firm enough to support small communities of people with huts and livestock. When the Uros need more land, they build another island.

▲ When the wind comes up, the Uros must anchor their islands to keep them from being swept away.

Peru's Three Geographic Regions

The Uros live on Lake Titicaca. Find Lake Titicaca on the map in the Country Profile. Lake Titicaca lies high in Peru's **altiplano** (al tih PLAH noh), a high plateau region in the Andes. The altiplano is about 12,000 feet (3,658 m) above sea level. It lies in the southern part of Peru near the Bolivian border.

Country Profile: Peru

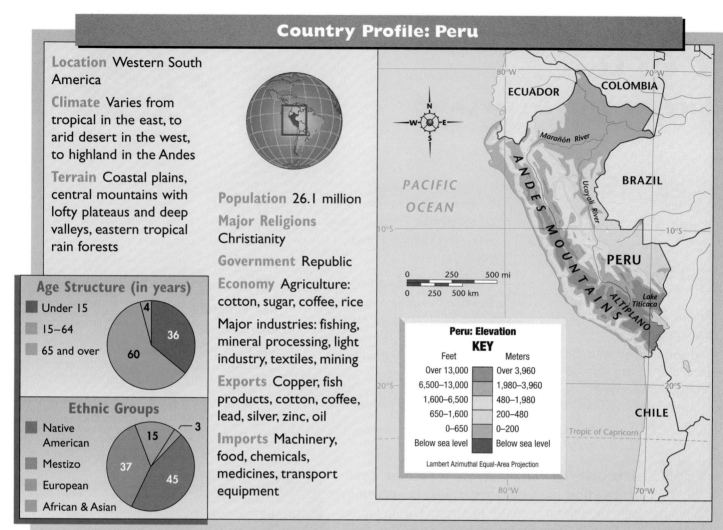

Location Western South America

Climate Varies from tropical in the east, to arid desert in the west, to highland in the Andes

Terrain Coastal plains, central mountains with lofty plateaus and deep valleys, eastern tropical rain forests

Population 26.1 million

Major Religions Christianity

Government Republic

Economy Agriculture: cotton, sugar, coffee, rice

Major industries: fishing, mineral processing, light industry, textiles, mining

Exports Copper, fish products, cotton, coffee, lead, silver, zinc, oil

Imports Machinery, food, chemicals, medicines, transport equipment

Age Structure (in years)

- Under 15
- 15–64
- 65 and over

4 / 36 / 60

Ethnic Groups

- Native American
- Mestizo
- European
- African & Asian

15 / 3 / 37 / 45

Peru: Elevation KEY

Feet		Meters
Over 13,000		Over 3,960
6,500–13,000		1,980–3,960
1,600–6,500		480–1,980
650–1,600		200–480
0–650		0–200
Below sea level		Below sea level

Lambert Azimuthal Equal-Area Projection

Map Study This map shows the elevation of land in Peru. The higher you climb in the mountains, the colder the climate gets. In the Andes Mountains, trees will not grow above 10,000 feet (3,048 m) because it is too cold. But east of the Andes, the elevation is lower. Much of the eastern lowlands is covered with a dense tropical rain forest. **Location** How high in the mountains is Lake Titicaca? What direction do the rivers on this map flow? How can you tell?

Peru's mountains divide the country into three geographic regions. The altiplano and Peru's highest mountains are in the **sierra,** the mountains that run from northwest to southeast Peru. The mountains are so high that the temperature can drop as low as 20°F (–7°C). People who live in this region must sleep under many blankets. They sometimes wear sweaters to bed.

Their life is far different from the lives of those who live on the coastal plain, which is Peru's second geographical region. This dry region is warmed by the sun and cooled by sea breezes. Several cities, including Trujillo (troo HEE yoh), Chimbote (chim BOH tay), and Lima (LEE muh), dot the coast.

The third region is called the **montaña.** The montaña is made of large stretches of tropical forests on the lower slopes of mountains in northeast Peru. Here the weather is warm and humid all year round.

Peru's People

Native Americans make up almost half of Peru's population. Most Native Americans living in Peru are Quechua. About 15 percent of Peruvians are of European descent. Another 37 percent are mestizo. The remaining Peruvians are of African and Asian descent.

Peru's Cities The altiplano contains cities and isolated towns. City life is very different from village life. Most city dwellers have electricity. The streets are paved, and there are telephones. But in Peru's cities, the old mixes with the new.

One Peruvian city, Cuzco, is the site of the ancient Incan capital. Parts of the old Incan wall that once surrounded the city are still standing. Today's modern houses are made of adobe, with red tile roofs. But their foundations are the remains of Incan stonework. There are buildings from the time of the Spanish colonists as well.

Spanish conquistador Francisco Pizarro founded Peru's largest city and capital, Lima, in 1535. Lima lies on the coastal plain. Like Cuzco, Lima is a mix of old and new. Historic Spanish cathedrals and government buildings from the 1600s and 1700s stand next to modern skyscrapers.

Bridging Canyons The Incas invented the technology for building suspension bridges. First, they built stone towers on each side of a canyon. They suspended cables woven from plants from the stone towers. Then, they laid wooden slats across the cables to make a bridge. They used smaller cables for railings. People still use Incan-style bridges today. Modern suspension bridges have steel cables and are reinforced with iron beams.

Open Air Market

◄ Lima is the busiest and most modern of Peru's cities. What details in the photo are modern? What details are more traditional?

Life in Rural Areas   In the isolated towns of the altiplano, life is very different from life in the city. There are no telephones to ring. Few buses drive through the villages. Most people are Quechua or Aymara.

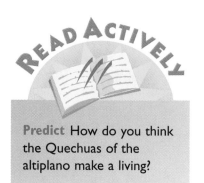

Predict How do you think the Quechuas of the altiplano make a living?

A Day in a Quechua Village   Modesto Mamani (moh DES toh muh MAN ee) is a 13-year-old Quechua boy. He wakes before dawn to the freezing mountain air. He eats breakfast as soon as the sun comes up. Breakfast is always the same: a couple of rolls, coffee with sugar, and whole wheat kernels that can be eaten like popcorn. The only other meal may be lunch. It is usually potato and barley soup with chunos—freeze-dried potato skins.

For much of the day, Modesto works in the field with his father and brothers. On other days, he looks after the sheep or goes with his mother to the market. Despite all of these chores, Modesto finds time to play soccer on the tundra in back of his house. A **tundra** is an area where no trees grow because the soil is always cold.

Modesto Mamani at School and at Work

Modesto's life mixes the modern and the traditional. He wants to study to become an engineer so that he can bring technology to the altiplano. But even when he is studying, Modesto is never far from his soccer ball. He also spends a lot of time tending sheep and knitting wool sweaters. Sometimes he even knits when he is playing soccer!

The Straw People Modesto's village is not far from the Uros islands on Lake Titicaca. The people there live on one of the 70 totora reed islands that float on the lake. The islanders use totora reeds for many other purposes besides building islands. They weave it to make boats. They use it as fuel for cooking. They eat the soft inside of the reeds. Most important, though, they use the reeds to repair the islands. Totora reeds last only a few months before they start to rot. A person who slipped through them could die in the lake's icy waters.

On the straw islands, women wake at dawn to get water from the lake for cooking and washing. They spend the rest of the day washing clothes, untangling fishing nets, and making new homes out of reeds. Once or twice a week they go to market to trade fish for rice, potatoes, and sugar. Meanwhile, the men fish and help to repair the straw islands.

A Modern Future Quechuas and other Native Americans living on the altiplano follow traditions that are hundreds of years old. Their communities, however, are slowly changing. Thousands of Native Americans have left for jobs in the city. Life is changing even for those who stay in the village. The future holds a promising mix of old and new ways.

Quechua Market Day

On market days, Quechua from several communities gather together to buy and sell goods. What kinds of goods are being sold at this market?

SECTION 2 REVIEW

1. **Define** (a) altiplano, (b) sierra, (c) montaña, (d) tundra.

2. **Identify** (a) Lake Titicaca, (b) Uros, (c) Quechua, (d) Cuzco.

3. How is the daily life of the Quechua affected by the high altitude of the altiplano?

4. Describe people's lives on the straw islands of Lake Titicaca.

Critical Thinking

5. **Recognizing Bias** Do you think the Quechua see their way of life as outsiders see it? Explain.

Activity

6. **Writing to Learn** Compare life in a Peruvian city with life in a rural Quechua or Uros community.

Using Isolines to Show Elevation

Climb straight up, hike over the side, or walk all the way around? That was the question Melissa and José faced.

They stared up at the huge hill in front of them. According to the map, the campsite they were hiking to was exactly on the opposite side of the hill. What was the best route to take?

Melissa spread the map out on a fallen log. "Look," she said, pointing at the map. "This hill is steep on this side, but we can climb it." She traced the route on the map. "But look what we'd run into on the other side!"

"A cliff!" José responded. "We'd never be able to get down. It's way too steep. I guess we'll have to walk around the hill."

"Not so fast. If we head to our left, we can climb up a gentle slope and work our way past the cliff down the hill on the other side. It's kind of steep, but at least we'll be going downhill!"

Get Ready

How could Melissa tell from the map how steep different parts of the hill were? The answer is that the map showed isolines. The word *isolines* comes from the Greek word *iso,* which means "equal," and our word *lines.* Isolines link together equal parts of a map. On the map Melissa and José used, every part of the hill that was the same elevation was linked by an isoline. By studying the pattern of the isolines, Melissa could figure out the best route to take.

Isolines that show elevation are also called contour lines, because their pattern shows the contour, or shape, of the land.

You can make your own contour map. To do this, you will need:

- an irregularly shaped rock, about the size of a cantaloupe
- a pan of water big enough and deep enough to submerge the rock
- a crayon or waterproof marker
- a sheet of blank paper and a pencil

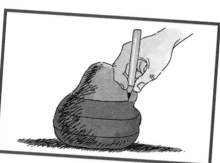
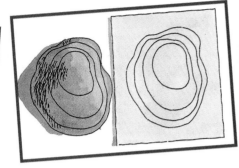

Try It Out

A. Fill the pan with water deep enough to cover the rock.

B. Holding the top of the rock, dip the bottom of it evenly about one inch into the water. Don't drop it! Remove the rock. Use the crayon or marker to trace the waterline all the way around the rock.

C. Dip the rock again, about one inch deeper. The waterline will now be about one inch higher up on the rock. Trace the new waterline with the crayon or marker, all the way around the rock.

D. Continue this process, dipping the rock about one inch deeper each time. Do this until you can go no farther.

E. Now, put the rock on the floor, and look at it from above. Can you see how each crayon or marker line connects the parts of the rock that are the same height? These are isolines. Using a pencil, copy the pattern you see looking down on the rock onto to your piece of paper. Next, label each of your isolines from the outside in. The outside line should be marked "1 inch," the next line "2 inches," and so on.

You have just drawn a map of the top of the rock using isolines.

Apply the Skill

The map on this page shows isolines of a region around the city of Lima, Peru. Use the map to visualize the shape of the land.

① **Remember that isolines connect places of equal elevation.** Just like the isolines you made on the rock, the isolines on this map connect places of equal elevation. The lines are numbered to show their elevation. What is the lowest elevation shown on the map? What is the highest elevation?

② **Use the isolines to get useful information from the map.** Remember that where the land is steep, isolines are close together. Where the land is flatter, isolines are farther apart. As you head east from Lima, does the elevation increase or decrease? Now sketch a side view of the map. What is the highest point? What is the lowest? How can you tell?

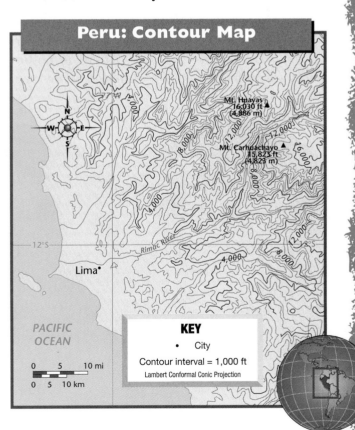

Peru: Contour Map

Mt. Huayas
16,030 ft
(4,886 m)

Mt. Carhuachayo
15,823 ft
(4,823 m)

Rimac River

Lima

PACIFIC
OCEAN

0   5   10 mi

0   5   10 km

KEY
• City
Contour interval = 1,000 ft
Lambert Conformal Conic Projection

SECTION 3

Chile

A GROWING ECONOMY BASED ON AGRICULTURE

BEFORE YOU READ

Reach Into Your Background

Do you like eating fresh fruit in summer? What if you could have fresh, juicy strawberries and peaches in the middle of winter? Think of ways to make this possible.

Questions to Explore

1. How does Chile's location affect the crops it grows?
2. How does producing more crops help Chile?

Key Terms
pesticide

Key Places
Santiago
Andes
Atacama Desert

▼ Maracas are normally used to play music.

It was a fairly quiet day at the airport of Santiago (san tee AH goh), the capital of Chile. Two passengers from Venezuela stepped off a plane. They had their carry-on luggage and a couple of maracas. A maraca is a musical instrument that sounds like a rattle. It is made from a hollow gourd filled with dried-out seeds or pebbles.

There is nothing very surprising about seeing maracas in South America. They are used in many orchestras and bands to play Latin music. So why was the customs officer staring at them suspiciously? Before the travelers had time to pass through customs, the officer grabbed the maracas and X-rayed them. Then he broke them open. Just as he thought, they did not contain dried-up seeds or pebbles. They were full of new seeds that were good for planting.

Life in Chile

Chile may be the only country in the world that inspects maracas brought into its borders. In recent years, Chile's agriculture has been booming. Chile makes millions of dollars a year by exporting peaches, grapes, cherries, and other

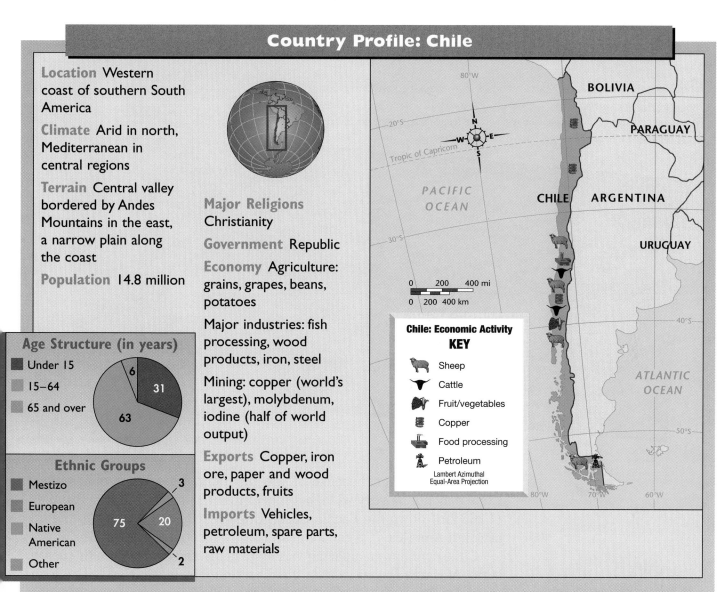

Country Profile: Chile

Location Western coast of southern South America

Climate Arid in north, Mediterranean in central regions

Terrain Central valley bordered by Andes Mountains in the east, a narrow plain along the coast

Population 14.8 million

Age Structure (in years)
- Under 15
- 15–64
- 65 and over

6
31
63

Ethnic Groups
- Mestizo
- European
- Native American
- Other

3
75
20
2

Major Religions Christianity

Government Republic

Economy Agriculture: grains, grapes, beans, potatoes

Major industries: fish processing, wood products, iron, steel

Mining: copper (world's largest), molybdenum, iodine (half of world output)

Exports Copper, iron ore, paper and wood products, fruits

Imports Vehicles, petroleum, spare parts, raw materials

Chile: Economic Activity
KEY
- Sheep
- Cattle
- Fruit/vegetables
- Copper
- Food processing
- Petroleum

Lambert Azimuthal Equal-Area Projection

BOLIVIA
PARAGUAY
PACIFIC OCEAN
CHILE ARGENTINA
URUGUAY
ATLANTIC OCEAN

0   200   400 mi
0   200   400 km

Map Study This map shows the major products of each region in Chile. Most of Chile's people live in its central valley. Read the description of the climate and terrain in central Chile. **Place** How do the climate and terrain of central Chile make it a good region for farming? **Movement** The Andes Mountains run down the whole length of Chile. What do you think would be the easiest way to ship Chile's products out of the country?

fruits and vegetables. Their country is protected by the Andes mountains, so some of the insect pests and animal diseases that plague other countries never reach Chile. That is why the government is so concerned about what enters now. Protecting Chile's crops is very important. No plant or animal matter from foreign places is allowed because it might bring disease to the crops.

The Geography of Chile Look at the physical map of Latin America in the Activity Atlas at the front of your book. Find the Andes Mountains. They run down the whole length of this long country like a giant spine. Chile is narrow. On average, it is about 100 miles (161 km) wide. If Chile were flat, it would take less than two hours to drive

The Atacama Desert looks barren and empty compared to Cerro Santa Lucia, a park in Santiago. But they are both in Chile. **Critical Thinking** What factors do you think make it possible for one country to have such different climates?

What Makes a Poem? What do you think is a proper topic for a poem? Chilean poet Pablo Neruda was willing to write a poem about anything. He wrote many poems about everyday subjects, like dusty wheels, sweat, and his socks. He even wrote a poem about a person wearing out a pair of shoes. He called it "You Flame Foot!"

across it. However, because of the mountains, it takes much longer. Chile may not be very wide, but it is extremely long. It runs 2,650 miles (4,265 km) down the Pacific Coast. Chile reaches all the way to the tip of South America. It is the longest, narrowest country in the world.

Chile contains an amazing variety of lands and climates. In the north is the Atacama Desert, one of the driest regions in the world. The long central valley near the coast has rolling hills, high grasses, and dense forests. This is the region where most of the people live.

The People of Chile Chile's early Spanish settlers married Native Americans already living there. Today, mestizos make up about 75 percent of the population. Only 3 percent of Chileans are Native Americans.

The lifestyles of Chileans vary from region to region. In the far south, sheep herders in heavy wool sweaters brave the strong winds. Farther north in the central valley, farmers grow wheat, potatoes, sugar beets, corn, tomatoes, and many fruits. In the cities, people in business suits hurry in and out of tall skyscrapers. Few people live in the Atacama Desert of the far north. Not many plants or animals can survive here either. But the desert is rich in copper, so the region is dotted with mines. Chile exports more copper than any country in the world.

A Chilean City A visit to Santiago is unforgettable. Old Spanish buildings stand near gleaming skyscrapers. The city is in the valley of the central plain, so the altitude is low enough to produce mild weather.

The sea makes the air humid. Palm trees grow in the public parks. The snowcapped Andes lie to the east.

The beautiful sights of Santiago are sometimes blocked by a thick layer of smog. Pollution has become so bad that it makes many small children and old people sick. The signs of pollution are everywhere. On a bad day, people wear surgical masks in order to breathe, or they press scarves to their faces. Few mothers bring their babies out on a day like this. If they do, the babies may have to be rushed to the hospital to receive oxygen.

The Problems of Industry How did pollution get to be so bad in Santiago? One cause is the city's location. It is surrounded by the Andes on three sides. The mountains trap the exhaust from vehicles and smoke from factories in the valley. This is especially true during the winter, when there is not much wind.

Another reason for the increase in pollution is the economy. Before the 1980s, Chile's economy depended mostly on its copper exports. Part of the copper industry was owned by the government. The profits went into projects that were supposed to help everyone in the country.

READ ACTIVELY

Connect What cities in the United States have problems with pollution? Which of these cities, like Santiago, are surrounded by mountains?

▼ German architecture can be found in many parts of southern Chile. German immigrants arrived here more than 100 years ago.

In northern Chile, the soil is not very good for farming. Many people here fish for a living. Chile's fishing industry is one of the largest in the world. **Critical Thinking** What difference do you see between people who fish for a living and those who fish for fun?

LINKS ACROSS THE WORLD

Falling Copper Prices Other countries besides Chile suffered when copper prices dropped in the 1980s. The Democratic Republic of Congo, in Central Africa, paid all its trade bills in 1980, mostly from the money it earned selling copper. By 1990, however, Congo was heavily in debt because of the fall in copper prices.

In the early 1980s, world copper prices began to drop. The government tried to solve the problem by encouraging industry. The government relaxed the laws that protected the environment from pollution. Government leaders thought that if the laws were too strict, some private industries would not survive. Encouraging private industry did save Chile's economy. It was easier to mine and process copper. Tons of steel, cement, glass, and electronic equipment were made and sold.

The standard of living rose. But so did pollution levels. Also, more people moved to the cities to get jobs in the new industries. More than 80 percent of Chile's people now live in cities.

During the 1990s, Chile's government took action to reduce the problems of pollution in the city. On days when the wind does not blow, industries are shut down. And only a limited number of cars may enter the city. Further, the government may also require new cars to have special exhaust systems that do not produce much pollution. No one knows how well these solutions will work. But most Chileans are hoping for a cleaner and healthier future.

Chile's Agricultural Revolution

The drop in copper prices in the early 1980s made it clear that Chile could not depend on copper to survive. Chile decided that one way to improve the economy was to sell more crops.

Pest-Free Produce   Chile's fruits and vegetables are free of many common plant pests. As a result, these products are welcome in many other countries. To supply the demands of these countries, about 15 percent of Chile's people farm. Chilean workers are also employed at packing plants for fruits and vegetables. Modern farming methods help grow even more crops.

By the late 1980s, agriculture was especially important for Chile. It had become a billion dollar industry, providing jobs for about 900,000 Chileans. Chile shipped wheat, potatoes, sugar beets, corn, grapes, melons, apples, peaches, apricots, cherries, and other fruits and vegetables around the world.

The United States, Japan, and Europe are an especially good market for Chilean produce from October through May. These months are winter in the Northern Hemisphere, but summer in the Southern Hemisphere. This means that Chile can provide fruits and vegetables to the United States, for example, during the months when American farmers cannot.

Although the Andes mountains protect Chile from many common plant pests and diseases, Chile has some pests of its own. To prevent them from destroying the fruits and vegetables, Chilean farmers use different kinds of pesticides. A **pesticide** (PES tuh syd) is a chemical used to kill insects and stop diseases that can hurt crops. Pesticides have helped farmers to increase crop production. But some people think that the pesticides may have caused certain kinds of illness in young children. As a result, Chilean scientists and farmers are trying to find ways to control pests without using chemicals. They want to make sure that Chilean fruits and vegetables are the tastiest and healthiest that people can buy.

SECTION 3 REVIEW

1. **Define** pesticide.

2. **Identify** (a) Santiago, (b) Andes, (c) Atacama Desert.

3. What aspect of Chile's location gives it an advantage in agriculture?

4. How has the growth of agriculture helped Chileans?

Critical Thinking

5. **Expressing Problems Clearly** Industries can cause pollution, but when industries close down, people lose their jobs. If you were the mayor of an industrial city with a pollution problem, what would you do?

Activity

6. **Writing to Learn** Like many places around the world, Chile is a popular tourist destination. Think about the reasons why a tourist might like to visit Chile. Describe the country's most interesting features. Present these paragraphs in the form of a tourist brochure.

SECTION 4

Venezuela

OIL POWERS THE ECONOMY

BEFORE YOU READ

Reach Into Your Background

There are some things in life that people can control and others that they cannot. Think of at least one thing in your life that you can control. Think of another thing that is beyond your control.

Questions to Explore

1. How was Venezuela affected by the oil boom?

2. How is Venezuela trying to change its economy for the future?

Key Terms
boom
privatization

Key Places
Caracas
Lake Maracaibo

Welcome to Caracas (kuh RAHK us), population about 3.3 million. The view from a high-rise apartment can be breathtaking. At night, thousands of lights dot the surrounding hills. Below, on the street, fashionable-looking people walk by on their way to dinner or a movie.

Outside, the air is balmy. You won't find much pollution in the air, either. The city is in a valley that runs from east to west. Winds blow through it. They sweep the exhaust of the many cars out of the city.

Why not visit one of the cafes? Or if you're lucky, you might find a party for teenagers going on right in the street. They may be listening to American-style rap music. But the words will be in Spanish. If you have the time, take the Caracas subway. It cost the government millions to build, more than any other subway in the world. You can get almost anywhere in the city on it, and the fare is only about 25 cents.

A Land Made Wealthy by Oil

Venezuela's government could pay for the subways because of money it made from the sale of oil. Venezuela has vast supplies of oil. The Country Profile map shows where Venezuela's oil is located. Venezuela's oil has earned millions of dollars on the world market. People migrated from the countryside to work for the oil companies.

▼ Many of Venezuela's largest petroleum deposits lie beneath the floor of Lake Maracaibo.

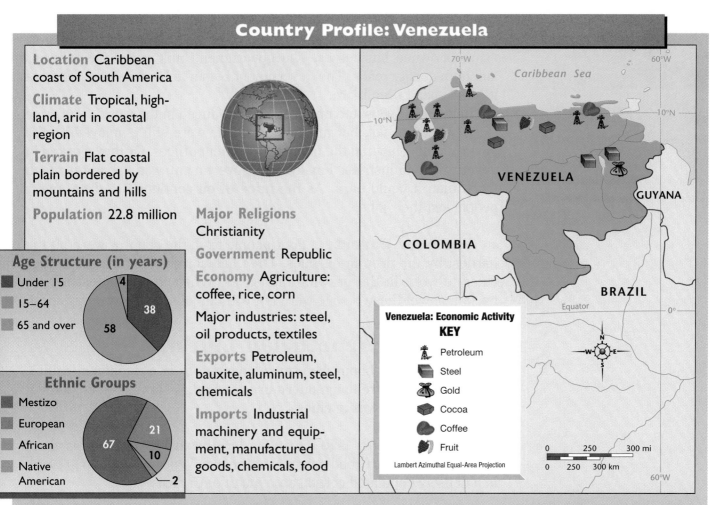

Country Profile: Venezuela

Location Caribbean coast of South America

Climate Tropical, highland, arid in coastal region

Terrain Flat coastal plain bordered by mountains and hills

Population 22.8 million

Major Religions Christianity

Government Republic

Economy Agriculture: coffee, rice, corn

Major industries: steel, oil products, textiles

Exports Petroleum, bauxite, aluminum, steel, chemicals

Imports Industrial machinery and equipment, manufactured goods, chemicals, food

Age Structure (in years)
- Under 15
- 15–64
- 65 and over

4
38
58

Ethnic Groups
- Mestizo
- European
- African
- Native American

21
67
10
2

Venezuela: Economic Activity
KEY
- Petroleum
- Steel
- Gold
- Cocoa
- Coffee
- Fruit

Lambert Azimuthal Equal-Area Projection

0   250   300 mi
0   250   300 km

Map Study This map shows the natural resources of Venezuela. Venezuela is famous for its deposits of petroleum. However, Venezuela also has many other resources, including soil that is good for farming and raising livestock. **Interaction** What part of Venezuela has the most natural resources? What area do you think has the most cities?

They helped maintain the giant oil rigs in Lake Maracaibo. They also worked in oil refineries.

Both the government and individuals own oil companies in Venezuela. They have grown rich mining, processing, and selling oil. By the early 1980s, Venezuela was the richest country in Latin America. Much of the money has gone to Caracas, where most Venezuelans live.

Ups and Downs of Oil Prices Venezuela's oil was discovered about 75 years ago. Since then, Venezuela has pumped about 67 billion barrels of oil. There seemed to be no end to the money that could be made in the oil industry. Except for the Persian Gulf region, Venezuela has the biggest oil reserves in the world.

During the 1970s, the price of oil went up. An oil boom began. A **boom** is a period of increased prosperity during which more of a product is produced and sold. The standard of living of many Venezuelans went up, too. That is when the government started spending huge sums

Predict Do you think that one resource, such as oil, can support a country forever? Why or why not?

of money. Many people were hired to run government agencies and government-owned businesses. The government built expensive subways and high-quality roads. The government began to borrow money so that it could spend even more.

In the mid-1980s, too much oil was produced in the world. The price of oil started to fall, but millions of people were still employed by the government. They ran the many government offices. Or they worked in government industries. Finally, the government was spending much more than it could earn. As the price of oil continued to drop, many people lost their jobs.

The New Poverty Poor people from the country were hit the hardest by the drop in oil sales. They had come to Caracas and other cities to work in the growing industries. When the oil industries cut back, many of these people were left without jobs.

Venezuelan Culture

During the oil boom, Venezuela changed from a traditional culture based on agriculture to a modern urban country. Now about 80 percent of the population lives in cities.

A Venezuelan Life Juan Varderi (hwahn var DEHR ee) is about 28 years old. He is a good example of the new Venezuelan. Juan grew up in a densely populated coastal area north of Caracas.

▼ Caracas is the largest city in Venezuela. It is also the country's capital.

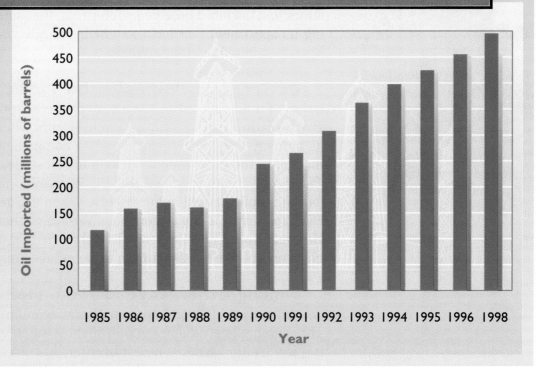

U.S. Petroleum Imports From Venezuela, 1985–1998

Chart Study The United States has several major petroleum deposits, but still uses more petroleum than it produces. The United States imports petroleum from Canada, Mexico, Nigeria, Saudi Arabia, and Venezuela.
Critical Thinking When did the United States import the least amount of petroleum from Venezuela? When did it import the most?

Oil Imported (millions of barrels)

Year

Juan's grandfather raised sheep on a ranch east of Lake Maracaibo. He made a fairly good living selling wool and meat to people in Caracas. He fully expected that his son, Juan's father, would work with him, so he never encouraged him to go to school. But in the 1970s, Juan's father was lured by the oil industry, which was beginning to boom.

Varderi's father left the ranch at age 16. He went to work on an oil rig that was owned by the government. By the time Juan was born, the family was living in Caracas in a small apartment. They had a radio but no telephone. Juan Varderi grew up playing baseball on the streets of Caracas. Baseball is very popular in Venezuela.

By the early 1980s, Juan's father was making more money. The family bought a television. Televisions had become popular. Varderi remembers those years as the most exciting time of his life.

ACROSS THE WORLD

Germany in Venezuela In 1843, the Venezuelan government recruited almost 400 Germans to live in the mountains west of Caracas. For over 100 years their colony, Colonia Tovar, was isolated. The people spoke German, ate German food, and married only Germans. The town is still so different from the rest of the country that it deserves its nickname, "Germany in Venezuela."

    " There were American programs you could watch on
      television, dubbed into Spanish. My friends and I
paid attention to the clothes that the Americans wore. We
tried to dress like them. We thought their music was the
coolest in the world. We used to watch rock videos and
try to learn the words of songs. In the early 1980s, we
thought we could live just like rich Americans seemed to
live. We didn't understand it was only taking place on TV.
We didn't know what was going to happen to us in just a
few years. "

Ask Questions If you had a chance to meet Juan Varderi, what questions would you ask? What questions do you think that Juan would ask you?

A few years later, when Juan Varderi turned 15, oil prices fell. His father lost his job. Three years after that, the family was in danger of losing its apartment. Varderi thought his family would have to move. But his father found another solution.

Government Businesses Go Public   The solution Juan's father found lay in a new government policy of privatization. **Privatization** (pry vuh tih ZAY shun) occurs when the government sells its industries to individuals or private companies. In the late 1980s and the 1990s, the government decided to sell some of its businesses to private corporations. It hoped that the corporations would make big profits. The profits would help workers. When the government turned over an oil refinery to a private company, Varderi's father applied for a job there. He was hired. The salary was less than he had earned working for the government, but it was enough to keep his family in their apartment.

Finding Other Ways to Make Money   Venezuela started new industries in an attempt to make its economy less dependent on oil. The country is producing goods such as steel, gold, cocoa, coffee, and tropical fruits. Varderi's oldest brother, Julio, received money from the government to start a small fruit orchard. This year he made enough money to support his family and help pay for a ticket for Juan to visit New York City. It was a trip Juan had always dreamed of.

Planting Corn in Venezuela

The Piaroa, one of Venezuela's Native American groups, farm on land they have cleared in Amazonas Territory. **Critical Thinking** What details from this photograph provide clues that these men are planting?

Many Venezuelans like to wear fashions from the United States, especially jeans. They also like to meet each other in plazas, or public squares. In fact, addresses in Caracas are given by plazas and corners, not streets.

A Changed Venezuela   Whatever Venezuela's economic fortune is, one thing is certain. The oil boom brought Venezuela into the modern world. When televisions, cellular phones, and other conveniences came into Venezuelan homes, life changed permanently. Juan Varderi dreams of having these things again in the future. And he is willing to work as hard as necessary to get them.

SECTION 4 REVIEW

1. **Define**   (a) boom, (b) privatization.

2. **Identify**   (a) Caracas, (b) Lake Maracaibo.

3. (a) What happened to many Venezuelans during the oil boom? (b) What happened to them after?

4. Explain how Venezuela is trying to improve its economy.

Critical Thinking
5. **Drawing Conclusions** (a) Why did the drop in oil prices affect Venezuela so much? (b) What do you think Venezuela should do to avoid economic problems in the future?

Activity
6. **Writing Activity**   Juan Varderi learned about United States culture from television programs. Describe America as shown on television.

Review and Activities

Reviewing Main Ideas

1. Why are the rain forests so important for the environment?
2. In what ways does the Brazilian economy depend upon the rain forest?
3. (a) What challenges does life on the altiplano present?
   (b) How do the people who live there overcome these challenges?
4. Why are many Quechua and Aymara moving to the cities of Peru?
5. Why does Chile have such strict customs laws?
6. (a) How does geography contribute to Chile's pollution problem?
   (b) How does it contribute to its agricultural boom?
7. What type of lifestyle changes did many Venezuelans make during the oil boom of the 1970s?
8. Why is it important for Venezuela to develop new ways to boost its economy?

Reviewing Key Terms

Use each key term below in a sentence that shows the meaning of the term.

1. canopy
2. photosynthesis
3. altiplano
4. sierra
5. montaña
6. tundra
7. pesticide
8. boom
9. privatization

Critical Thinking

1. **Making Comparisons** In what ways have Chile's and Venezuela's economic histories been similar? How have they differed?
2. **Recognizing Cause and Effect** How do you think the coming of modern conveniences like electricity will change life for the Quechua?

Graphic Organizer

Copy the chart onto a piece of paper. Then fill in the empty boxes to complete the chart.

	Brazil	Peru	Chile	Venezuela
Important exports				
Major cities				

Map Activity

For each place listed below, write the letter from the map that shows its location.

1. Amazon River
2. Rio de Janeiro
3. Brasília
4. Cuzco
5. Lake Titicaca
6. Santiago
7. Andes
8. Caracas
9. Orinoco River

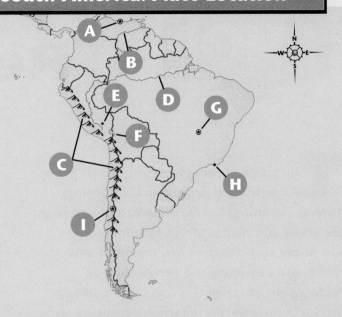

South America: Place Location

Writing Activity

Writing a Test

Write your own test about the economies of Chile and Venezuela. You may include multiple choice, true/false, fill in the blank, and essay questions on your test. Ask questions about how natural resources are important in each country's economy. Ask about benefits and problems that have affected each economy. Write an answer key to go with your test. Then trade tests with a partner. Take each other's tests. How did you do?

Internet Activity

Use a search engine to find the site **Rainforest Action Network.** Click on **Kid's Corner.** Here you can learn about life in the rain forest, issues of concern, and action that you can take. After exploring, click the BACK button on your browser. Click on **Rainforest Information.** Click on **Kids' Art Gallery.** Make your own drawing based on ideas you've gotten from the site.

Skills Review

Turn to the Skill Activity.

Review the steps for making a contour map. Then answer the following: (a) What are isolines? (b) Explain in your own words how you can use isolines to get useful information from a map.

How Am I Doing?

Answer these questions to help you check your progress.

1. Can I explain how changes in Brazil's rain forests affect the rest of the world?
2. Do I understand how geography has affected the lifestyles of Native Americans in Peru?
3. Can I explain why agriculture is important to Chile's economy?
4. Do I understand how the oil boom affected Venezuela's economy?
5. What information from this chapter can I use in my book project?

Rain Forest Resources

The tropical rain forests of South America are in danger. Lumbering, mining, ranching, and farming are destroying the trees and plants of the rain forests. As you know, some people are trying to save the rain forests by using the renewable, or replaceable, parts of the trees and plants in products for sale. For example, cashews and brazil nuts from rain forest trees can be harvested without harming the trees themselves. Oils from rain forest plants and nuts can be used in lotions and shampoos. If people can make money from a rain forest without cutting or burning it, people will have reasons to preserve the forests.

Purpose

In this activity, you will invent a new rain forest product. As you work on this activity, you will discover how rain forest products can be used without destroying rain forest resources.

Invent a Product

Think of a product that can be made with a renewable rain forest resource. Rain forest nuts are used in candy, ice cream, and cookies. Natural rubber from rubber trees is used to make bath toys. Use encyclopedias and other references to find out about the fruits of the assai tree, the oil of the babacu tree, and the resin of the copaiba tree. Think of something from the rain forest that many people need. Once you decide on your product, give it a name that people will remember.

Design a Package

When you have a product in mind, decide how it should look in a store. Should it come in a bag, a box, a can, or a bottle? Design the package, including art work and a product description.

Set a Price

Do some research to find out what products like yours cost. Visit or call a store. Then decide on the price for your product that is in the range of similar products. Put the price on your package.

Figure Your Costs

Now figure out how much money is needed to make your product. Assume that your costs are half of the selling price. For example, if your selling price is $6.50, then your manufacturing cost is $3.25. Divide your total manufacturing cost into the categories listed below.

- 50 percent for labor
- 25 percent for materials
- 10 percent for transportation
- 10 percent for advertising
- 5 percent for taxes

Then make a circle graph showing the percentage and dollar amount for each type of expense.

Make a Poster

Make a poster showing the layers of rain forest life: herb layer, shrub layer, understory, canopy, and emergent layer. Use encyclopedias and reference books such as *Usborne Science and Experiments: Ecology* (Usborne Publishing, 1988). Show the different kinds of creatures that live at each level and explain how they survive.

Links to Other Subjects

Designing a package for a new product	**Art**
Making a circle graph	**Math**
Doing research on the layers of the rain forest	**Science**
Writing a script	**Language Arts**
Writing a song	**Music**

Create a Commercial

You can make a commercial to advertise your rain forest product. Use the poster you made as a prop for your commercial. Write a short script that explains why it is important to protect rain forests and how your product helps in that effort. Write and perform an original jingle or music for the commercial. You can produce your commercial on computer or shoot it with a video camera. Or, you can perform your commercial for the rest of the class. Remember that your commercial should make people want to buy your product.

ANALYSIS AND CONCLUSION

Write a summary that describes the process you used to create your product. Be sure to answer the following questions in your summary.

1. What did you learn about using rain forest resources?

2. How can rain forest resources be used without destroying them?

3. Do you think it is possible for people to protect rain forests by using their renewable resources?

Question Book

BY PABLO NERUDA

BEFORE YOU READ

Reach Into Your Background

Do you pay close attention to the world around you? Describe a plant, a building, or a person that you saw on your way to school today. Remember as many details as you can. If you saw a tree, try to remember the shape of its leaves and whether its roots were visible above the ground. If you saw a person, try to remember what the person was wearing and how old the person seemed to be.

Many of Pablo Neruda's poems help readers pay more attention to the world around them. Neruda, who lived in Chile, often wrote about subjects that people take for granted. The following poem is from a book of Neruda's poetry called *Question Book*.

Questions to Explore

1. How does this poem help you look more closely at the changes of the seasons?
2. Because Chile is in the Southern Hemisphere, its seasons are the reverse of the seasons in the United States. Does knowing this change your understanding of the poem? Why or why not?

Ask Questions If you were going to write a poem of questions, what questions would you ask?

LXXII

Si todos los ríos son dulces
de dónde saca sal el mar?

Cómo saben las estaciones
que deben cambiar de camisa?

Por qué tan lentas en invierno
y tan palpitantes después?

Y cómo saben las raíces
que deben subir a la luz?

Y luego saludar al aire
con tantas flores y colores?

Siempre es la misma
        primavera
la que repite su papel?

LXXII

If all rivers are sweet
where does the sea get its salt?

How do the seasons discover
it's time to change shirts?

Why are winters so slow
and the aftermaths, volatile?

How do the roots know
they must climb toward the light?

And then greet the air
with such colors and flowers?

Is it always the same spring,
repeating the same role?

aftermath (AF ter math) *n.:*
the period that comes after
an event
volatile (VOL a til) *adj.:*
explosive
role (roll) *n.:* a part played
by an actor

◀▲ These photos show
winter and summer in
Chile's Patagonian Andes.
How can you tell which
season is which?

READ ACTIVELY

Visualize What does a
root look like as it pushes
away from a seed and up
toward the sky?

EXPLORING YOUR READING

Look Back

1. What do all the questions
in this poem have in
common?

Think It Over

2. Seasons don't wear shirts.
What does Neruda mean
when he refers to the seasons changing their shirts?

3. How is spring like an actor
playing a role in a play?

4. Based on this poem, does
Neruda seem to think
that nature is friendly or
unfriendly? Explain your
answer.

Go Beyond

5. How can paying attention
to details around you help
you appreciate nature?

Ideas for Writing:
Answer Poem

6. The questions that Neruda
asks all have scientific
explanations. Find out
the scientific answer to
Neruda's questions. Then,
write an answer poem in
response to Neruda's.

LATIN AMERICA
PROJECT POSSIBILITIES

As you study Latin America, you will be reading and thinking about these important questions.

☞ **What are the main physical features of Latin America?**

☞ **What factors have affected cultures in Latin America?**

☞ **Why have many Latin Americans been moving to cities in recent years?**

☞ **What is the relationship of the nations of Latin America with the United States and the world?**

☞ **How has geography influenced the ways in which Latin Americans make a living?**

Doing a project shows what you know! Are you doing this project? Muy bueno!

GEO LEO

Project Menu

The chapters in this book have some answers to these questions. Now it's time for you to find your own answers by doing projects on your own or with a group. Here are some ways to make your own discoveries about Latin America.

A Latin American Concert As you study Latin America, find out about the music of each region. Find out what kinds of instruments people play and what the instruments are made of. Then try to find examples of each kind of music. You might find some in public libraries, which usually have a music collection. Play the music for your class. You might explain how history and geography had an effect on the development of each kind of music. For example, in the Andes, people make a kind of rattle out of llamas' hooves. Talk about the roles of different types of music. For example, merengue is dance music, and reggae often serves as political protest.

From Questions to Careers

INTERPRETER

When people who speak different languages need to talk to each other, they often need an interpreter. An interpreter is someone who speaks both languages and can translate for both people as they talk.

In the United States, most interpreters work for the government. They translate during meetings between U.S. officials and visitors from other countries. Interpreters are especially important when there is an emergency. For example, when a major earthquake struck San Francisco in 1989, interpreters helped Spanish speakers get medical attention and talk to telephone operators.

Interpreters also work for companies doing business in other countries. Large corporations often have a whole team of interpreters.

Many interpreters have a degree in their second language and additional training in interpreting. However, some bilingual people are able to become interpreters for small companies or agencies without training.

Visions of Latin America
Create a diorama showing the effect of geography on the way people live in Latin America. Your diorama can be realistic or it can show a symbol. Work in groups of three or four.

After you finish your diorama, write a short report to explain how the subject of your diorama affects the people of Latin America today. Display the whole set of dioramas with the reports. Invite other students to look at them. You might also display them at parents' night.

Latin America in the News
As you read about Latin America, keep a bulletin board display called *Latin America in the News*. Look in magazines and newspapers for articles that describe life in Latin America. For example, when you study Mexico, you can collect articles about Mexican culture, politics, or economics.

When you have finished your study of Latin America, choose the articles that you want to keep. Make a scrapbook to contain the articles. Display the scrapbook in the school library or resource center.

Explorer's Dictionary
Many languages are spoken in Latin America. As you work on this book, create a dictionary of important terms. Use a foreign-language dictionary to translate your terms into Spanish or another Latin American language.

Illustrate your dictionary with drawings or pictures cut out from magazines or travel brochures. Bind the pages together with yarn or staples. Display your dictionary so other students can use it.

Reference

TABLE OF CONTENTS

MAP AND GLOBE Handbook

This Map and Globe Handbook is designed to help you develop some of the skills you need to be a world explorer. These can help you whether you explore from the top of an elephant in India or from a computer at school.

You can use the information in this handbook to improve your map and globe skills. But the best way to sharpen your skills is to practice. The more you practice, the better you'll get.

GEO CLEO and GEO LEO

Table of Contents

Five Themes of Geography

Studying the geography of the entire world can be a huge task. You can make that task easier by using the five themes of geography: location, place, human-environment interaction, movement, and regions. The themes are tools you can use to organize information and to answer the where, why, and how of geography.

1 Location answers the question, "Where is it?" You can think of the location of a continent or a country as its address. You might give an absolute location such as "22 South Lake Street" or "40°N and 80°W." You might also use a relative address, telling where one place is by referring to another place. "Between school and the mall" and "eight miles east of Pleasant City" are examples of relative locations.

2 Place identifies the natural and human features that make one place different from every other place. You can identify a specific place by its landforms, climate, plants, animals, people, or cultures. You might even think of place as a geographic signature. Use the signature to help you understand the natural and human features that make one place different from every other place.

1. Location
Chicago, Illinois, occupies one location on the Earth. No other place has exactly the same absolute location.

2. Place
Ancient cultures in Egypt built distinctive pyramids. Use the theme of place to help you remember features that exist only in Egypt.

3 Human-Environment Interaction focuses on the relationship between people and the environment. As people live in an area, they often begin to make changes to it, usually to make their lives easier. For example, they might build a dam to control flooding during rainy seasons. Also, the environment can affect how people live, work, dress, travel, and communicate.

4 Movement answers the question "How do people, goods, and ideas move from place to place?" Remember that, often, what happens in one place can affect what happens in another. Use the theme of movement to help you trace the spread of goods, people, and ideas from one location to the next.

5 Regions is the last geographic theme. A region is a group of places that share common features. Geographers divide the world into many types of regions. For example, countries, states, and cities are political regions. The people in these places live under the same type of government. Other features can be used to define regions. Places that have the same climate belong to a particular climate region. Places that share the same culture belong to a cultural region. The same place can be found in more than one region. The state of Hawaii is in the political region of the United States. Because it has a tropical climate, Hawaii is also part of a tropical climate region.

PRACTICE YOUR WORLD EXPLORER SKILLS

1. What is the absolute location of your school? What is one way to describe its relative location?

2. What might be a "geographic signature" of the town or city you live in?

3. Give an example of human-environment interaction where you live.

4. Name at least one thing that comes into your town or city and one that goes out. How is each moved? Where does it come from? Where does it go?

5. What are several regions you think your town or city belongs in?

3. Human-Environment Interaction
Peruvians have changed steep mountain slopes into terraces suitable for farming. Think how this environment looked before people made changes.

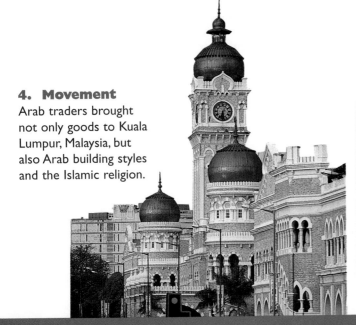

4. Movement
Arab traders brought not only goods to Kuala Lumpur, Malaysia, but also Arab building styles and the Islamic religion.

5. Regions
Wheat farming is an important activity in Kansas. This means that Kansas is part of a farming region.

Understanding Movements of the Earth

lanet Earth is part of our solar system. The Earth revolves around the sun in a nearly circular path called an orbit. A revolution, or one complete orbit around the sun, takes 365 1/4 days, or a year. As the Earth revolves around the sun, it is also spinning around in space. This movement is called a rotation. The Earth rotates on its axis—an invisible line through the center of the Earth from the North Pole to the South Pole. The Earth makes one full rotation about every 24 hours. As the Earth rotates, it is daytime on the side facing the sun. It is night on the side away from the sun.

The Earth's axis is tilted at an angle. Because of this tilt, sunlight strikes different parts of the Earth at certain points in the year, creating different seasons.

Earth's Revolution and the Seasons

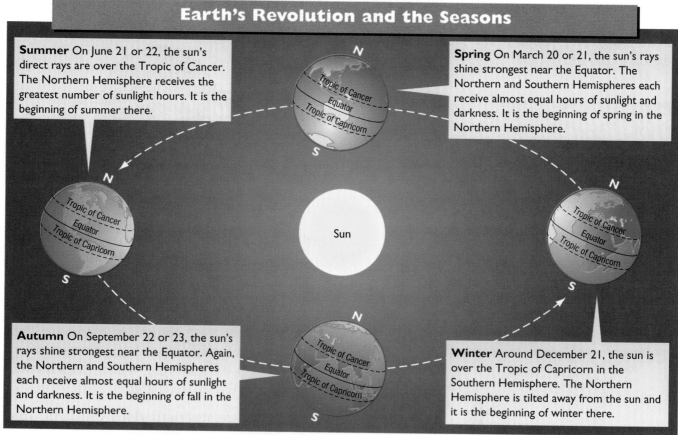

Summer On June 21 or 22, the sun's direct rays are over the Tropic of Cancer. The Northern Hemisphere receives the greatest number of sunlight hours. It is the beginning of summer there.

Spring On March 20 or 21, the sun's rays shine strongest near the Equator. The Northern and Southern Hemispheres each receive almost equal hours of sunlight and darkness. It is the beginning of spring in the Northern Hemisphere.

Autumn On September 22 or 23, the sun's rays shine strongest near the Equator. Again, the Northern and Southern Hemispheres each receive almost equal hours of sunlight and darkness. It is the beginning of fall in the Northern Hemisphere.

Winter Around December 21, the sun is over the Tropic of Capricorn in the Southern Hemisphere. The Northern Hemisphere is tilted away from the sun and it is the beginning of winter there.

▲ **Location** This diagram shows how the Earth's tilt and orbit around the sun combine to create the seasons. Remember, in the Southern Hemisphere the seasons are reversed.

PRACTICE YOUR WORLD EXPLORER SKILLS

1 What causes the seasons in the Northern Hemisphere to be the opposite of those in the Southern Hemisphere?

2 During which two months of the year do the Northern and Southern Hemispheres have about equal hours of daylight and darkness?

Maps and Globes Represent the Earth

Globes

A globe is a scale model of the Earth. It shows the actual shapes, sizes, and locations of all the Earth's landmasses and bodies of water. Features on the surface of the Earth are drawn to scale on a globe. This means a smaller unit of measure on the globe stands for a larger unit of measure on the Earth.

Because a globe is made in the true shape of the Earth, it offers these advantages for studying the Earth.

- The shape of all land and water bodies are accurate.
- Compass directions from one point to any other point are correct.
- The distance from one location to another is always accurately represented.

However, a globe presents some disadvantages for studying the Earth. Because a globe shows the entire Earth, it cannot show small areas in great detail. Also, a globe is not easily folded and carried from one place to another. For these reasons, geographers often use maps to learn about the Earth.

Maps

A map is a drawing or representation, on a flat surface, of a region. A map can show details too small to be seen on a globe. Floor plans, mall directories, and road maps are among the maps we use most often.

While maps solve some of the problems posed by globes, they have some disadvantages of their own. Maps flatten the real round world. Mapmakers cut, stretch, push, and pull some parts of the Earth to get it all flat on paper. As a result, some locations may be distorted. That is, their size, shape, and relative location may not be accurate. For example, on most maps of the entire world, the size and shape of the Antarctic and Arctic regions are not accurate.

PRACTICE YOUR WORLD EXPLORER SKILLS

1. What is the main difference between a globe and a map?

2. What is one advantage of using a globe instead of a map?

Global Gores

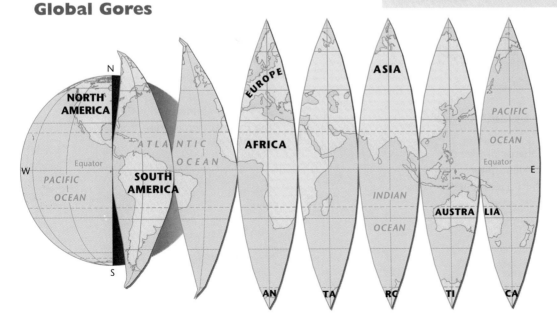

◀ **Location**
When mapmakers flatten the surface of the Earth, curves become straight lines. As a result, size, shape, and distance are distorted.

Locating Places on a Map or a Globe

The Hemispheres

Another name for a round ball like a globe is a sphere. The Equator, an imaginary line halfway between the North and South Poles, divides the globe into two hemispheres. (The prefix *hemi* means "half.") Land and water south of the Equator are in the Southern Hemisphere. Land and water north of the Equator are in the Northern Hemisphere.

Mapmakers sometimes divide the globe along an imaginary line that runs from North Pole to South Pole. This line, called the Prime Meridian, divides the globe into the Eastern and Western Hemispheres.

Northern Hemisphere

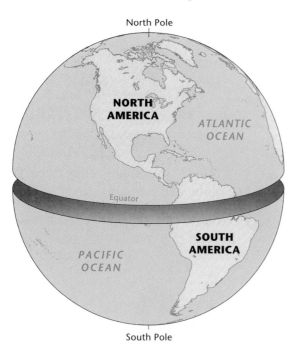

Southern Hemisphere

▲ The Equator divides the Northern Hemisphere from the Southern Hemisphere.

Western Hemisphere **Eastern Hemisphere**

▲ The Prime Meridian divides the Eastern Hemisphere from the Western Hemisphere.

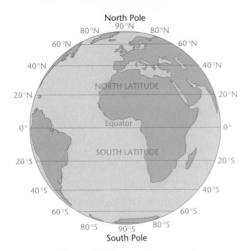

Parallels of Latitude

The Equator, at 0° latitude, is the starting place for measuring latitude or distances north and south. Most globes do not show every parallel of latitude. They may show every 10, 20, or even 30 degrees.

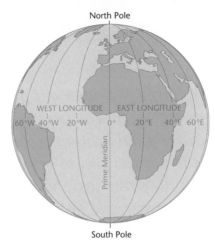

Meridians of Longitude

The Prime Meridian, at 0° longitude, runs from pole to pole through Greenwich, England. It is the starting place for measuring longitude or distances east and west. Each meridian of longitude meets its opposite longitude at the North and South Poles.

The Global Grid

Two sets of lines cover most globes. One set of lines runs parallel to the Equator. These lines, including the Equator, are called *parallels of latitude.* They are measured in degrees (°). One degree of latitude represents a distance of about 70 miles (112 km). The Equator has a location of 0°. The other parallels of latitude tell the direction and distance from the Equator to another location.

The second set of lines runs north and south. These lines are called *meridians of longitude.* Meridians show the degrees of longitude east or west of the Prime Meridian, which is located at 0°. A meridian of longitude tells the direction and distance from the Prime Meridian to another location. Unlike parallels, meridians are not the same distance apart everywhere on the globe.

Together the pattern of parallels of latitude and meridians of longitude is called the global grid. Using the lines of latitude and longitude, you can locate any place on Earth. For example, the location of 30° north latitude and 90° west longitude is usually written as 30°N, 90°W. Only one place on Earth has these coordinates—the city of New Orleans, in the state of Louisiana.

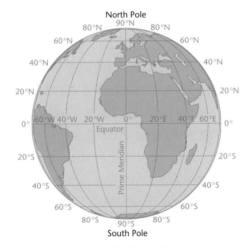

The Global Grid

By using lines of latitude and longitude, you can give the absolute location of any place on the Earth.

1 Which continents lie completely in the Northern Hemisphere? The Western Hemisphere?

2 Is there land or water at 20°S latitude and the Prime Meridian? At the Equator and 60°W longitude?

Map Projections

*I*magine trying to flatten out a complete orange peel. The peel would split. The shape would change. You would have to cut the peel to get it to lie flat. In much the same way, maps cannot show the correct size and shape of every landmass or body of water on the Earth's curved surface. Maps shrink some places and stretch others. This shrinking and stretching is called distortion—*a change made to a shape.*

To make up for this disadvantage, mapmakers use different map projections. Each map projection is a way of showing the round Earth on flat paper. Each type of projection has some distortion. No one projection can accurately show the correct area, shape, distance, and direction for the Earth's surface. Mapmakers use the projection that has the least distortion for the information they are studying.

Same-Shape Maps

Some map projections can accurately show the shapes of landmasses. However, these projections often greatly distort the size of landmasses as well as the distance between them.

One of the most common same-shape maps is a Mercator projection, named for the mapmaker who invented it. The Mercator projection accurately shows shape and direction, but it distorts distance and size. In this projection, the northern and southern areas of the globe appear stretched more than areas near the Equator. Because the projection shows true directions, ships' navigators use it to chart a straight line course between two ports.

Mercator Projection

Equal-Area Maps

Some map projections can show the correct size of landmasses. Maps that use these projections are called equal-area maps. In order to show the correct size of landmasses, these maps usually distort shapes. The distortion is usually greater at the edges of the map and less at the center.

Robinson Maps

Many of the maps in this book use the Robinson projection. This is a compromise between the Mercator and equal-area projections. It gives a useful overall picture of the world. The Robinson projection keeps the size and shape relationships of most continents and oceans but does distort size of the polar regions.

Azimuthal Maps

Another kind of projection shows true compass direction. Maps that use this projection are called azimuthal maps. Such maps are easy to recognize—they are usually circular. Azimuthal maps are often used to show the areas of the North and South Poles. However, azimuthal maps distort scale, area, and shape.

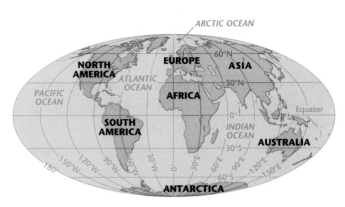

Equal-Area Projection

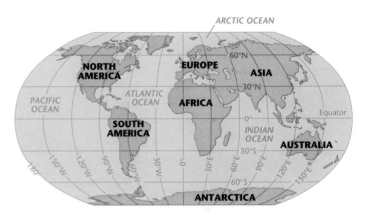

Robinson Projection

Azimuthal Projection

1. What feature is distorted on an equal-area map?

2. Would you use a Mercator projection to find the exact distance between two locations? Tell why or why not.

3. Which would be a better choice for studying the Antarctic—an azimuthal projection or a Robinson projection? Explain.

Parts of a Map

Mapmakers provide several clues to help you understand the information on a map. As an explorer, it is your job to read and interpret these clues.

Compass

Many maps show north at the top of the map. One way to show direction on a map is to use an arrow that points north. There may be an N shown with the arrow. Many maps give more information about direction by displaying a compass showing the directions, north, east, south, and west. The letters N, E, S, and W are placed to indicate these directions.

Title

The title of a map is the most basic clue. It signals what kinds of information you are likely to find on the map. A map titled *West Africa: Population Density* will be most useful for locating information about where people live in West Africa.

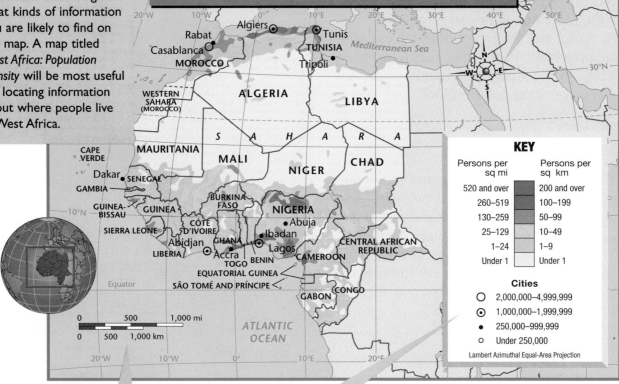

West Africa: Population Density

KEY

Persons per sq mi	Persons per sq km
520 and over	200 and over
260–519	100–199
130–259	50–99
25–129	10–49
1–24	1–9
Under 1	Under 1

Cities

- ○ 2,000,000–4,999,999
- ◉ 1,000,000–1,999,999
- ● 250,000–999,999
- ○ Under 250,000

Lambert Azimuthal Equal-Area Projection

Scale

A map scale helps you find the actual distances between points shown on the map. You can measure the distance between any two points on the map, compare them to the scale, and find out the actual distance between the points. Most map scales show distances in both miles and kilometers.

Key

Often a map has a key, or legend, that shows the symbols used on the map and what each one means. On some maps, color is used as a symbol. On those maps, the key also tells the meaning of each color.

PRACTICE YOUR WORLD EXPLORER SKILLS

1. What part of a map tells you what the map is about?

2. Where on the map should you look to find out the meaning of this symbol? •

3. What part of the map can you use to find the distance between two cities?

Comparing Maps of Different Scale

Here are three maps drawn to three different scales. The first map shows Moscow's location in the northeastern portion of Russia. This map shows the greatest area—a large section of northern Europe. It has the smallest scale (1 inch = about 900 miles) and shows the fewest details. This map can tell you what direction to travel to reach Moscow from Finland.

Find the red box on Map 1. It shows the whole area covered by Map 2. Study Map 2. It gives a closer look at the city of Moscow. It shows the features around the city, the city's boundary, and the general shape of the city. This map can help you find your way from the airport to the center of town.

Now find the red box on Map 2. This box shows the area shown on Map 3. This map moves you closer into the city. Like the zoom on a computer or camera, Map 3 shows the smallest area but has the greatest detail. This map has the largest scale (1 inch = about 0.8 miles). This is the map to use to explore downtown Moscow.

Map 1

KEY

—— National boundary

0   500   1,000 mi
0   500 1,000 km

One inch = about 900 miles

Map 2

KEY

▢ Built-up area

═══ Road or street

0   5   10 mi
0   5   10 km

One inch = about 12.5 miles

Map 3

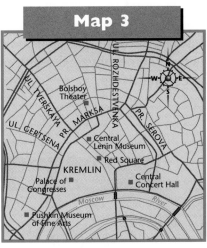

KEY

═══ Road or street

■ Point of interest

0   .5   1 mi
0   .5   1 km

One inch = about 0.8 miles

PRACTICE YOUR WORLD EXPLORER SKILLS

1 Which map would be best for finding the location of Red Square? Why?

2 Which map best shows Moscow's location relative to Poland? Explain.

3 Which map best shows the area immediately surrounding the city?

Political Maps

Mapmakers create maps to show all kinds of information. The kind of information presented affects the way a map looks. One type of map is called a political map. Its main purpose is to show continents, countries, and divisions within countries such as states or provinces. Usually different colors are used to show different countries or divisions within a country. The colors do not have any special meaning. They are used only to make the map easier to read.

Political maps also show where people have built towns and cities. Symbols can help you tell capital cities from other cities and towns. Even though political maps do not give information that shows what the land looks like, they often include some physical features such as oceans, lakes, and rivers.

Political maps usually have many labels. They give country names, and the names of capital and major cities. Bodies of water such as lakes, rivers, oceans, seas, gulfs, and bays are also labeled.

PRACTICE YOUR WORLD EXPLORER SKILLS

1. What symbol shows the continental boundary?

2. What symbol is used to indicate a capital city? A major city?

3. What kinds of landforms are shown on this map?

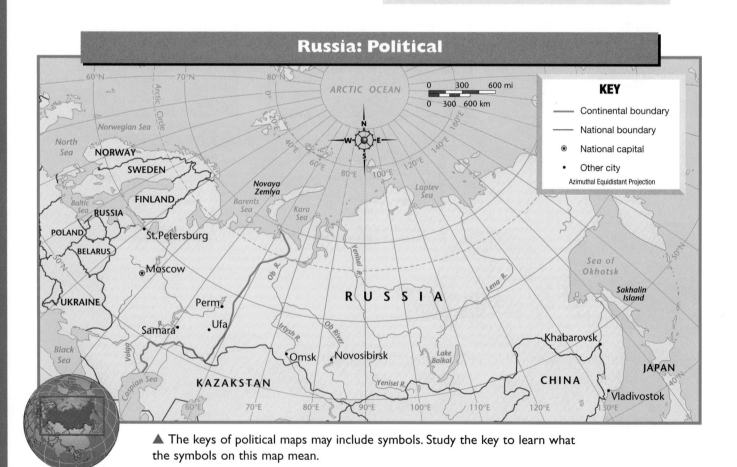

Russia: Political

KEY
— Continental boundary
— National boundary
⊛ National capital
• Other city
Azimuthal Equidistant Projection

▲ The keys of political maps may include symbols. Study the key to learn what the symbols on this map mean.

Physical Maps

Like political maps, physical maps show country labels and labels for capital cities. However, physical maps also show what the land of a region looks like by showing the major physical features such as plains, hills, plateaus, or mountains. Labels give the names of features such as mountain peaks, mountains, plateaus, and river basins.

In order to tell one landform from another, physical maps often show elevation and relief.

Elevation is the height of the land above sea level. Physical maps in this book use color to show elevation. Browns and oranges show higher lands while blues and greens show lands that are at or below sea level.

Relief shows how quickly the land rises or falls. Hills, mountains, and plateaus are shown on relief maps using shades of gray. Level or nearly level land is shown without shading. Darkly shaded areas indicate steeper lands.

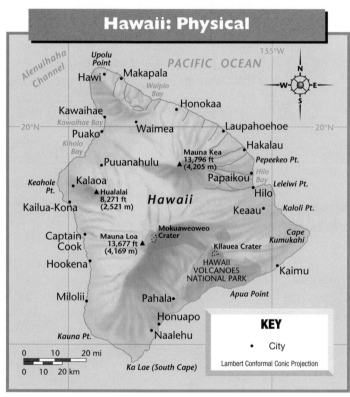

Hawaii: Physical

PRACTICE YOUR WORLD EXPLORER SKILLS

1. How is relief shown on the map to the left?

2. How can you use relief to decide which areas will be the most difficult to climb?

3. What information is given with the name of a mountain peak?

▲ On a physical map, shading is sometimes used to show relief. Use the shading to locate the mountains in Hawaii.

▼ Mauna Kea, an extinct volcano, is the highest peak in the state of Hawaii. Find Mauna Kea on the map.

Special Purpose Maps

As you explore the world, you will encounter many different kinds of special purpose maps. For example, a road map is a special purpose map. The title of each special purpose map tells the purpose and content of the map. Usually a special purpose map highlights only one kind of information. Examples of special purpose maps include land use, population distribution, recreation, transportation, natural resources, or weather.

The key on a special purpose map is very important. Even though a special purpose map shows only one kind of information, it may present many different pieces of data. This data can be shown in symbols, colors, or arrows. In this way, the key acts like a dictionary for the map.

Reading a special purpose map is a skill in itself. Look at the map below. First, try to get an overall sense of what it shows. Then, study the map to identify its main ideas. For example, one main idea of this map is that much of the petroleum production in the region takes place around the Persian Gulf.

PRACTICE YOUR WORLD EXPLORER SKILLS

1. What part of a special purpose map tells what information is contained on the map?

2. What part of a special purpose map acts like a dictionary for the map?

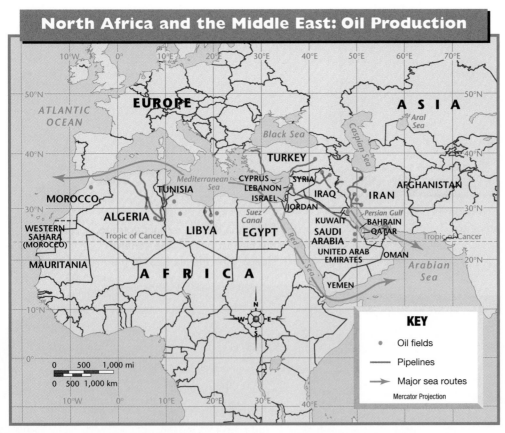

North Africa and the Middle East: Oil Production

ATLANTIC OCEAN
EUROPE
ASIA
Aral Sea
Black Sea
Caspian Sea
TURKEY
Mediterranean Sea
CYPRUS
LEBANON
SYRIA
IRAQ
IRAN
AFGHANISTAN
ISRAEL
JORDAN
MOROCCO
Suez Canal
Persian Gulf
WESTERN SAHARA (MOROCCO)
ALGERIA
LIBYA
EGYPT
Tropic of Cancer
KUWAIT
SAUDI ARABIA
BAHRAIN
QATAR
UNITED ARAB EMIRATES
OMAN
Tropic of Cancer
MAURITANIA
AFRICA
Red Sea
YEMEN
Arabian Sea
TUNISIA

0   500   1,000 mi
0   500 1,000 km

KEY
• Oil fields
— Pipelines
→ Major sea routes
Mercator Projection

◀ The title on a special purpose map indicates what information can be found on the map. The symbols used on the map are explained in the map's key.

Landforms, Climate Regions, and Natural Vegetation Regions

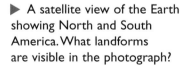

aps that show landforms, climate, and vegetation regions are special purpose maps. Unlike the boundary lines on a political map, the boundary lines on these maps do not separate the land into exact divisions. A tropical wet climate gradually changes to a tropical wet and dry climate. A tundra gradually changes to an ice cap. Even though the boundaries between regions may not be exact, the information on these maps can help you understand the region and the lives of people in it.

Landforms

Understanding how people use the land requires an understanding of the shape of the land itself. The four most important landforms are mountains, hills, plateaus, and plains. Human activity in every region in the world is influenced by these landforms.

- **Mountains** are high and steep. Most are wide at the bottom and rise to a narrow peak or ridge. Most geographers classify a mountain as land that rises at least 2,000 feet (610 m) above sea level. A series of mountains is called a mountain range.

- **Hills** rise above surrounding land and have rounded tops. Hills are lower and usually less steep than mountains. The elevation of surrounding land determines whether a landform is called a mountain or a hill.

- A **plateau** is a large, mostly flat area of land that rises above the surrounding land. At least one side of a plateau has a steep slope.

- **Plains** are large areas of flat or gently rolling land. Plains have few changes in elevation. Many plains areas are located along coasts. Others are located in the interior regions of some continents.

▶ A satellite view of the Earth showing North and South America. What landforms are visible in the photograph?

Climate Regions

Another important influence in the ways people live their lives is the climate of their region. Climate is the weather of a given location over a long period of time. Use the descriptions in the table below to help you visualize the climate regions shown on maps.

Climate	Temperatures	Precipitation
Tropical		
Tropical wet	Hot all year round	Heavy all year round
Tropical wet and dry	Hot all year round	Heavy when sun is overhead, dry other times
Dry		
Semiarid	Hot summers, mild to cold winters	Light
Arid	Hot days, cold nights	Very light
Mild		
Mediterranean	Hot summers, cool winters	Dry summers, wet winters
Humid subtropical	Hot summers, cool winters	Year round, heavier in summer than in winter
Marine west coast	Warm summers, cool winters	Year round, heavier in winter than in summer
Continental		
Humid continental	Hot summers, cold winters	Year round, heavier in summer than in winter
Subarctic	Cool summers, cold winters	Light
Polar		
Tundra	Cool summers, very cold winters	Light
Ice Cap	Cold all year round	Light
Highlands	Varies, depending on altitude and direction of prevailing winds	Varies, depending on altitude and direction of prevailing winds

Natural Vegetation Regions

Natural vegetation is the plant life that grows wild without the help of humans. A world vegetation map tells what the vegetation in a place would be if people had not cut down forests or cleared grasslands. The table below provides descriptions of natural vegetation regions shown on maps. Comparing climate and vegetation regions can help you see the close relationship between climate and vegetation.

Vegetation	Description
Tropical rain forest	Tall, close-growing trees forming a canopy over smaller trees, dense growth in general
Deciduous forest	Trees and plants that regularly lose their leaves after each growing season
Mixed forest	Both leaf-losing and cone-bearing trees, no type of tree dominant
Coniferous forest	Cone-bearing trees, evergreen trees and plants
Mediterranean vegetation	Evergreen shrubs and small plants
Tropical savanna	Tall grasses with occasional trees and shrubs
Temperate grassland	Tall grasses with occasional stands of trees
Desert scrub	Low shrubs and bushes, hardy plants
Desert	Little or no vegetation
Tundra	Low shrubs, mosses, lichens; no trees
Ice Cap	Little or no vegetation
Highlands	Varies, depending on altitude and direction of prevailing winds

PRACTICE YOUR WORLD EXPLORER SKILLS

1 How are mountains and hills similar? How are they different?

2 What is the difference between a plateau and a plain?

REGIONAL Data Bank

Use the Regional Data Bank to gather information about the geography, culture, and economy of the regions of Latin America.

Sources: The Microsoft® Encarta® '98 Encyclopedia, the CIA World Factbook, and the New York Times 1999 World Almanac. Map Sources: the National Geographic Atlas of the World, the Hammond Gold Medallion World Atlas, and the Macmillan Centennial Atlas of the World.

Latin America

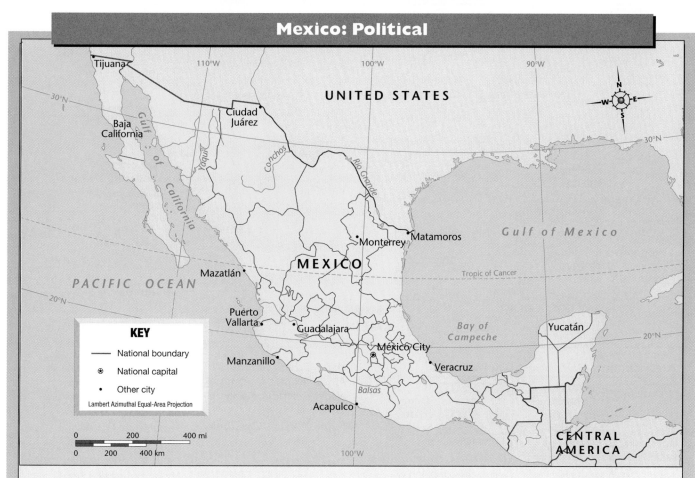

Mexico

Terrain Large central plateau, bordered by the Sierra Madre Occidental mountain range in the west and the Sierra Madre Oriental in the east; dense forests in south; lowlands on Pacific coast; plains on Gulf Coast

Climate Hot and dry north; temperate central; tropical south, with rainy and dry seasons

Population 98.5 million

Agriculture Corn, beans, wheat, coffee, cotton, citrus fruit, sugar, tomatoes, barley, rice, soybeans; cattle, chickens

Major Industries Steel, chemicals, food and beverages, textiles, electronic goods

Major Ethnic Groups Mestizo, European, Native American groups

Major Religion Christianity

Mexico

Highest Mountain Pico de Orizaba, 18,700 ft (5,700 m)

Longest River Rio Grande (source: Colorado, U.S.), 1,885 mi (3,035 km)

Largest City Mexico City, 8,236,960 people

1. What body of water borders Mexico on the west?

2. In what direction would you travel to reach the Mexican capital from Tijuana?

3. About how many miles apart are the cities of Guadalajara and Monterrey?

4. What kind of terrain would you expect to find near the city of Veracruz?

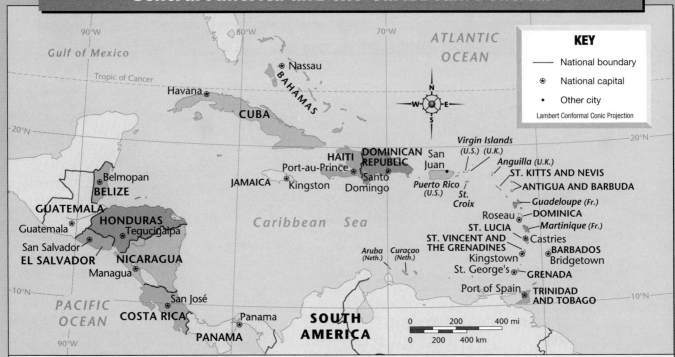

Gulf of Mexico

Tropic of Cancer

90°W   80°W   70°W

ATLANTIC OCEAN

Nassau

Havana

BAHAMAS

CUBA

20°N

20°N

HAITI
Port-au-Prince

DOMINICAN REPUBLIC
Santo Domingo

San Juan

Virgin Islands (U.S.) (U.K.)

Anguilla (U.K.)

ST. KITTS AND NEVIS

ANTIGUA AND BARBUDA

JAMAICA
Kingston

Belmopan
BELIZE

GUATEMALA

Guatemala

HONDURAS
Tegucigalpa

San Salvador
EL SALVADOR

NICARAGUA
Managua

Caribbean Sea

Puerto Rico (U.S.)
St. Croix

Guadeloupe (Fr.)

Roseau DOMINICA

ST. LUCIA Martinique (Fr.)

ST. VINCENT AND THE GRENADINES Castries

Aruba (Neth.) Curaçao (Neth.)

Kingstown BARBADOS
Bridgetown

St. George's GRENADA

Port of Spain TRINIDAD AND TOBAGO

10°N

PACIFIC OCEAN

San José

COSTA RICA

Panama

PANAMA

SOUTH AMERICA

90°W

0   200   400 mi

0   200   400 km

10°N

Antigua and Barbuda

Terrain Antigua: Island of coastal lowlands rising to central highland; Barbuda: flat coral island

Climate Tropical dry

Population 60,000

Agriculture Cotton, fruits and vegetables, sugar

Major Industries Tourism, construction, light manufacturing

Major Ethnic Group African

Major Religion Christianity

Bahamas

Terrain 700 low-lying islands

Climate Subtropical

Population 280,000

Agriculture Citrus fruit, vegetables; poultry

Major Industries Tourism, international banking, cement

Major Ethnic Group African

Major Religion Christianity

Barbados

Terrain Coral island of coastal lowlands and central hills

Climate Tropical; rainy season

Population 260,000

Agriculture Sugar, vegetables, cotton

Major Industries Tourism, sugar, light manufacturing

Major Ethnic Group African

Major Religion Christianity

Belize

Terrain Swampy lowlands in north; mountainous south dominated by Maya Mountains; coral barrier reefs along coast

Climate Subtropical; long rainy season

Population 230,000

Agriculture Sugar, citrus fruit, bananas

Major Industries Food processing, wood products, clothing

Major Ethnic Groups African or part African; Native American, mainly Carib and Maya

Major Religion Christianity

Costa Rica

Terrain Mainly highlands with several mountain ranges

Climate Tropical along coast; mild in interior; long rainy season

Population 3.6 million

Agriculture Coffee, bananas, cacao, sugar, pineapples, corn, rice, cotton; cattle, hogs

Major Industries Food processing, wood products, textiles, chemicals

Major Ethnic Groups European, mestizo

Major Religion Christianity

Cuba

Terrain Island mainly of flat land and rolling hills; three mountain ranges with fertile valleys

Climate Semitropical; rainy, hot summers

Population 11.1 million

Agriculture Sugar, tobacco, citrus fruit, rice, coffee; cattle

Major Industries Sugar, petroleum, food and tobacco processing, cement

Major Ethnic Groups European, mixed European and African

Major Religion Christianity

Dominica

Terrain Mountainous; forested

Climate Tropical; rainy summers and dry winters

Population 70,000

Agriculture Bananas, citrus fruit, mangoes, coconuts, cacao, cinnamon, vanilla beans, vegetables; fish

Major Industries Soap, coconut oil, fruit juices, tourism

Major Ethnic Group African

Major Religion Christianity

Dominican Republic

Terrain Mountainous; fertile central valley and southeastern coastal plain

Climate Semitropical; warm in lowlands, much cooler and wetter in highlands; rainy season

Population 8 million

Agriculture Sugar, rice, coffee, bananas, cacao, tobacco, cotton; cattle, pigs

Major Industries Tourism, sugar, textiles, ferronickel and gold mining

Major Ethnic Group Mixed European and African

Major Religion Christianity

El Salvador

Terrain Dominated by volcanic mountain ranges; plateaus and valleys in central region; narrow Pacific coastal plain

Climate Tropical; very hot along coastal plain but cooler in mountains; rainy summers and dry winters

Population 5.8 million

Agriculture Coffee, sugar, corn, rice, beans, oilseeds, cereal grains, fruit; cattle, dairy products

Major Industries Food processing, chemicals, textiles, clothing, leather goods, tobacco, furniture, wood and metal products

Major Ethnic Group Mestizo (mix of European with Maya and Nahuatl)

Major Religion Christianity

Grenada

Terrain Mountainous; fertile valleys with swift-flowing streams

Climate Tropical; rainy season

Population 100,000

Agriculture Bananas, cacao, nutmeg, mace, citrus fruit

Major Industries Tourism, food and beverages, textiles

Major Ethnic Group African

Major Religion Christianity

Guatemala

Terrain Mountain ranges running east-west; lowlands in north; Pacific coastal plain

Climate Ranges from hot and humid at coast to cold in mountains; rainy summers and dry winters

Population 12 million

Agriculture Sugar, bananas, corn, coffee, cotton; cattle, sheep, pigs

Major Industries Sugar, textiles and clothing, food processing, furniture

Major Ethnic Groups Mestizo (mix of European and Native American called ladino), Maya

Major Religions Christianity, traditional Mayan

Haiti

Terrain Mountainous; fertile central plains and river valley

Climate Tropical; rainfall heavy in southwest, much lighter in northwest; hot in lowlands, much cooler in highlands

Population 6.8 million

Agriculture Coffee, sugar, grains, sisal, cotton; chickens

Major Industries Sugar refining, textiles, flour and cement milling

Major Ethnic Group African

Major Religion Christianity, sometimes combined with African traditional beliefs

Honduras

Terrain Mainly plateau, with plains and valleys; some volcanic mountain ranges

Climate Tropical; hot, humid coastal lowlands; rainy summers, dry winters

Population 5.9 million

Agriculture Coffee, bananas, sugar, palm oil, corn, beans, rice; cattle, pigs; shrimp

Major Industries Food processing, textiles, cement and wood products, chemicals

Major Ethnic Group Mestizo

Major Religion Christianity

Jamaica

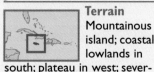

Terrain Mountainous island; coastal lowlands in south; plateau in west; several natural harbors

Climate Tropical; hot and humid in coastal lowlands; rain heavy in northeast mountains

Population 2.6 million

Agriculture Sugar, bananas, coffee, citrus fruit, potatoes, tobacco, cacao; poultry, goats, milk

Major Industries Tourism, bauxite mining, textiles

Major Ethnic Group African

Major Religion Christianity

Nicaragua

Terrain Lowlands on Pacific and Caribbean coasts; volcanic mountains just inland from Pacific coast; central highland plateau

Climate Tropical; hottest at coasts; rainy summers

Population 4.6 million

Agriculture Coffee, cereal grains, cotton, sugar, bananas; cattle; shrimp

Major Industries Food processing, textiles, chemicals, metal processing

Major Ethnic Group Mestizo

Major Religion Christianity

Panama

Terrain Mountainous; dense rain forest in east; narrow coastal plains in central region

Climate Tropical; warm and humid

Population 2.7 million

Agriculture Bananas, rice, sugar, coffee, corn

Major Industries Manufacturing and construction, oil refining, international banking

Major Ethnic Groups Mestizo, mixed European and African

Major Religion Christianity

Saint Kitts and Nevis

Terrain Islands with mountainous central regions
Climate Tropical; rainy season
Population 40,000
Agriculture Sugar, rice, yams, vegetables, bananas
Major Industries sugar processing, tourism, cotton
Major Ethnic Group African
Major Religion Christianity

Saint Lucia

Terrain Island with forested mountain range; fertile valleys
Climate Tropical; rainy season
Population 150,000
Agriculture Bananas, coconuts, vegetables, root crops, citrus fruit, cacao
Major Industries Clothing, electrical parts, beverages, cardboard boxes, food processing, tourism
Major Ethnic Group African
Major Religion Christianity

Saint Vincent and the Grenadines

Terrain Island group; main island (St. Vincent) crossed by volcanic mountains
Climate Tropical; rainy season
Population 120,000
Agriculture Bananas, coconuts, sweet potatoes, spices; livestock; fish
Major Industries Food processing, cement, furniture, clothing, starch
Major Ethnic Group African
Major Religion Christianity

Trinidad and Tobago

Terrain Trinidad: Hilly island with plains; rocky northern coast, steep southern coast; Tobago: island of single volcanic mountain
Climate Tropical; rainy season
Population 1.1 million
Agriculture Sugar, cacao, coffee, citrus fruit; poultry
Major Industries Petroleum, chemicals, tourism
Major Ethnic Groups African, East Indian
Major Religions Christianity, Hinduism

GEOFACTS

Caribbean
Highest Mountain Duarte Peak (Dominican Republic), 10,400 ft (3,170 m)
Longest River Cauto (source: Cuba's Sierra Maestro), 230 mi (370 km)
Largest City Havana (Cuba), 2,175,995 people
Largest Country Cuba, 42,805 sq mi (110,860 sq km)
Smallest Country St. Kitts and Nevis, 104 sq mi (269 sq km)

PRACTICE YOUR WORLD EXPLORER SKILLS

1. What is the northernmost nation in the region?
2. What two nations in the region occupy the same island?
3. Use the country descriptions to answer these questions: What is the dominant religion throughout the region? What is the one other major religion in the region?
4. In what direction would an airplane head to travel from Panama to El Salvador?

Brazil

Terrain Thickly forested lowlands of the Amazon River Basin in north; semiarid interior region in northeast; mainly open highlands to south, including grasslands, plateaus, and mountains; narrow coastal plain

Climate Tropical to subtropical; north rainy, hot, and humid all year; central seasonal rains and temperatures; northeast long dry season; south more moderate temperatures and rainfall

Population 169.8 million

Agriculture Coffee, soybeans, sugar, wheat, rice, corn, citrus fruit; cattle

Major Industries Textiles, shoes, chemicals, mining, steel, automobiles, machinery, appliances

Major Ethnic Groups European, mixed European and African

Major Religion Christianity

KEY

—— National boundary

⊛ National capital

• Other city

Lambert Azimuthal Equal Area Projection

Brazil

Highest Mountain Pico da Neblina, 9,888 ft (3,014 m)

Longest River Amazon (source: Andes Mountains, Peru), 4,000 mi (6,400 km)

Largest City São Paulo, 9,842,059 people

WORLD EXPLORER

1 What is the capital of Brazil?

2 Into what major body of water does the Amazon River empty?

3 In what direction would you travel to go from São Paulo to Brasília?

4 Use the map and the country description to answer this question: How does the climate differ in Manaus and Rio de Janeiro?

KEY

—— National boundary

⊛ National capital

• Other city

Lambert Azimuthal Equal-Area Projection

Colombia

Terrain Dominated by three ranges of Andes mountain chain in central and western regions; plateaus and fertile valleys between ranges; dense rain forests in the southeast; vast plains (called *llanos*) in the northeast

Climate Tropical along coasts and river valleys; subtropical to cold in the mountains; rainy and dry periods alternate

Population 38.6 million

Agriculture Coffee, cut flowers, bananas, rice, tobacco

Major Industries Textiles, food processing, oil, mining

Major Ethnic Groups Mestizo, European

Major Religion Christianity

French Guiana

(a territory of France)

Terrain Mostly dense forests covering central plateau; marshy lowlands along coast; highlands in south

Climate Tropical; hot and humid; dry summers, rainy winters

Population 160,000

Agriculture Rice, corn, cassava; cattle, pigs, poultry; shrimp

Major Industries Construction, shrimp processing, forest products

Major Ethnic Groups African or mixed African and European (also known as Creole)

Major Religion Christianity

GEOFACTS

Northern South America

Highest Mountain Pico Cristóbal Colón (Colombia), 18,950 ft (5,776 m)

Longest River Orinoco (source: Venezuela), 1,590 mi (2560 km)

Largest City Bogotá, 5,237,635 people

Largest Country Colombia, 440,831 sq mi (1,141,748 sq km)

Smallest Country French Guiana (a territory of France), 35,135 sq mi (91,000 sq km)

Guyana

Terrain Dense forest; coastal lowlands; central highland and grasslands

Climate Tropical; rainy season

Population 710,000

Agriculture Sugar, rice; cattle, hogs, chickens

Major Industries Bauxite mining, sugar, rice milling

Major Ethnic Groups East Indian, African

Major Religions Christianity, Hinduism

Suriname

Terrain Swampy coastal plain; central plateau of grasslands, sand dunes, and forests; thickly forested highlands in the south

Climate Tropical; rainy season

Population 430,000

Agriculture Rice, bananas; timber

Major Industries Bauxite mining, alumina and aluminum processing, lumbering

Major Ethnic Groups Asian (mainly from India and Indonesia), mixed African and Native American

Major Religions Christianity, Hinduism, Islam

Venezuela

Terrain Highlands in north and northwest and in south and southeast; lowlands near northwest coast; Orinoco River flows through grasslands (or llanos) of north central region

Climate Tropical along coast and in grasslands; milder in highlands

Population 22.8 million

Agriculture Corn, sorghum, sugar, rice, bananas, vegetables, coffee

Major Industries Petroleum, steel, iron-ore mining, textiles

Major Ethnic Groups Mestizo, European

Major Religion Christianity

PRACTICE YOUR
WORLD EXPLORER
SKILLS

1 Which capital city in this region is *not* located near the coast?

2 What country borders Suriname on the west?

3 Which city is farther from Caracas: Bogotá or Paramaribo? Use the scale on the map to estimate.

4 Use the country descriptions to answer this question: Which countries have large Asian ethnic populations?

Bolivia

Terrain Dominated by two Andes mountain ranges, in west and in central region; plateau between the ranges has forested and well-watered valleys; lowland plains (llanos) in east have dense forests and grasslands

Climate Varies with elevation, from hot and wet to cold and dry; rainy season

Population 7.8 million

Agriculture Coffee, cotton, corn, sugar, rice, potatoes; timber

Major Industries Mining, smelting, petroleum, food and beverages, tobacco, handicrafts, clothing

Major Ethnic Groups Quechua, Aymara, mestizo

Major Religion Christianity

Chile

Terrain Dominated by Andes Mountains in east; low coastal range in west; plateau region, between the mountain ranges, includes Atacama Desert and Central Valley

Climate Arid desert in north; mild, dry central; cool, rainy south

Population 14.8 million

Agriculture Wheat, corn, grapes, beans, sugar beets, potatoes

Major Industries Copper, other minerals, foodstuffs, fish processing, iron and steel, wood and wood products

Major Ethnic Group Mestizo (mix of Spanish and mainly Araucanian)

Major Religion Christianity

Ecuador

Terrain Coastal plain; central highlands, two Andes mountain chains enclosing a central plateau; rain forest east of the Andes; mountainous Galápagos Islands

Climate Tropical along coast; hotter and more humid in rain forest; moderate in central region

Population 12.3 million

Agriculture Bananas, coffee, cacao, rice; cattle, sheep, pigs

Major Industries Petroleum, food processing, textiles

Major Ethnic Groups Mestizo, Native American

Major Religion Christianity

Peru

Terrain Coastal plain; Andes Mountains, lying east of and parallel to coast, contain plateaus, gorges, and valleys; dense rain forests in northeast

Climate Arid along coast; tropical in northeast; temperate to cold in the mountains, where rainfall varies

Population 26.1 million

Agriculture Coffee, cotton, sugar, rice; poultry, red meat, dairy products, wool; fish

Major Industries Mining, petroleum, fishing, textiles, clothing, food processing

Major Ethnic Groups Native American, mestizo

Major Religion Christianity

GEOFACTS

Andean Countries

Highest Mountain Tupungato (Chile-Argentina border), 22,310 ft (6,800 m)

Longest River Amazon (source: Andes Mountains, Peru), 4,000 mi (6,400 km)

Largest City Lima (Peru), 5,706,127 people

Largest Country Peru, 494,200 sq mi (1,280,000 sq km)

Smallest Country Ecuador, 105,037 sq mi (272,045 sq km)

Argentina

Terrain Central and east dominated by rolling plains, including the treeless Pampas; arid steppes (Patagonia) in south; Andes Mountains in west

Climate Mainly temperate; tropical area in northeast; cold in mountains; north wetter than south and west

Population 36.3 million

Agriculture Wheat, corn, sorghum, soybeans, sugar beets; livestock

Major Industries Food processing, motor vehicles, durable consumer goods, textiles, chemicals

Major Ethnic Group European

Major Religion Christianity

Paraguay

Terrain Grassy plains, swamps, and scrub forest in west; plateau with grassy foothills in east

Climate Subtropical; rainy in east; semiarid in parts of west

KEY

—— National boundary

⊛ National capital

• Other city

Lambert Azimuthal Equal Area Projection

0   250   500 mi

0   250   500 km

Population 5.3 million

Agriculture Sugar, soybeans, cotton, corn, wheat, cassava; cattle, pigs; timber

Major Industries Meat packing, oilseed crushing, lumber milling

Major Ethnic Group Mestizo

Major Religion Christianity

Uruguay

Terrain Grassy, rolling plains in south; tidal marshland along coast; low plateau in north and northwest; highlands in east

Climate Temperate; ample rainfall all year

Population 3.3 million

Agriculture Wheat, rice, corn, sorghum; livestock; fishing

Major Industries Meat processing, wool and hides, sugar

Major Ethnic Group European

Major Religion Christianity

GEOFACTS

Southern South America

Highest Mountain Aconcagua (Argentina), 22,834 ft (6,960 m)

Longest River Paraná (source: central Brazil), 1,740 mi (2,800 km)

Largest City Buenos Aires (Argentina), 12,960,976 people

Largest Country Argentina, 1,073,518 sq mi (2,780,400 sq km)

Smallest Country Uruguay, 68,037 sq mi (176,215 sq km)

PRACTICE YOUR WORLD EXPLORER SKILLS

1 About how many kilometers apart are the cities of Montevideo and Buenos Aires?

2 Which country in the region extends farthest east?

3 What rivers would lead you from the capital of Paraguay to that of Argentina?

4 Use the country descriptions to answer this question: Where in this region do the Andes Mountains lie?

Atlas

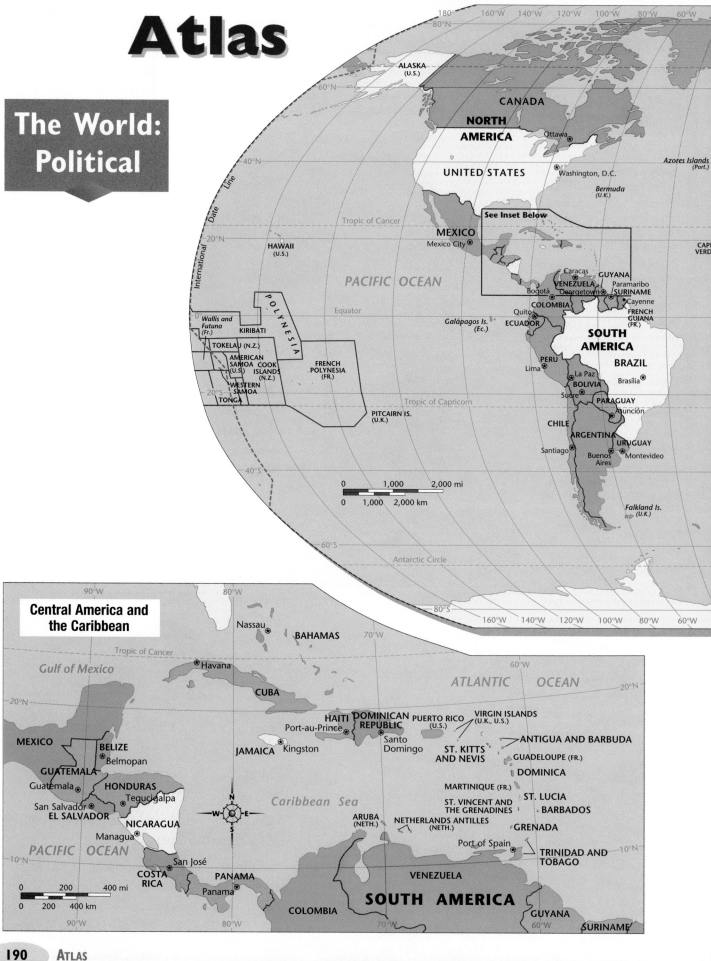

The World: Political

ALASKA (U.S.)

CANADA

NORTH AMERICA

Ottawa ⊛

UNITED STATES

Washington, D.C. ⊛

Azores Islands (Port.)

Bermuda (U.K.)

See Inset Below

Tropic of Cancer

MEXICO

Mexico City ⊛

CAPE VERDE

HAWAII (U.S.)

PACIFIC OCEAN

Caracas ⊛

VENEZUELA

GUYANA

Paramaribo •

SURINAME

Bogotá ⊛

Georgetown ⊛

COLOMBIA

• Cayenne

FRENCH GUIANA (FR.)

Equator

Galápagos Is. (Ec.)

Quito ⊛

ECUADOR

P O L Y N E S I A

Wallis and Futuna (Fr.)

KIRIBATI

TOKELAU (N.Z.)

AMERICAN SAMOA (U.S.)

COOK ISLANDS (N.Z.)

FRENCH POLYNESIA (FR.)

WESTERN SAMOA

TONGA

International Date Line

PERU

Lima ⊛

SOUTH AMERICA

BRAZIL

La Paz ⊛

BOLIVIA

Sucre ⊛

Brasília ⊛

PARAGUAY

Asunción ⊛

Tropic of Capricorn

PITCAIRN IS. (U.K.)

CHILE

ARGENTINA

URUGUAY

Santiago ⊛

Buenos Aires ⊛

Montevideo ⊛

Falkland Is. (U.K.)

| 0 | 1,000 | 2,000 mi |
| 0 | 1,000 | 2,000 km |

Antarctic Circle

Central America and the Caribbean

Nassau ⊛

BAHAMAS

Tropic of Cancer

Gulf of Mexico

Havana ⊛

CUBA

ATLANTIC OCEAN

HAITI

Port-au-Prince ⊛

DOMINICAN REPUBLIC

PUERTO RICO (U.S.)

VIRGIN ISLANDS (U.K., U.S.)

JAMAICA

Kingston ⊛

Santo Domingo ⊛

ANTIGUA AND BARBUDA

MEXICO

BELIZE

Belmopan ⊛

ST. KITTS AND NEVIS

GUADELOUPE (FR.)

DOMINICA

GUATEMALA

Guatemala ⊛

HONDURAS

Tegucigalpa ⊛

MARTINIQUE (FR.)

ST. LUCIA

San Salvador ⊛

EL SALVADOR

Caribbean Sea

ST. VINCENT AND THE GRENADINES

BARBADOS

NICARAGUA

ARUBA (NETH.)

NETHERLANDS ANTILLES (NETH.)

GRENADA

PACIFIC OCEAN

Managua ⊛

San José ⊛

Port of Spain ⊛

TRINIDAD AND TOBAGO

COSTA RICA

PANAMA

Panama ⊛

VENEZUELA

SOUTH AMERICA

COLOMBIA

GUYANA

SURINAME

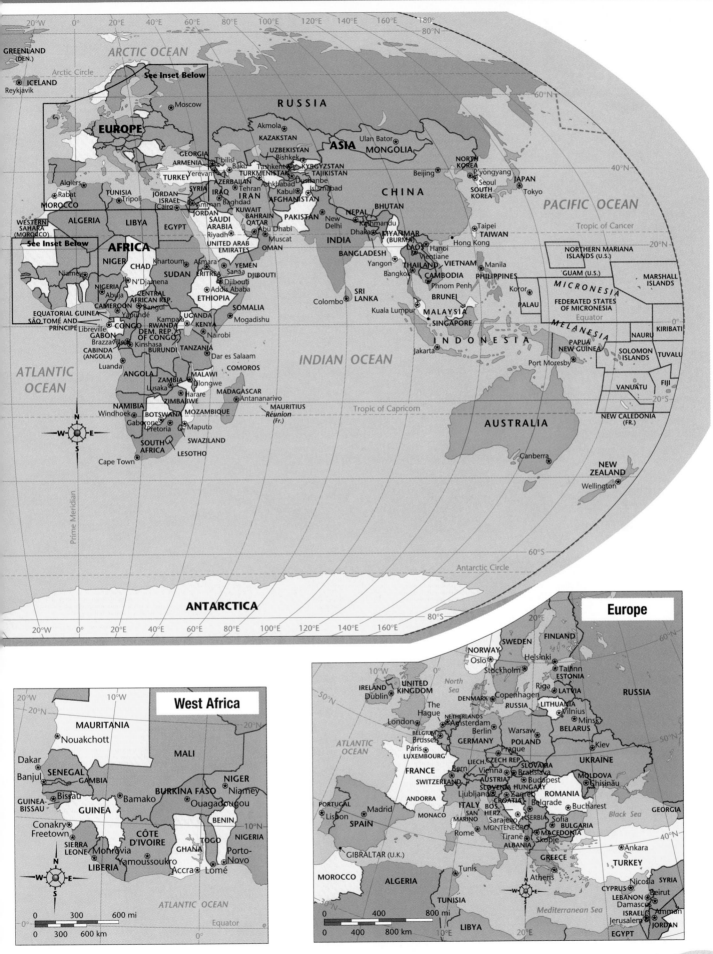

ATLAS **191**

The World: Physical

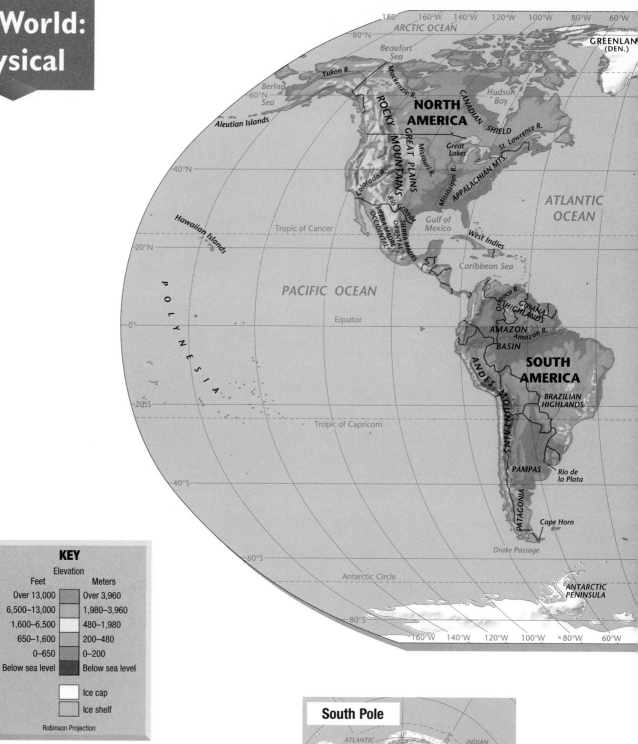

KEY

Elevation

Feet		Meters
Over 13,000		Over 3,960
6,500–13,000		1,980–3,960
1,600–6,500		480–1,980
650–1,600		200–480
0–650		0–200
Below sea level		Below sea level

Ice cap

Ice shelf

Robinson Projection

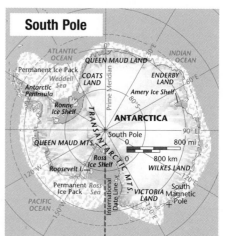

South Pole

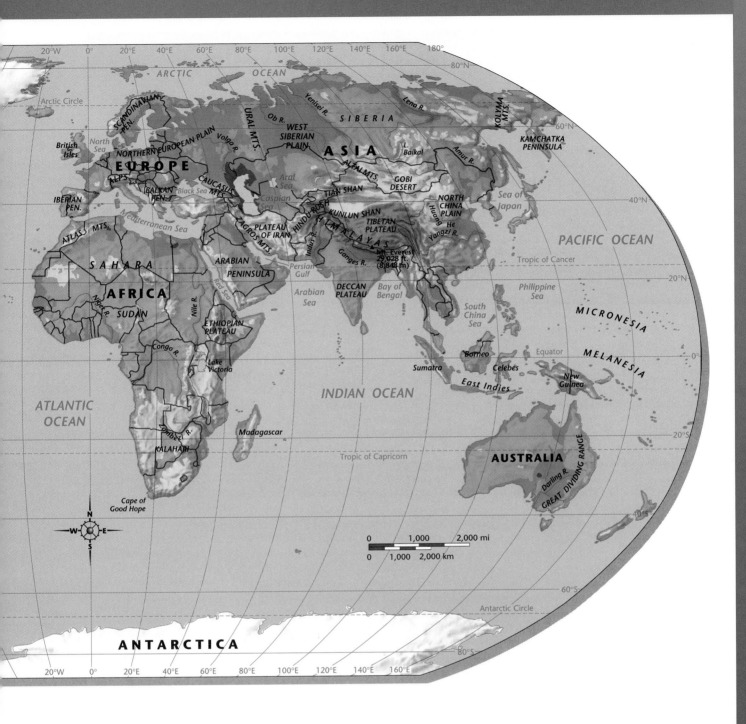

20°W | 0° | 20°E | 40°E | 60°E | 80°E | 100°E | 120°E | 140°E | 160°E | 180°

Arctic Circle

ARCTIC OCEAN

80°N

SCANDINAVIAN PEN.

British Isles

North Sea

NORTHERN EUROPEAN PLAIN

EUROPE

URAL MTS.

Ob R.

Volga R.

Yenisei R.

SIBERIA

Lena R.

60°N

KOLYMA MTS.

KAMCHATKA PENINSULA

ALPS

CAUCASUS MTS.

Black Sea

Aral Sea

WEST SIBERIAN PLAIN

ASIA

ALTAI MTS.

L. Baikal

Amur R.

Sea of Japan

40°N

IBERIAN PEN.

BALKAN PEN.

Caspian Sea

TIAN SHAN

GOBI DESERT

NORTH CHINA PLAIN

ATLAS MTS.

Mediterranean Sea

ZAGROS MTS.

PLATEAU OF IRAN

HINDU KUSH

KUNLUN SHAN

TIBETAN PLATEAU

HIMALAYAS

Huang He

Yangzi R.

PACIFIC OCEAN

SAHARA

ARABIAN PENINSULA

Red Sea

Indus R.

Ganges R.

Mt. Everest 29,028 ft (8,848 m)

Tropic of Cancer

20°N

AFRICA

Nile R.

Persian Gulf

Arabian Sea

DECCAN PLATEAU

Bay of Bengal

South China Sea

Philippine Sea

MICRONESIA

Niger R.

SUDAN

ETHIOPIAN PLATEAU

Congo R.

Borneo

Celebes

New Guinea

MELANESIA

0°

Lake Victoria

Sumatra

East Indies

Equator

INDIAN OCEAN

ATLANTIC OCEAN

Zambezi R.

Madagascar

20°S

KALAHARI

Tropic of Capricorn

AUSTRALIA

Darling R.

GREAT DIVIDING RANGE

Cape of Good Hope

N W E S

0   1,000   2,000 mi
0   1,000   2,000 km

40°S

60°S

Antarctic Circle

ANTARCTICA

80°S

20°W | 0° | 20°E | 40°E | 60°E | 80°E | 100°E | 120°E | 140°E | 160°E

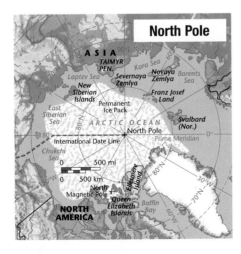

North Pole

ASIA

TAIMYR PEN.

Laptev Sea

Kara Sea

Novaya Zemlya

Barents Sea

New Siberian Islands

Severnaya Zemlya

Franz Josef Land

East Siberian Sea

Permanent Ice Pack

ARCTIC OCEAN

Svalbard (Nor.)

International Date Line

North Pole

Prime Meridian

Chukchi Sea

0   500 mi
0   500 km

North Magnetic Pole

Ellesmere Island

NORTH AMERICA

Queen Elizabeth Islands

Baffin Bay

United States: Political

ARCTIC OCEAN

RUSSIA

ALASKA

CANADA

Anchorage

Juneau

Bering Sea

Gulf of Alaska

Arctic Circle

Bering Strait

Yukon River

70°N

60°N

0 250 500 mi
0 250 500 km

160°W 140°W

Seattle
Olympia
WASHINGTON
Spokane

Columbia
Portland
Salem

OREGON

Klamath Falls

Eureka

Winnemucca

Carson City

Sacramento

San Francisco

NEVADA

CALIFORNIA

Los Angeles

San Diego

PACIFIC OCEAN

IDAHO
Boise

Snake River

Twin Falls

Great Salt Lake

Salt Lake City

UTAH

Cedar City

Las Vegas

ARIZONA

Phoenix

Tucson

Helena

MONTANA

Billings

Sheridan

Jackson

WYOMING

Cheyenne

Denver

Grand Junction

COLORADO

Pueblo

Colorado River

Albuquerque

Santa Fe

NEW MEXICO

Roswell

Rio Grande

El Paso

Missouri River

Mino

Bismar

Pi
Rapid C

NEBRAS

Ark

MEXICO

120°W 110°W

50°N

40°N

Tropic of Cancer

120°W 110°W

160°W 155°W

Honolulu

PACIFIC OCEAN

HAWAII

Hilo

20°N

20°N

155°W

0 50 100 mi
0 50 100 km

CANADA

90°W 80°W 70°W

0 150 300 mi
0 150 300 km

NORTH DAKOTA

Lake Superior

Duluth

Sault Ste. Marie

Presque Isle

MAINE

Augusta

MINNESOTA

MICHIGAN

Portland

Lake Huron

Montpelier

VERMONT

NEW HAMPSHIRE

Concord

Boston

SOUTH DAKOTA

Minneapolis St. Paul

WISCONSIN

Lansing

Lake Michigan

Lake Ontario

NEW YORK

Albany

MASSACHUSETTS

Providence

Hartford

RHODE ISLAND

40°N

Mississippi River

Milwaukee

Madison

Detroit

Lake Erie

Buffalo

New Haven

CONNECTICUT

Missouri

Chicago

Cleveland

PENNSYLVANIA

New York City

Trenton

IOWA

Cedar Rapids

INDIANA

OHIO

Harrisburg

Pittsburgh

NEW JERSEY

Philadelphia

Omaha

Des Moines

Columbus

Indianapolis

Baltimore

Dover

DELAWARE

Lincoln

ILLINOIS

Springfield

Cincinnati

WEST VIRGINIA

Washington, D.C.

Annapolis

Topeka

Kansas City

Louisville

Frankfort

Charleston

Richmond

MARYLAND

KANSAS

Jefferson City

St. Louis

VIRGINIA

Norfolk

River

MISSOURI

Ohio River

KENTUCKY

Wichita

Tennessee River

Raleigh

NORTH CAROLINA

ATLANTIC OCEAN

Tulsa

Nashville

TENNESSEE

Charlotte

OKLAHOMA

ARKANSAS

Memphis

Columbia

Oklahoma City

Little Rock

Atlanta

SOUTH CAROLINA

Red River

Pine Bluff

Birmingham

GEORGIA

Charleston

30°N

MISSISSIPPI

ALABAMA

Columbus

Savannah

Dallas

Jackson

Montgomery

Hattiesburg

Jacksonville

TEXAS

Shreveport

Tallahassee

Austin

Baton Rouge

LOUISIANA

FLORIDA

San Antonio

Houston

New Orleans

Tampa

Lake Okeechobee

Gulf of Mexico

Rio Grande

Miami

KEY

——— National boundary
——— State boundary
⊛ National capital
✧ State capital
• Other city

Transverse Mercator Projection

90°W 80°W

ATLAS **195**

North and South America: Political

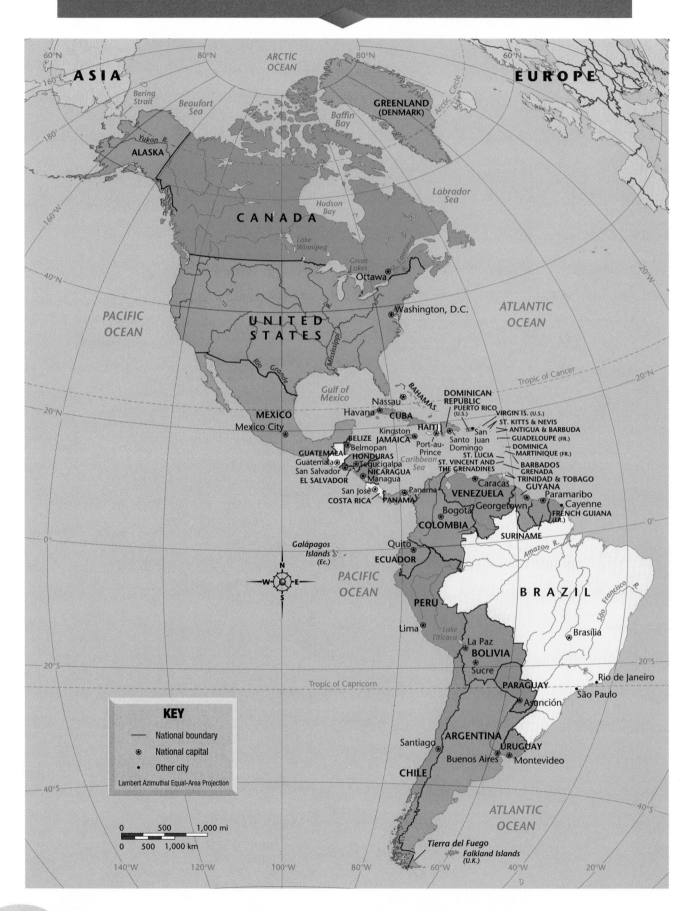

KEY

— National boundary

⊛ National capital

• Other city

Lambert Azimuthal Equal-Area Projection

0   500   1,000 mi

0   500   1,000 km

North and South America: Physical

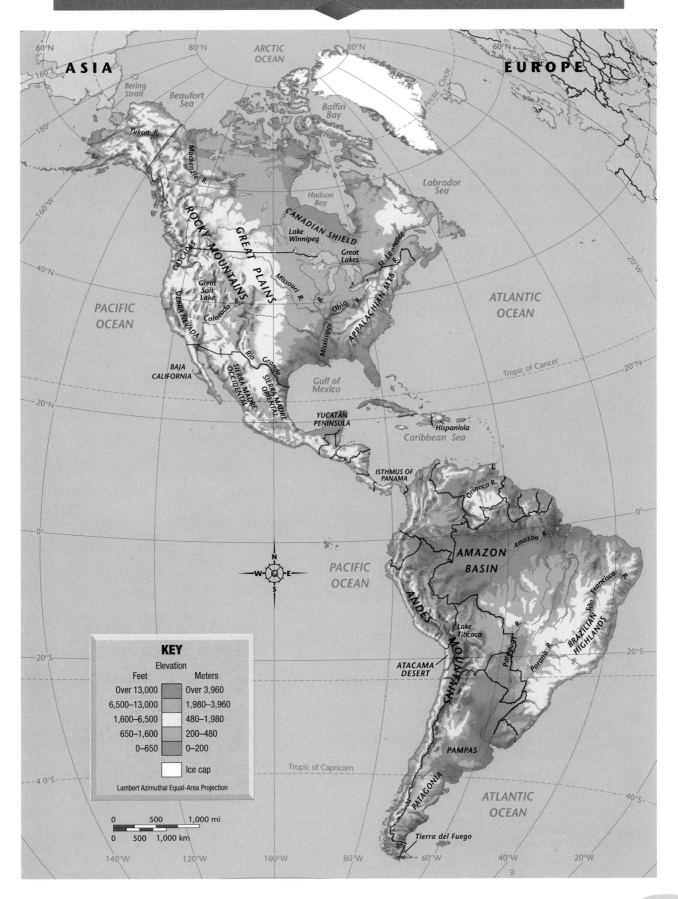

ASIA

EUROPE

60°N 80°N ARCTIC OCEAN 80°N 60°N

160°E 180° Bering Strait Beaufort Sea Baffin Bay Arctic Circle 0°

Yukon R. Mackenzie R. Labrador Sea 20°W

160°W Hudson Bay CANADIAN SHIELD

ROCKY MOUNTAINS Lake Winnipeg Great Lakes St. Lawrence R.

40°N CASCADES GREAT PLAINS Missouri R. ATLANTIC OCEAN 20°W

PACIFIC OCEAN SIERRA NEVADA Great Salt Lake Missouri R. Ohio R. APPALACHIAN MTS.

Colorado R. Mississippi R.

BAJA CALIFORNIA Rio Grande SIERRA MADRE OCCIDENTAL SIERRA MADRE ORIENTAL Tropic of Cancer 20°N

20°N Gulf of Mexico

YUCATÁN PENINSULA Hispaniola Caribbean Sea

ISTHMUS OF PANAMA Orinoco R.

0° PACIFIC OCEAN AMAZON BASIN Amazon R. 0°

ANDES MOUNTAINS São Francisco R.

Lake Titicaca BRAZILIAN HIGHLANDS

ATACAMA DESERT Paraguay R. Paraná R. 20°S

20°S

PAMPAS

Tropic of Capricorn

PATAGONIA ATLANTIC OCEAN 40°S

40°S

Tierra del Fuego

140°W 120°W 100°W 80°W 60°W 40°W 20°W

KEY

Elevation

Feet	Meters
Over 13,000	Over 3,960
6,500–13,000	1,980–3,960
1,600–6,500	480–1,980
650–1,600	200–480
0–650	0–200

Ice cap

Lambert Azimuthal Equal-Area Projection

0   500   1,000 mi

0   500   1,000 km

Europe: Political

KEY

—— National boundary

⊛ National capital

• Other city

Lambert Azimuthal Equal-Area Projection

ARCTIC OCEAN

Arctic Circle

30°W   20°W   10°W   0°   10°E   20°E   30°E   40°E   50°E

Reykjavik ⊛   **ICELAND**

60°N

Faeroe Is.
(Den.)

Shetland Is.
(U.K.)

ATLANTIC
OCEAN

Prime Meridian

FINLAND

SWEDEN

Gulf of Bothnia

NORWAY
Lillehammer •

Turku •   Helsinki ⊛   • St. Petersburg

Oslo ⊛   Stockholm ⊛   Tallinn ⊛   **ESTONIA**

60°N   **RUSSIA**

• Göteborg   *Baltic Sea*   Riga ⊛   Moscow ⊛

LATVIA

North
Sea

DENMARK   **LITHUANIA**
Copenhagen ⊛   Vilnius ⊛   **BELARUS**

IRELAND   **RUSSIA**   Minsk ⊛
Dublin ⊛   **UNITED**
KINGDOM   Gdańsk •

• Manchester   **POLAND**

Amsterdam ⊛   Berlin ⊛   Warsaw ⊛   Kiev ⊛
The Hague ⊛   Łódź •

London •   **NETHERLANDS**   50°N

Brussels ⊛   **GERMANY**   Katowice •   **UKRAINE**
English Channel   **BELGIUM**   Cologne •   Kraków •
Bonn •

• Frankfurt   Prague ⊛   **CZECH**
LUXEMBOURG   Luxembourg ⊛   **REPUBLIC**   **MOLDOVA**
Brno •   Chişinău •

⊛ Paris   Danube R.   Munich •   **SLOVAKIA**
LIECHTENSTEIN   Bratislava ⊛   Cluj •

Bay   **FRANCE**   Vienna ⊛   • Budapest   **ROMANIA**
of   Bern ⊛   **AUSTRIA**   **HUNGARY**
Biscay   **SWITZERLAND**
Ljubljana ⊛   Bucharest ⊛   *Black*
• Milan   **SLOVENIA**   Zagreb ⊛   *Sea*
CROATIA   Belgrade ⊛

SAN MARINO   **BOSNIA &**   **BULGARIA**
HERZEGOVINA   **SERBIA**
Marseille •   **MONACO**   Sarajevo •   Sophia ⊛
ITALY   Adriatic   Podgorica •
PORTUGAL   **ANDORRA**   *Corsica*   **VATICAN**   Rome ⊛   **MONTENEGRO**   Skopje ⊛
CITY   Sea   **ALBANIA**   **MACEDONIA**
Lisbon ⊛   • Madrid   • Barcelona   Naples •   Tiranë ⊛   *Aegean*
40°N   *Sea*
SPAIN   *Sardinia*   Tyrrhenian   **GREECE**
Balearic Is.   Sea   Ionian   Athens ⊛
Sea

Strait of   **GIBRALTAR**   Mediterranean   *Crete*
Gibraltar   **(U.K.)**
Sea   N
Sicily   W ⊛ E
AFRICA   **MALTA**   S

0   250   500 mi

0   250   500 km

0°   10°E   20°E

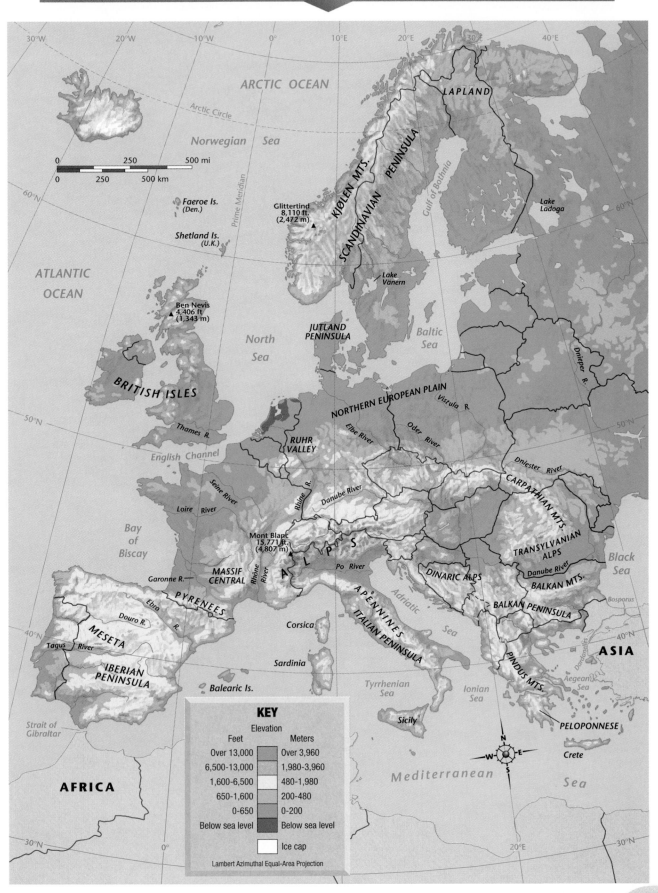

ARCTIC OCEAN

Arctic Circle

Norwegian Sea

LAPLAND

KJØLEN MTS.

SCANDINAVIAN PENINSULA

Gulf of Bothnia

Lake Ladoga

Glittertind
8,110 ft.
(2,472 m)

Faeroe Is.
(Den.)

Shetland Is.
(U.K.)

ATLANTIC OCEAN

Lake Vänern

Ben Nevis
4,406 ft
(1,343 m)

JUTLAND PENINSULA

North Sea

Baltic Sea

BRITISH ISLES

NORTHERN EUROPEAN PLAIN

Vistula R.

Dnieper R.

Thames R.

RUHR VALLEY

Elbe River

Oder River

English Channel

Seine River

Rhine R.

Danube River

Dniester River

CARPATHIAN MTS.

Loire River

Bay of Biscay

Mont Blanc
15,771 ft.
(4,807 m)

A L P S

Po River

TRANSYLVANIAN ALPS

MASSIF CENTRAL

Rhône River

A P E N N I N E S

DINARIC ALPS

Danube River

BALKAN MTS.

Garonne R.

PYRENEES

Adriatic Sea

BALKAN PENINSULA

Black Sea

Ebro R.

Douro R.

MESETA

Corsica

ITALIAN PENINSULA

Bosporus

Tagus River

IBERIAN PENINSULA

Sardinia

PINDUS MTS.

ASIA

Dardanelles

Aegean Sea

Balearic Is.

Tyrrhenian Sea

Ionian Sea

PELOPONNESE

Strait of Gibraltar

Sicily

Crete

AFRICA

Mediterranean Sea

KEY

Elevation

Feet		Meters
Over 13,000		Over 3,960
6,500–13,000		1,980–3,960
1,600–6,500		480–1,980
650–1,600		200–480
0–650		0–200
Below sea level		Below sea level
Ice cap		

Lambert Azimuthal Equal-Area Projection

N
W E
S

Africa: Political

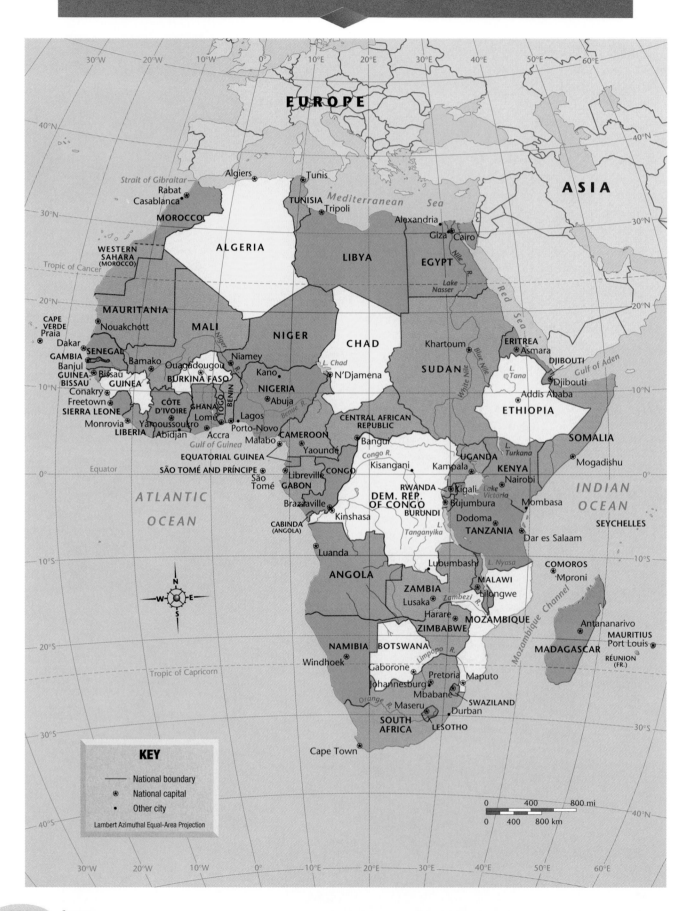

EUROPE

ASIA

Strait of Gibraltar
Algiers ⊛   Tunis ⊛
Rabat   TUNISIA   *Mediterranean Sea*
Casablanca •   Tripoli ⊛
MOROCCO   Alexandria •
                    Giza • ⊛ Cairo

WESTERN
SAHARA   ALGERIA   LIBYA   EGYPT
(MOROCCO)

Tropic of Cancer   Lake Nasser

MAURITANIA   MALI   NIGER   CHAD   Khartoum ⊛   ERITREA
CAPE   Nouakchott ⊛   ⊛ Asmara   DJIBOUTI
VERDE
Praia ·   Niamey   L. Chad   SUDAN   L. Tana   Djibouti ⊛
Dakar ·   Bamako ⊛   ⊛ Niamey   N'Djamena ⊛   Addis Ababa ⊛
GAMBIA SENEGAL   Ouagadougou   Kano ·
Banjul ⊛   BURKINA FASO   NIGERIA   CENTRAL AFRICAN   ETHIOPIA
GUINEA- Bissau ⊛   GHANA ·   Abuja ⊛   REPUBLIC
BISSAU   GUINEA   CÔTE   TOGO BENIN   SOMALIA
Conakry ⊛   D'IVOIRE   Benue R.   Bangui ⊛
Freetown ⊛   Lomé   CAMEROON   UGANDA   Mogadishu ·
SIERRA LEONE   Yamoussoukro   Porto-Novo   Yaoundé ⊛   Kisangani ·   Kampala ⊛ KENYA
Monrovia ⊛   Abidjan · Accra   Malabo ⊛   EQUATORIAL GUINEA   Nairobi ⊛
LIBERIA   Gulf of Guinea   CONGO   RWANDA Kigali ⊛   Mombasa ·
Equator   SÃO TOMÉ AND PRÍNCIPE ⊛   Libreville ⊛   DEM. REP.   Bujumbura ⊛   INDIAN
                    São   GABON   OF CONGO   BURUNDI   Dodoma ⊛   OCEAN
                    Tomé   Brazzaville ⊛   L. Tanganyika   TANZANIA   SEYCHELLES
ATLANTIC   CABINDA   Kinshasa ⊛   Dar es Salaam ·
OCEAN   (ANGOLA)
                    Luanda ⊛   Lubumbashi ·   L. Nyasa   COMOROS
                                                                    Moroni ·
                    ANGOLA   ZAMBIA   MALAWI
                              Lusaka ⊛ Lilongwe ⊛   MOZAMBIQUE   Antananarivo ⊛
                                   Zambezi R.   Harare ⊛   MAURITIUS
                    NAMIBIA   BOTSWANA   ZIMBABWE   MADAGASCAR   Port Louis ⊛
Tropic of Capricorn   Windhoek ⊛   Limpopo R.   RÉUNION (FR.)
                    Gaborone ⊛   Pretoria ⊛ Maputo ⊛
                    Johannesburg ·   Mbabane ⊛
                    Orange R.   Maseru ⊛ SWAZILAND
                    SOUTH   Durban ·
                    AFRICA   LESOTHO
                    Cape Town ·

KEY

— National boundary
⊛ National capital
· Other city

Lambert Azimuthal Equal-Area Projection

0   400   800 mi
0   400 800 km

Africa: Physical

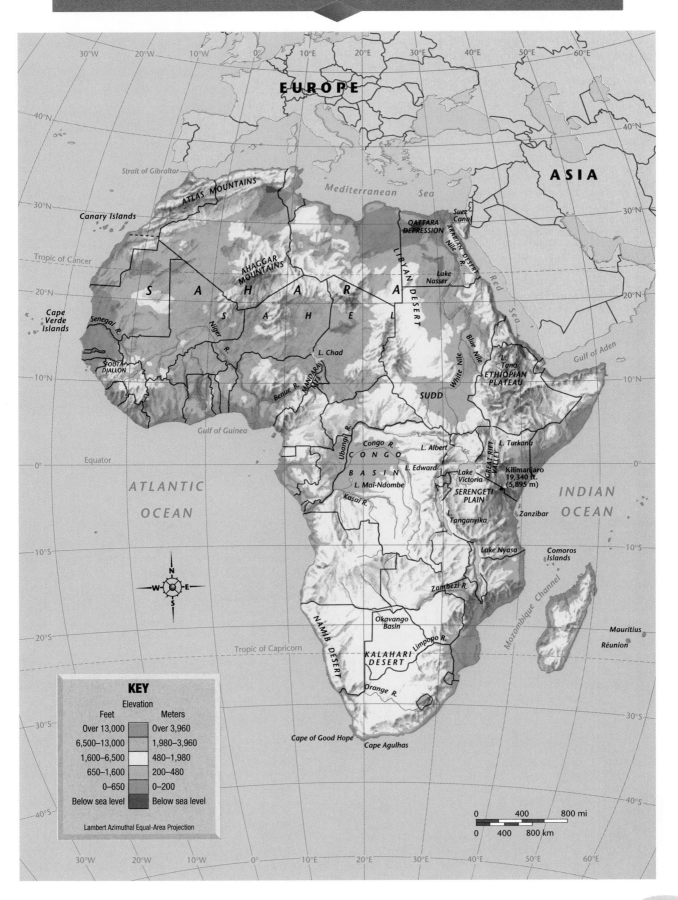

KEY

Elevation

Feet		Meters
Over 13,000		Over 3,960
6,500–13,000		1,980–3,960
1,600–6,500		480–1,980
650–1,600		200–480
0–650		0–200
Below sea level		Below sea level

Lambert Azimuthal Equal-Area Projection

0   400   800 mi

0   400   800 km

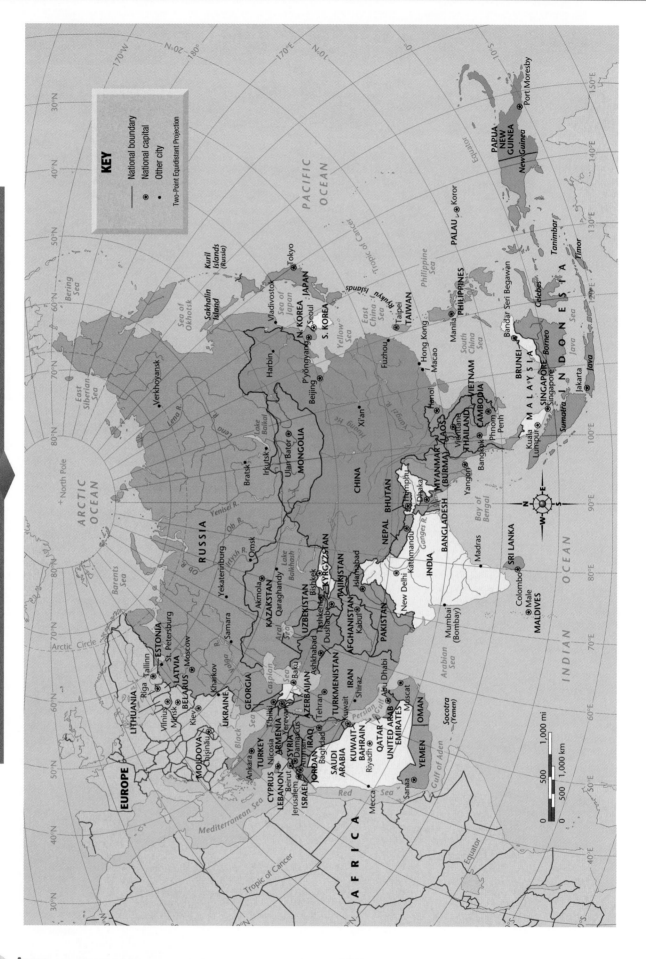

Asia: Political

KEY
—— National boundary
⊛ National capital
• Other city

Two-Point Equidistant Projection

ARCTIC OCEAN

North Pole

PACIFIC OCEAN

Bering Sea

Sea of Okhotsk

Kuril Islands (Russia)

Sakhalin Island

Sea of Japan

Vladivostok

Tokyo

JAPAN

N. KOREA ⊛ Seoul

Pyŏngyang ⊛ ⊛ S. KOREA

Yellow Sea

East China Sea

Ryukyu Islands

Taipei

TAIWAN

Hong Kong

Macao

Fuzhou

PHILIPPINES

Manila ⊛

Philippine Sea

South China Sea

Bandar Seri Begawan

BRUNEI

Borneo

Celebes Sea

INDONESIA

Java Sea

Jakarta ⊛

Java

Sumatra

MALAYSIA

Kuala Lumpur ⊛

SINGAPORE ⊛ Singapore

PALAU ⊛ Koror

PAPUA NEW GUINEA

New Guinea

Port Moresby

Tanimbar

Timor

Tropic of Cancer

Equator

East Siberian Sea

Verkhoyansk

Lena R.

Harbin

Beijing ⊛

Huang He

Xi'an

CHINA

Yangzi R.

Hanoi ⊛

VIETNAM

LAOS Vientiane ⊛

CAMBODIA

Phnom Penh ⊛

MYANMAR (BURMA)

Yangon ⊛

THAILAND ⊛ Bangkok

RUSSIA

Yenisei R.

Ob R.

Irtysh R.

Omsk

Yekaterinburg

Volga

Samara

Bratsk

Irkutsk

Lake Baikal

Ulan Bator ⊛

MONGOLIA

Arctic Circle

St. Petersburg

Moscow ⊛

Kharkov

BELARUS

Minsk ⊛

Kiev ⊛

UKRAINE

ESTONIA

LATVIA

Riga ⊛

LITHUANIA

Vilnius ⊛

Tallinn ⊛

MOLDOVA Chişinău ⊛

Aral Sea

KAZAKSTAN

Akmola ⊛

Qaraghandy

Lake Balkhash

UZBEKISTAN

Tashkent ⊛

Bishkek ⊛

KYRGYZSTAN

TAJIKISTAN

Dushanbe ⊛

Ashkhabad ⊛

TURKMENISTAN

Kabul ⊛

AFGHANISTAN

Islamabad ⊛

PAKISTAN

Ganges R.

New Delhi ⊛

INDIA

NEPAL

Kathmandu ⊛

Thimphu ⊛

BHUTAN

Dhaka ⊛

BANGLADESH

Bay of Bengal

Madras

SRI LANKA

Colombo ⊛

⊛ Male

MALDIVES

Mumbai (Bombay)

Arabian Sea

Caspian Sea

Black Sea

GEORGIA

Tbilisi ⊛

ARMENIA

Yerevan ⊛

Baku ⊛

AZERBAIJAN

Tehran ⊛

IRAN

Shiraz

Abu Dhabi ⊛

UNITED ARAB EMIRATES

Persian Gulf

Gulf of Oman

Muscat ⊛

OMAN

Socotra (Yemen)

Gulf of Aden

TURKEY

Ankara ⊛

Nicosia ⊛

CYPRUS

LEBANON Beirut ⊛

SYRIA Damascus ⊛

ISRAEL

Jerusalem ⊛

JORDAN Amman ⊛

IRAQ Baghdad ⊛

Kuwait ⊛

KUWAIT

BAHRAIN

QATAR

SAUDI ARABIA

Riyadh ⊛

YEMEN

Sanaa ⊛

Mecca

Red Sea

EUROPE

AFRICA

Mediterranean Sea

Barents Sea

INDIAN OCEAN

Equator

Tropic of Cancer

1,000 mi

1,000 km

500

500

0

0

170°W

180°

170°E

160°E

150°E

140°E

130°E

120°E

110°E

100°E

90°E

80°E

70°E

60°E

50°E

40°E

30°E

20°E

80°N

70°N

60°N

50°N

40°N

30°N

20°N

10°N

0°

10°S

N
W E
S

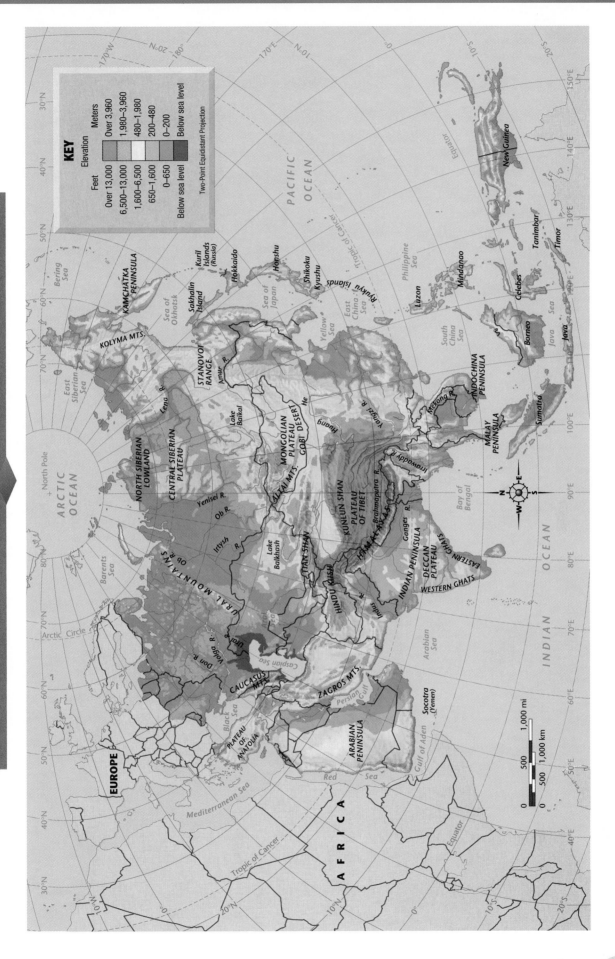

Asia: Physical

KEY

Elevation

Feet	Meters
Over 13,000	Over 3,960
6,500–13,000	1,980–3,960
1,600–6,500	480–1,980
650–1,600	200–480
0–650	0–200
Below sea level	Below sea level

Two-Point Equidistant Projection

North Pole

ARCTIC OCEAN

Arctic Circle

EUROPE

AFRICA

Barents Sea

East Siberian Sea

Bering Sea

KAMCHATKA PENINSULA

KOLYMA MTS.

Sea of Okhotsk

STANOVOI RANGE

Sakhalin Island

Kuril Islands (Russia)

Hokkaido

Honshu

Shikoku

Kyushu

Ryukyu Islands

Amur R.

Lena R.

Lake Baikal

NORTH SIBERIAN LOWLAND

CENTRAL SIBERIAN PLATEAU

MONGOLIAN PLATEAU

GOBI DESERT

ALTAI MTS.

Huang He

Yenisei R.

Ob R.

Irtysh R.

URAL MOUNTAINS

Ural R.

Volga R.

Don R.

Lake Balkhash

TIAN SHAN

KUNLUN SHAN

PLATEAU OF TIBET

HINDU KUSH

HIMALAYAS

Indus R.

Ganges R.

Brahmaputra R.

INDIAN PENINSULA

DECCAN PLATEAU

WESTERN GHATS

EASTERN GHATS

Yangzi R.

Mekong R.

Irrawaddy R.

INDOCHINA PENINSULA

MALAY PENINSULA

CAUCASUS MTS.

ZAGROS MTS.

Caspian Sea

Black Sea

PLATEAU OF ANATOLIA

Mediterranean Sea

Red Sea

Persian Gulf

Gulf of Aden

ARABIAN PENINSULA

Socotra (Yemen)

Arabian Sea

Bay of Bengal

INDIAN OCEAN

PACIFIC OCEAN

Sea of Japan

Yellow Sea

East China Sea

South China Sea

Philippine Sea

Luzon

Mindanao

Celebes

Borneo

Celebes Sea

Java Sea

Java

Sumatra

Timor

Tanimbar

New Guinea

Equator

Tropic of Cancer

Tropic of Cancer

1,000 mi

1,000 km

500

500

Australia, New Zealand, and the Pacific Islands: Physical–Political

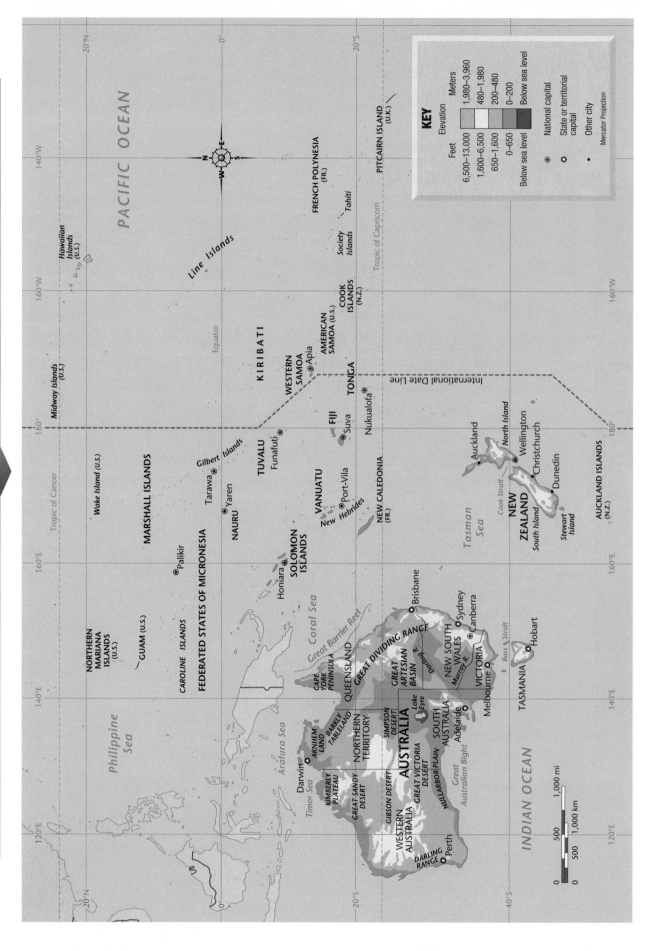

PACIFIC OCEAN

KEY

Elevation	
Feet	Meters
6,500–13,000	1,980–3,960
1,600–6,500	480–1,980
650–1,600	200–480
0–650	0–200
Below sea level	Below sea level

⊛ National capital
⊕ State or territorial capital
• Other city

Mercator Projection

Midway Islands (U.S.)

Hawaiian Islands (U.S.)

Line Islands

French Polynesia (Fr.)

Society Islands — Tahiti

Tropic of Capricorn

PITCAIRN ISLAND (U.K.)

Tropic of Cancer

Wake Island (U.S.)

MARSHALL ISLANDS

NORTHERN MARIANA ISLANDS (U.S.)

GUAM (U.S.)

CAROLINE ISLANDS

FEDERATED STATES OF MICRONESIA

• Palikir

Gilbert Islands

Tarawa ⊛

NAURU ⊛ Yaren

KIRIBATI

Equator

Apia ⊛
WESTERN SAMOA

AMERICAN SAMOA (U.S.)

COOK ISLANDS (N.Z.)

International Date Line

TUVALU
Funafuti ⊛

FIJI
• Suva

TONGA
Nukualofa ⊛

VANUATU
⊛ Port-Vila
New Hebrides

SOLOMON ISLANDS
Honiara ⊛

NEW CALEDONIA (Fr.)

Philippine Sea

Arafura Sea

Timor Sea

Coral Sea

Great Barrier Reef

CAPE YORK PENINSULA

QUEENSLAND

Brisbane •

GREAT DIVIDING RANGE

GREAT ARTESIAN BASIN

Darling R.

NEW SOUTH WALES

Sydney •
⊕ Canberra

Darwin •

ARNHEM LAND

KIMBERLY PLATEAU

NORTHERN TERRITORY

BARKLY TABLELAND

SIMPSON DESERT

AUSTRALIA

Lake Eyre

SOUTH AUSTRALIA

Adelaide •

Murray R.

VICTORIA
Melbourne •

GREAT SANDY DESERT

GIBSON DESERT

WESTERN AUSTRALIA

GREAT VICTORIA DESERT

NULLARBOR PLAIN

Great Australian Bight

Perth •
DARLING RANGE ⊛

INDIAN OCEAN

Bass Strait

TASMANIA
Hobart •

Tasman Sea

North Island
Auckland •
Wellington ⊛

NEW ZEALAND

South Island
Christchurch •
Dunedin •

Cook Strait

Stewart Island

AUCKLAND ISLANDS (N.Z.)

0	500	1,000 mi
0	500	1,000 km

The Arctic

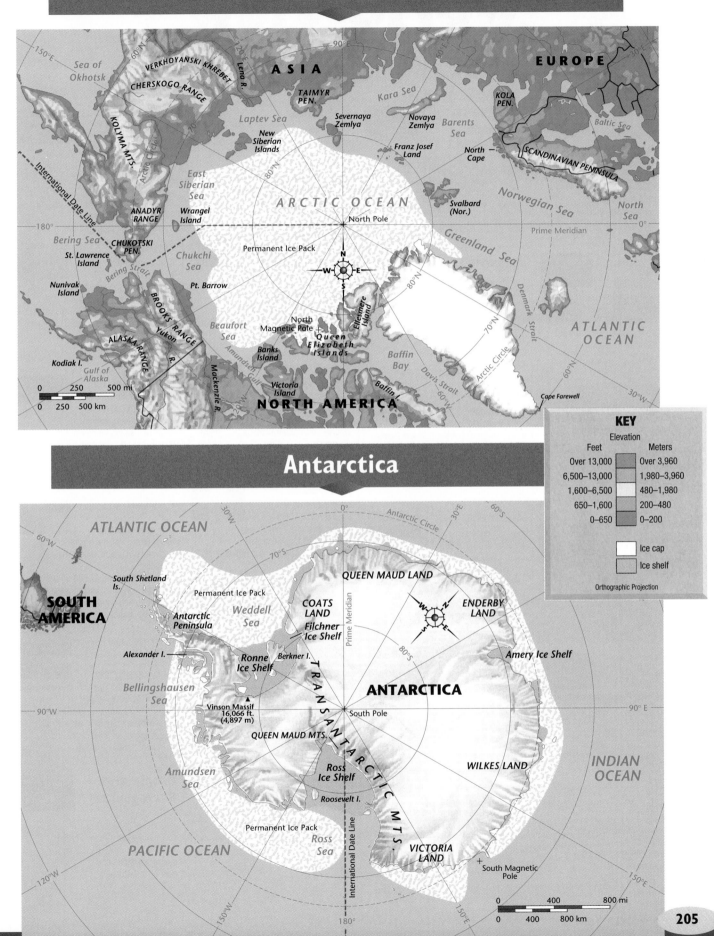

Sea of Okhotsk

VERKHOYANSKI KHREBET

CHERSKOGO RANGE

KOLYMA MTS.

ASIA

Lena R.

EUROPE

TAIMYR PEN.

Kara Sea

KOLA PEN.

Laptev Sea

Severnaya Zemlya

Novaya Zemlya

Barents Sea

Baltic Sea

New Siberian Islands

Franz Josef Land

North Cape

SCANDINAVIAN PENINSULA

ANADYR RANGE

East Siberian Sea

Wrangel Island

ARCTIC OCEAN

Svalbard (Nor.)

Norwegian Sea

North Sea

International Date Line

Bering Sea

CHUKOTSKI PEN.

North Pole

Greenland Sea

Prime Meridian

St. Lawrence Island

Chukchi Sea

Permanent Ice Pack

Denmark Strait

ATLANTIC OCEAN

Nunivak Island

BROOKS RANGE

Pt. Barrow

ALASKA RANGE

Yukon R.

Beaufort Sea

North Magnetic Pole

Ellesmere Island

Queen Elizabeth Islands

Baffin Bay

Arctic Circle

Kodiak I.

Gulf of Alaska

Mackenzie R.

Amundsen Gulf

Banks Island

Victoria Island

Baffin I.

Davis Strait

Cape Farewell

0   250   500 mi

0   250   500 km

NORTH AMERICA

Antarctica

ATLANTIC OCEAN

South Shetland Is.

Permanent Ice Pack

QUEEN MAUD LAND

Antarctic Circle

SOUTH AMERICA

Antarctic Peninsula

Weddell Sea

COATS LAND

Filchner Ice Shelf

ENDERBY LAND

Alexander I.

Ronne Ice Shelf

Berkner I.

Amery Ice Shelf

Bellingshausen Sea

Vinson Massif 16,066 ft. (4,897 m)

TRANSANTARCTIC MTS.

ANTARCTICA

Prime Meridian

Amundsen Sea

QUEEN MAUD MTS.

South Pole

WILKES LAND

INDIAN OCEAN

Ross Ice Shelf

Roosevelt I.

Permanent Ice Pack

PACIFIC OCEAN

Ross Sea

VICTORIA LAND

South Magnetic Pole

International Date Line

0   400   800 mi

0   400   800 km

KEY

Elevation

Feet		Meters
Over 13,000		Over 3,960
6,500–13,000		1,980–3,960
1,600–6,500		480–1,980
650–1,600		200–480
0–650		0–200

Ice cap

Ice shelf

Orthographic Projection

World View

Afghanistan
CAPITAL: Kabul
POPULATION: 24,792,375
MAJOR LANGUAGES: Pashtu, Afghan Persian, Turkic, and 30 various languages
AREA: 250,010 sq mi; 647,500 sq km
LEADING EXPORTS: fruits and nuts, handwoven carpets, and wool
CONTINENT: Asia

Albania
CAPITAL: Tiranë
POPULATION: 3,330,754
MAJOR LANGUAGES: Albanian, Tosk dialect, and Greek
AREA: 11,101 sq mi; 28,750 sq km
LEADING EXPORTS: asphalt, metals and metallic ores, and electricity
CONTINENT: Europe

Algeria
CAPITAL: Algiers
POPULATION: 30,480,793
MAJOR LANGUAGES: Arabic (official), French, and Berber dialects
AREA: 919,626 sq mi; 2,381,740 sq km
LEADING EXPORTS: petroleum and natural gas
CONTINENT: Africa

Andorra
CAPITAL: Andorra La Vella
POPULATION: 64,716
MAJOR LANGUAGES: Catalan (official), French, and Castilian
AREA: 174 sq mi; 450 sq km
LEADING EXPORTS: electricity, tobacco products, and furniture
CONTINENT: Europe

Angola
CAPITAL: Luanda
POPULATION: 10,864,512
MAJOR LANGUAGES: Portuguese (official), Bantu, and various languages
AREA: 481,370 sq mi; 1,246,700 sq km
LEADING EXPORTS: oil, diamonds, and refined petroleum products
CONTINENT: Africa

Anguilla
CAPITAL: The Valley
POPULATION: 11,147
MAJOR LANGUAGE: English (official)
AREA: 35 sq mi; 91 sq km
LEADING EXPORTS: lobster and salt
LOCATION: Caribbean Sea

Antigua and Barbuda
CAPITAL: Saint John's
POPULATION: 64,006
MAJOR LANGUAGES: English (official) and various dialects
AREA: 170 sq mi; 440 sq km
LEADING EXPORTS: petroleum products and manufactures
LOCATION: Caribbean Sea

Argentina
CAPITAL: Buenos Aires
POPULATION: 36,265,463
MAJOR LANGUAGES: Spanish (official), English, Italian, German, and French
AREA: 1,068,339 sq mi; 2,766,890 sq km
LEADING EXPORTS: meat, wheat, corn, oilseed, and manufactures
CONTINENT: South America

Armenia
CAPITAL: Yerevan
POPULATION: 3,421,775
MAJOR LANGUAGES: Armenian and Russian
AREA: 11,506 sq mi; 29,800 sq km
LEADING EXPORTS: gold and jewelry, and aluminum
CONTINENT: Asia

Australia
CAPITAL: Canberra
POPULATION: 18,613,087
MAJOR LANGUAGES: English and various languages
AREA: 2,968,010 sq mi; 7,686,850 sq km
LEADING EXPORTS: coal, gold, meat, wool, and alumina
CONTINENT: Australia

Austria
CAPITAL: Vienna
POPULATION: 8,133,611
MAJOR LANGUAGE: German
AREA: 32,376 sq mi; 83,850 sq km
LEADING EXPORTS: machinery and equipment, and iron and steel
CONTINENT: Europe

Azerbaijan
CAPITAL: Baku
POPULATION: 7,855,576
MAJOR LANGUAGES: Azeri, Russian, Armenian, and various languages
AREA: 33,438 sq mi; 86,600 sq km
LEADING EXPORTS: oil and gas, chemicals, and oil field equipment
CONTINENT: Asia

Bahamas
CAPITAL: Nassau
POPULATION: 279,833
MAJOR LANGUAGES: English and Creole
AREA: 5,382 sq mi; 13,940 sq km
LEADING EXPORTS: pharmaceuticals, cement, rum, and crawfish
LOCATION: Caribbean Sea

Bahrain
CAPITAL: Manama
POPULATION: 616,342
MAJOR LANGUAGES: Arabic, English, Farsi, and Urdu
AREA: 239 sq mi; 620 sq km
LEADING EXPORTS: petroleum and petroleum products
CONTINENT: Asia

Bangladesh
CAPITAL: Dhaka
POPULATION: 127,567,002
MAJOR LANGUAGES: Bangla and English
AREA: 55,600 sq mi; 144,000 sq km
LEADING EXPORTS: garments, jute and jute goods, and leather
CONTINENT: Asia

Barbados
CAPITAL: Bridgetown
POPULATION: 259,025
MAJOR LANGUAGE: English
AREA: 166 sq mi; 430 sq km
LEADING EXPORTS: sugar and molasses, and rum
LOCATION: Caribbean Sea

Belarus
CAPITAL: Minsk
POPULATION: 10,409,050
MAJOR LANGUAGES: Byelorussian and Russian
AREA: 79,926 sq mi; 207,600 sq km
LEADING EXPORTS: machinery and transportation equipment
CONTINENT: Europe

Belgium
CAPITAL: Brussels
POPULATION: 10,174,922
MAJOR LANGUAGES: Dutch, French, and German
AREA: 11,780 sq mi; 30,510 sq km
LEADING EXPORTS: iron and steel, and transportation equipment
CONTINENT: Europe

Belize
CAPITAL: Belmopan
POPULATION: 230,160
MAJOR LANGUAGES: English (official), Spanish, Maya, and Garifuna
AREA: 8,865 sq mi; 22,960 sq km
LEADING EXPORTS: sugar, citrus fruits, bananas, and clothing
CONTINENT: North America

Benin
CAPITAL: Porto-Novo
POPULATION: 6,100,799
MAJOR LANGUAGES: Fon, Yoruba, and at least 6 various languages
AREA: 43,484 sq mi; 112,620 sq km
LEADING EXPORTS: cotton, crude oil, palm products, and cocoa
LOCATION: Atlantic Ocean

Bermuda
CAPITAL: Hamilton
POPULATION: 62,009
MAJOR LANGUAGE: English
AREA: 19.3 sq mi; 50 sq km
LEADING EXPORTS: semitropical produce and light manufactures
LOCATION: Atlantic Ocean

Bhutan
CAPITAL: Thimphu
POPULATION: 1,908,307
MAJOR LANGUAGES: Dzongkha (official), Tibetan dialects, and Nepalese dialects
AREA: 18,147 sq mi; 47,000 sq km
LEADING EXPORTS: cardamon, gypsum, timber, and handicrafts
CONTINENT: Asia

Bolivia
CAPITAL: La Paz
POPULATION: 7,826,352
MAJOR LANGUAGES: Spanish, Quechua, and Aymara
AREA: 424,179 sq mi; 1,098,580 sq km
LEADING EXPORTS: metals, natural gas, soybeans, jewelry, and wood
CONTINENT: South America

Bosnia and Herzegovina

CAPITAL: Sarajevo
POPULATION: 3,365,727
MAJOR LANGUAGE: Serbo-Croatian
AREA: 19,782 sq mi; 51,233 sq km
LEADING EXPORTS: none
CONTINENT: Europe

Botswana

CAPITAL: Gaborone
POPULATION: 1,448,454
MAJOR LANGUAGES: English and Setswana
AREA: 231,812 sq mi; 600,370 sq km
LEADING EXPORTS: diamonds, copper and nickel, and meat
CONTINENT: Africa

Brazil

CAPITAL: Brasília
POPULATION: 169,806,557
MAJOR LANGUAGES: Portuguese, Spanish, English, and French
AREA: 3,286,600 sq mi; 8,511,965 sq km
LEADING EXPORTS: iron ore, soybean, bran, and orange juice
CONTINENT: South America

British Virgin Islands

CAPITAL: Road Town
POPULATION: 13,368
MAJOR LANGUAGE: English
AREA: 58 sq mi; 150 sq km
LEADING EXPORTS: rum, fresh fish, gravel, sand, and fruits
LOCATION: Caribbean Sea

Brunei

CAPITAL: Bandar Seri Begawan
POPULATION: 315,292
MAJOR LANGUAGES: Malay, English, and Chinese
AREA: 2,228 sq mi; 5,770 sq km
LEADING EXPORTS: crude oil and liquefied natural gas
LOCATION: South China Sea

Bulgaria

CAPITAL: Sofia
POPULATION: 8,240,426
MAJOR LANGUAGE: Bulgarian
AREA: 42,824 sq mi; 110,910 sq km
LEADING EXPORTS: machinery and agricultural products
CONTINENT: Europe

Burkina Faso

CAPITAL: Ouagadougou
POPULATION: 11,266,393
MAJOR LANGUAGES: French (official) and Sudanic languages
AREA: 105,873 sq mi; 274,200 sq km
LEADING EXPORTS: cotton, gold, and animal products
CONTINENT: Africa

Burundi

CAPITAL: Bujumbura
POPULATION: 5,537,387
MAJOR LANGUAGES: Kirundi, French, and Swahili
AREA: 10,746 sq mi; 27,830 sq km
LEADING EXPORTS: coffee, tea, cotton, and hides and skins
CONTINENT: Africa

Cambodia

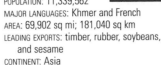

CAPITAL: Phnom Penh
POPULATION: 11,339,562
MAJOR LANGUAGES: Khmer and French
AREA: 69,902 sq mi; 181,040 sq km
LEADING EXPORTS: timber, rubber, soybeans, and sesame
CONTINENT: Asia

Cameroon

CAPITAL: Yaounde
POPULATION: 15,029,433
MAJOR LANGUAGES: 24 various languages, English, and French
AREA: 183,574 sq mi; 475,440 sq km
LEADING EXPORTS: petroleum products and lumber
CONTINENT: Africa

Canada

CAPITAL: Ottawa
POPULATION: 30,675,398
MAJOR LANGUAGES: English and French
AREA: 3,851,940 sq mi; 9,976,140 sq km
LEADING EXPORTS: newsprint, wood pulp, timber, and crude petroleum
CONTINENT: North America

Cape Verde

CAPITAL: Praia
POPULATION: 399,857
MAJOR LANGUAGES: Portuguese and Crioulo
AREA: 1,556 sq mi; 4,030 sq km
LEADING EXPORTS: fish, bananas, and hides and skins
CONTINENT: Africa

Cayman Islands

CAPITAL: George Town
POPULATION: 37,716
MAJOR LANGUAGE: English
AREA: 100 sq mi; 260 sq km
LEADING EXPORTS: turtle products and manufactured goods
LOCATION: Caribbean Sea

Central African Republic

CAPITAL: Bangui
POPULATION: 3,375,771
MAJOR LANGUAGES: French, Sangho, Arabic, Hunsa, and Swahili
AREA: 240,542 sq mi; 622,980 sq km
LEADING EXPORTS: diamonds, timber, cotton, coffee, and tobacco
CONTINENT: Africa

Chad

CAPITAL: N'Djamena
POPULATION: 7,359,512
MAJOR LANGUAGES: French, Arabic, Sara, Songo, and over 100 various languages and dialects
AREA: 495,772 sq mi; 1,284,000 sq km
LEADING EXPORTS: cotton, cattle, textiles, and fish
CONTINENT: Africa

Chile

CAPITAL: Santiago
POPULATION: 14,787,781
MAJOR LANGUAGE: Spanish
AREA: 292,269 sq mi; 756,950 sq km
LEADING EXPORTS: copper and other metals and minerals
CONTINENT: South America

China

CAPITAL: Beijing
POPULATION: 1,236,914,658
MAJOR LANGUAGES: Mandarin, Putonghua, Yue, Wu, Minbei, Minnan, Xiang, and Gan and Hakka dialects
AREA: 3,705,533 sq mi; 9,596,960 sq km
LEADING EXPORTS: textiles, garments, footwear, and toys
CONTINENT: Asia

Colombia

CAPITAL: Bogota
POPULATION: 38,580,949
MAJOR LANGUAGE: Spanish
AREA: 439,751 sq mi; 1,138,910 sq km
LEADING EXPORTS: petroleum, coffee, coal, and bananas
CONTINENT: South America

Comoros

CAPITAL: Moroni
POPULATION: 545,528
MAJOR LANGUAGES: Arabic, French, and Comoran
AREA: 838 sq mi; 2,170 sq km
LEADING EXPORTS: vanilla, ylang-ylang, cloves, and perfume oil
LOCATION: Indian Ocean

Congo (Democratic Republic of)

CAPITAL: Kinshasa
POPULATION: 49,000,511
MAJOR LANGUAGES: French, Lingala, Swahili, Kingwana, Kikongo, and Tshiluba
AREA: 905,599 sq mi; 2,345,410 sq km
LEADING EXPORTS: copper, coffee, diamonds, cobalt, and crude oil
CONTINENT: Africa

Congo (Republic of the)

CAPITAL: Brazzaville
POPULATION: 2,658,123
MAJOR LANGUAGES: French, Lingala, Kikongo, and other languages
AREA: 132,051 sq mi; 342,000 sq km
LEADING EXPORTS: crude oil, lumber, plywood, sugar, and cocoa
CONTINENT: Africa

Cook Islands

CAPITAL: Avarua
POPULATION: 19,989
MAJOR LANGUAGES: English and Maori
AREA: 95 sq mi; 240 sq km
LEADING EXPORTS: copra, fresh and canned fruit, and clothing
LOCATION: Pacific Ocean

Costa Rica

CAPITAL: San José
POPULATION: 3,604,642
MAJOR LANGUAGES: Spanish and English
AREA: 19,730 sq mi; 51,100 sq km
LEADING EXPORTS: coffee, bananas, textiles, and sugar
CONTINENT: North America

Côte d'Ivoire

CAPITAL: Yamoussoukro
POPULATION: 15,446,231
MAJOR LANGUAGES: French, Dioula, and 59 other dialects
AREA: 124,507 sq mi; 322,460 sq km
LEADING EXPORTS: cocoa, coffee, tropical woods, and petroleum
CONTINENT: Africa

Croatia

CAPITAL: Zagreb
POPULATION: 4,671,584
MAJOR LANGUAGE: Serbo-Croatian
AREA: 21,830 sq mi; 56,538 sq km
LEADING EXPORTS: machinery and transportation equipment
CONTINENT: Europe

Cuba

CAPITAL: Havana
POPULATION: 11,050,729
MAJOR LANGUAGE: Spanish
AREA: 42,805 sq mi; 110,860 sq km
LEADING EXPORTS: sugar, nickel, shellfish, and tobacco
LOCATION: Caribbean Sea

Cyprus

CAPITAL: Nicosia
POPULATION: 748,982
MAJOR LANGUAGES: Greek, Turkish, and English
AREA: 3,572 sq mi; 9,250 sq km
LEADING EXPORTS: citrus, potatoes, grapes, wines, and cement
LOCATION: Mediterranean Sea

Czech Republic

CAPITAL: Prague
POPULATION: 10,286,470
MAJOR LANGUAGES: Czech and Slovak
AREA: 30,388 sq mi; 78,703 sq km
LEADING EXPORTS: manufactured goods
CONTINENT: Europe

Denmark

CAPITAL: Copenhagen
POPULATION: 5,333,617
MAJOR LANGUAGES: Danish, Faroese, Greenlandic, and German
AREA: 16,630 sq mi; 43,070 sq km
LEADING EXPORTS: meat and meat products, and dairy products
CONTINENT: Europe

Djibouti

CAPITAL: Djibouti
POPULATION: 440,727
MAJOR LANGUAGES: French, Arabic, Somali, and Afar
AREA: 8,495 sq mi; 22,000 sq km
LEADING EXPORTS: hides and skins, and coffee (in transit)
CONTINENT: Africa

Dominica

CAPITAL: Roseau
POPULATION: 65,777
MAJOR LANGUAGES: English and French patois
AREA: 290 sq mi; 750 sq km
LEADING EXPORTS: bananas, soap, bay oil, and vegetables
LOCATION: Caribbean Sea

Dominican Republic

CAPITAL: Santo Domingo
POPULATION: 7,998,776
MAJOR LANGUAGE: Spanish
AREA: 18,815 sq mi; 48,730 sq km
LEADING EXPORTS: ferronickel, sugar, gold, coffee, and cocoa
LOCATION: Caribbean Sea

Ecuador

CAPITAL: Quito
POPULATION: 12,336,572
MAJOR LANGUAGES: Spanish, Quechua, and various languages
AREA: 109,487 sq mi; 283,560 sq km
LEADING EXPORTS: petroleum, bananas, shrimp, and cocoa
CONTINENT: South America

Egypt

CAPITAL: Cairo
POPULATION: 66,050,004
MAJOR LANGUAGES: Arabic, English, and French
AREA: 386,675 sq mi; 1,001,450 sq km
LEADING EXPORTS: crude oil and petroleum products
CONTINENT: Africa

El Salvador

CAPITAL: San Salvador
POPULATION: 5,752,067
MAJOR LANGUAGES: Spanish and Nahua
AREA: 8,124 sq mi; 21,040 sq km
LEADING EXPORTS: coffee, sugar cane, and shrimp
CONTINENT: North America

Equatorial Guinea

CAPITAL: Malabo
POPULATION: 454,001
MAJOR LANGUAGES: Spanish, Pidgin English, Fang, Bubi, and Ibo
AREA: 10,831 sq mi; 28,050 sq km
LEADING EXPORTS: coffee, timber, and cocoa beans
CONTINENT: Africa

Eritrea

CAPITAL: Asmara
POPULATION: 3,842,436
MAJOR LANGUAGES: Tigre, Kunama, Cushitic dialects, Nora Bana, and Arabic
AREA: 46,844 sq mi; 121,320 sq km
LEADING EXPORTS: salt, hides, cement, and gum arabic
CONTINENT: Africa

Estonia

CAPITAL: Tallinn
POPULATION: 1,421,335
MAJOR LANGUAGES: Estonian, Latvian, Lithuanian, and Russian
AREA: 17,414 sq mi; 45,100 sq km
LEADING EXPORTS: textiles, food products, vehicles, and metals
CONTINENT: Europe

Ethiopia

CAPITAL: Addis Ababa
POPULATION: 58,390,351
MAJOR LANGUAGES: Amharic, Tigrinya, Orominga, Guaraginga, Somali, Arabic, English, and various languages
AREA: 435,201 sq mi; 1,127,127 sq km
LEADING EXPORTS: coffee, leather products, and gold
CONTINENT: Africa

Fiji

CAPITAL: Suva
POPULATION: 802,611
MAJOR LANGUAGES: English, Fijian, and Hindustani
AREA: 7,054 sq mi; 18,270 sq km
LEADING EXPORTS: sugar, clothing, gold, processed fish, and lumber
LOCATION: Pacific Ocean

Finland

CAPITAL: Helsinki
POPULATION: 5,149,242
MAJOR LANGUAGES: Finnish, Swedish, Lapp, and Russian
AREA: 130,132 sq mi; 337,030 sq km
LEADING EXPORTS: paper and pulp, machinery, and chemicals
CONTINENT: Europe

France

CAPITAL: Paris
POPULATION: 58,804,944
MAJOR LANGUAGES: French and regional dialects and languages
AREA: 211,217 sq mi; 547,030 sq km
LEADING EXPORTS: machinery and transportation equipment
CONTINENT: Europe

Gabon

CAPITAL: Libreville
POPULATION: 1,207,844
MAJOR LANGUAGES: French, Fang, Myene, Bateke, Bapounou/Eschira, and Bandjabi
AREA: 103,351 sq mi; 267,670 sq km
LEADING EXPORTS: crude oil, timber, manganese, and uranium
CONTINENT: Africa

The Gambia

CAPITAL: Banjul
POPULATION: 1,291,858
MAJOR LANGUAGES: English, Mandinka, Wolof, Fula, and various languages
AREA: 4,363 sq mi; 11,300 sq km
LEADING EXPORTS: peanuts and peanut products, and fish
CONTINENT: Africa

Georgia

CAPITAL: T'bilisi
POPULATION: 5,108,527
MAJOR LANGUAGES: Armenian, Azeri, Georgian, Russian, and various languages
AREA: 26,912 sq mi; 69,700 sq km
LEADING EXPORTS: citrus fruits, tea, and wine
CONTINENT: Asia

Germany

CAPITAL: Berlin
POPULATION: 82,079,454
MAJOR LANGUAGE: German
AREA: 137,808 sq mi; 356,910 sq km
LEADING EXPORTS: machines and machine tools, and chemicals
CONTINENT: Europe

Ghana

CAPITAL: Accra
POPULATION: 18,497,206
MAJOR LANGUAGES: English, Akan, Moshi-Dagomba, Ewe, Ga, and various languages
AREA: 92,104 sq mi; 238,540 sq km
LEADING EXPORTS: cocoa, gold, timber, tuna, and bauxite
CONTINENT: Africa

Greece

CAPITAL: Athens
POPULATION: 10,662,138
MAJOR LANGUAGES: Greek, English, and French
AREA: 50,944 sq mi; 131,940 sq km
LEADING EXPORTS: manufactured goods, foodstuffs, and fuels
CONTINENT: Europe

Grenada

CAPITAL: Saint George's
POPULATION: 96,217
MAJOR LANGUAGES: English and French patois
AREA: 131 sq mi; 340 sq km
LEADING EXPORTS: bananas, cocoa, nutmeg, and fruits and vegetables
LOCATION: Caribbean Sea

Guatemala

CAPITAL: Guatemala
POPULATION: 12,007,580
MAJOR LANGUAGES: Spanish, Quiche, Cakchiquel, Kekchi, and various languages and dialects
AREA: 42,044 sq mi; 108,890 sq km
LEADING EXPORTS: coffee, sugar, bananas, cardamom, and beef
CONTINENT: North America

Guinea

CAPITAL: Conakry
POPULATION: 7,477,110
MAJOR LANGUAGES: French and various languages
AREA: 94,930 sq mi; 245,860 sq km
LEADING EXPORTS: bauxite, alumina, diamonds, gold, and coffee
CONTINENT: Africa

Guinea-Bissau

CAPITAL: Bissau
POPULATION: 1,206,311
MAJOR LANGUAGES: Portuguese, Criolo, and various languages
AREA: 13,946 sq mi; 36,210 sq km
LEADING EXPORTS: cashews, fish, peanuts, and palm kernels
CONTINENT: Africa

Guyana

CAPITAL: Georgetown
POPULATION: 707,954
MAJOR LANGUAGES: English and various dialects
AREA: 83,003 sq mi; 214,970 sq km
LEADING EXPORTS: sugar, bauxite/alumina, rice, and shrimp
CONTINENT: South America

Haiti

CAPITAL: Port-au-Prince
POPULATION: 6,780,501
MAJOR LANGUAGES: French and Creole
AREA: 8,784 sq mi; 22,750 sq km
LEADING EXPORTS: light manufactures and coffee
LOCATION: Caribbean Sea

Holy See (Vatican City)

CAPITAL: Vatican City
POPULATION: 840
MAJOR LANGUAGES: Italian, Latin, and various languages
AREA: 0.17 sq mi; 0.44 sq km
LEADING EXPORTS: none
CONTINENT: Europe

Honduras

CAPITAL: Tegucigalpa
POPULATION: 5,861,955
MAJOR LANGUAGES: Spanish and various dialects
AREA: 43,280 sq mi; 112,090 sq km
LEADING EXPORTS: bananas, coffee, shrimp, lobsters, and minerals
CONTINENT: North America

Hungary

CAPITAL: Budapest
POPULATION: 10,208,127
MAJOR LANGUAGES: Hungarian and various languages
AREA: 35,920 sq mi; 93,030 sq km
LEADING EXPORTS: raw materials and semi-finished goods
CONTINENT: Europe

Iceland

CAPITAL: Reykjavik
POPULATION: 271,033
MAJOR LANGUAGE: Icelandic
AREA: 39,770 sq mi; 103,000 sq km
LEADING EXPORTS: fish and fish products, and animal products
LOCATION: Atlantic Ocean

India

CAPITAL: New Delhi
POPULATION: 984,003,683
MAJOR LANGUAGES: English, Hindi, Bengali, Telugu, Marathi, Tamil, Urdu, Gujarati, Malayam, Kannada, Oriya, Punjabi, Assamese, Kashmiri, Sindhi, Sanskrit, and Hindustani (all official)
AREA: 1,269,389 sq mi; 3,287,590 sq km
LEADING EXPORTS: clothing, and gems and jewelry
CONTINENT: Asia

Indonesia

CAPITAL: Jakarta
POPULATION: 212,941,810
MAJOR LANGUAGES: Bahasa Indonesia, English, Dutch, Javanese, and various dialects
AREA: 741,052 sq mi; 1,919,251 sq km
LEADING EXPORTS: manufactures, fuels, and foodstuffs
CONTINENT: Asia

Iran

CAPITAL: Tehran
POPULATION: 68,959,931
MAJOR LANGUAGES: Farsi (official) and Turkic languages
AREA: 634,562 sq mi; 1,643,452 sq km
LEADING EXPORTS: petroleum, carpets, fruit, nuts, and hides
CONTINENT: Asia

Iraq

CAPITAL: Baghdad
POPULATION: 21,722,287
MAJOR LANGUAGES: Arabic, Kurdish, Assyrian, and Armenian
AREA: 168,760 sq mi; 437,072 sq km
LEADING EXPORTS: crude oil and refined products, and fertilizers
CONTINENT: Asia

Ireland

CAPITAL: Dublin
POPULATION: 3,619,480
MAJOR LANGUAGES: Irish Gaelic and English
AREA: 27,136 sq mi; 70,280 sq km
LEADING EXPORTS: chemicals and data processing equipment
CONTINENT: Europe

Israel

CAPITAL: Jerusalem
POPULATION: 5,643,966
MAJOR LANGUAGES: Hebrew, Arabic, and English
AREA: 8,019 sq mi; 20,849 sq km
LEADING EXPORTS: machinery and equipment, and cut diamonds
CONTINENT: Asia

Italy

CAPITAL: Rome
POPULATION: 56,782,748
MAJOR LANGUAGES: Italian, German, French, and Slovene
AREA: 116,310 sq mi; 301,230 sq km
LEADING EXPORTS: metals, and textiles and clothing
CONTINENT: Europe

Jamaica

CAPITAL: Kingston
POPULATION: 2,634,678
MAJOR LANGUAGES: English and Creole
AREA: 4,243 sq mi; 10,990 sq km
LEADING EXPORTS: alumina, bauxite, sugar, bananas, and rum
LOCATION: Caribbean Sea

Japan

CAPITAL: Tokyo
POPULATION: 125,931,533
MAJOR LANGUAGE: Japanese
AREA: 145,888 sq mi; 377,835 sq km
LEADING EXPORTS: machinery, motor vehicles, and electronics
CONTINENT: Asia

Jordan

CAPITAL: Amman
POPULATION: 4,434,978
MAJOR LANGUAGES: Arabic and English
AREA: 34,447 sq mi; 89,213 sq km
LEADING EXPORTS: phosphates, fertilizers, and potash
CONTINENT: Asia

Kazakstan

CAPITAL: Akmola
POPULATION: 16,846,808
MAJOR LANGUAGES: Kazakh and Russian
AREA: 1,049,191 sq mi; 2,717,300 sq km
LEADING EXPORTS: oil, and ferrous and nonferrous metals
CONTINENT: Asia

Kenya

CAPITAL: Nairobi
POPULATION: 28,337,071
MAJOR LANGUAGES: English, Swahili, and various languages
AREA: 224,970 sq mi; 582,650 sq km
LEADING EXPORTS: tea, coffee, and petroleum products
CONTINENT: Africa

Kiribati

CAPITAL: Tarawa
POPULATION: 83,976
MAJOR LANGUAGES: English and Gilbertese
AREA: 277 sq mi; 717 sq km
LEADING EXPORTS: copra, seaweed, and fish
LOCATION: Pacific Ocean

Korea, North

CAPITAL: P'yongyang
POPULATION: 21,234,387
MAJOR LANGUAGE: Korean
AREA: 46,542 sq mi; 120,540 sq km
LEADING EXPORTS: minerals and metallurgical products
CONTINENT: Asia

Korea, South

CAPITAL: Seoul
POPULATION: 46,416,796
MAJOR LANGUAGES: Korean and English
AREA: 38,025 sq mi; 98,480 sq km
LEADING EXPORTS: electronic and electrical equipment
CONTINENT: Asia

Kuwait

CAPITAL: Kuwait
POPULATION: 1,913,285
MAJOR LANGUAGES: Arabic and English
AREA: 6,881 sq mi; 17,820 sq km
LEADING EXPORT: oil
CONTINENT: Asia

Kyrgyzstan

CAPITAL: Bishkek
POPULATION: 4,522,281
MAJOR LANGUAGES: Kyrgyz and Russian
AREA: 76,644 sq mi; 198,500 sq km
LEADING EXPORTS: wool, chemicals, cotton, metals, and shoes
CONTINENT: Asia

Laos

CAPITAL: Vientiane
POPULATION: 5,260,842
MAJOR LANGUAGES: Lao, French, English, and various languages
AREA: 91,432 sq mi; 236,800 sq km
LEADING EXPORTS: electricity, wood products, coffee, and tin
CONTINENT: Asia

Latvia

CAPITAL: Riga
POPULATION: 2,385,396
MAJOR LANGUAGES: Lettish, Lithuanian, Russian, and various languages
AREA: 24,750 sq mi; 64,100 sq km
LEADING EXPORTS: oil products, timber, and ferrous metals
CONTINENT: Europe

Lebanon

CAPITAL: Beirut
POPULATION: 3,505,794
MAJOR LANGUAGES: Arabic, French, Armenian, and English
AREA: 4,016 sq mi; 10,400 sq km
LEADING EXPORTS: agricultural products, chemicals, and textiles
CONTINENT: Asia

Lesotho

CAPITAL: Maseru
POPULATION: 2,089,829
MAJOR LANGUAGES: Sesotho, English, Zulu, and Xhosa
AREA: 11,719 sq mi; 30,350 sq km
LEADING EXPORTS: wool, mohair, wheat, cattle, and peas
CONTINENT: Africa

Liberia

CAPITAL: Monrovia
POPULATION: 2,771,901
MAJOR LANGUAGES: English and Niger-Congo
AREA: 43,002 sq mi; 111,370 sq km
LEADING EXPORTS: iron ore, rubber, timber, and coffee
CONTINENT: Africa

Libya

CAPITAL: Tripoli
POPULATION: 5,690,727
MAJOR LANGUAGES: Arabic, Italian, and English
AREA: 679,385 sq mi; 1,759,540 sq km
LEADING EXPORTS: crude oil and refined petroleum products
CONTINENT: Africa

Liechtenstein

CAPITAL: Vaduz
POPULATION: 31,717
MAJOR LANGUAGES: German and Alemannic
AREA: 62 sq mi; 160 sq km
LEADING EXPORTS: small specialty machinery and dental products
CONTINENT: Europe

Lithuania

CAPITAL: Vilnius
POPULATION: 3,600,158
MAJOR LANGUAGES: Lithuanian, Polish, and Russian
AREA: 25,175 sq mi; 65,200 sq km
LEADING EXPORTS: electronics, petroleum products, and food
CONTINENT: Europe

Luxembourg

CAPITAL: Luxembourg
POPULATION: 425,017
MAJOR LANGUAGES: Luxembourgisch, German, French, and English
AREA: 998 sq mi; 2,586 sq km
LEADING EXPORTS: finished steel products and chemicals
CONTINENT: Europe

Macedonia

CAPITAL: Skopje
POPULATION: 2,009,387
MAJOR LANGUAGES: Macedonian, Albanian, Turkish, Serb, Gypsy, and various languages
AREA: 9,781 sq mi; 25,333 sq km
LEADING EXPORTS: manufactured goods and machinery
CONTINENT: Europe

Madagascar

CAPITAL: Antananarivo
POPULATION: 14,462,509
MAJOR LANGUAGES: French and Malagasy
AREA: 226,665 sq mi; 587,040 sq km
LEADING EXPORTS: coffee, vanilla, cloves, shellfish, and sugar
CONTINENT: Africa

Malawi

CAPITAL: Lilongwe
POPULATION: 9,840,474
MAJOR LANGUAGES: English, Chichewa, and various languages
AREA: 45,747 sq mi; 118,480 sq km
LEADING EXPORTS: tobacco, tea, sugar, coffee, and peanuts
CONTINENT: Africa

Malaysia

CAPITAL: Kuala Lumpur
POPULATION: 20,932,901
MAJOR LANGUAGES: Malay, English, Mandarin, Tamil, Chinese dialects, and various languages and dialects
AREA: 127,322 sq mi; 329,750 sq km
LEADING EXPORTS: electronic equipment
CONTINENT: Asia

Maldives

CAPITAL: Male
POPULATION: 290,211
MAJOR LANGUAGES: Divehi dialect and English
AREA: 116 sq mi; 300 sq km
LEADING EXPORTS: fish and clothing
CONTINENT: Asia

Mali

CAPITAL: Bamako
POPULATION: 10,108,569
MAJOR LANGUAGES: French, Bambara, and various languages
AREA: 478,783 sq mi; 1,240,000 sq km
LEADING EXPORTS: cotton, livestock, and gold
CONTINENT: Africa

Malta

CAPITAL: Valletta
POPULATION: 379,563
MAJOR LANGUAGES: Maltese and English
AREA: 124 sq mi; 320 sq km
LEADING EXPORTS: machinery and transportation equipment
LOCATION: Mediterranean Sea

Marshall Islands

CAPITAL: Majuro
POPULATION: 63,031
MAJOR LANGUAGES: English, Marshallese dialects, and Japanese
AREA: 70 sq mi; 181.3 sq km
LEADING EXPORTS: coconut oil, fish, live animals, and trichus shells
LOCATION: Pacific Ocean

Mauritania

CAPITAL: Nouakchott
POPULATION: 2,511,473
MAJOR LANGUAGES: Hasaniya Arabic, Wolof, Pular, and Soninke
AREA: 397,969 sq mi; 1,030,700 sq km
LEADING EXPORTS: iron ore, and fish and fish products
CONTINENT: Africa

Mauritius

CAPITAL: Port Louis
POPULATION: 1,168,256
MAJOR LANGUAGES: English (official), Creole, French, Hindi, Urdu, Hakka, and Bojpoori
AREA: 718 sq mi; 1,860 sq km
LEADING EXPORTS: textiles, sugar, and light manufactures
LOCATION: Indian Ocean

Mayotte

CAPITAL: Mamoutzou
POPULATION: 141,944
MAJOR LANGUAGES: Mahorian and French
AREA: 145 sq mi; 375 sq km
LEADING EXPORTS: ylang-ylang and vanilla
CONTINENT: Africa

Mexico

CAPITAL: Mexico City
POPULATION: 98,552,776
MAJOR LANGUAGES: Spanish and Mayan dialects
AREA: 761,632 sq mi; 1,972,550 sq km
LEADING EXPORTS: crude oil, oil products, coffee, and silver
CONTINENT: North America

Micronesia

CAPITAL: Federated states of Kolonia (on the Island of Pohnpei)
*a new capital is being built about 10 km southwest in the Palikir Valley
POPULATION: 129,658
MAJOR LANGUAGES: English, Turkese, Pohnpeian, Yapese, and Kosrean
AREA: 271 sq mi; 702 sq km
LEADING EXPORTS: fish, copra, bananas, and black pepper
LOCATION: Pacific Ocean

Moldova

CAPITAL: Chisinau
POPULATION: 4,457,729
MAJOR LANGUAGES: Moldovan (official), Russian, and Gagauz dialect
AREA: 13,012 sq mi; 33,700 sq km
LEADING EXPORTS: foodstuffs, wine, and tobacco
CONTINENT: Europe

Monaco

CAPITAL: Monaco
POPULATION: 32,035
MAJOR LANGUAGES: French (official), English, Italian, and Monegasque
AREA: .73 sq mi; 1.9 sq km
LEADING EXPORTS: exports through France
CONTINENT: Europe

Mongolia

CAPITAL: Ulaanbaatar
POPULATION: 2,578,530
MAJOR LANGUAGES: Khalkha Mongol, Turkic, Russian, and Chinese
AREA: 604,270 sq mi; 1,565,000 sq km
LEADING EXPORTS: copper, livestock, animal products, and cashmere
CONTINENT: Asia

Morocco

CAPITAL: Rabat
POPULATION: 29,114,497
MAJOR LANGUAGES: Arabic (official), Berber dialects, and French
AREA: 172,420 sq mi; 446,550 sq km
LEADING EXPORTS: food and beverages
CONTINENT: Africa

Mozambique

CAPITAL: Maputo
POPULATION: 18,641,469
MAJOR LANGUAGES: Portuguese and various dialects
AREA: 309,506 sq mi; 801,590 sq km
LEADING EXPORTS: shrimp, cashews, cotton, sugar, copra, and citrus
CONTINENT: Africa

Myanmar (Burma)

CAPITAL: Rangoon
POPULATION: 47,305,319
MAJOR LANGUAGE: Burmese
AREA: 261,979 sq mi; 678,500 sq km
LEADING EXPORTS: pulses and beans, teak, rice, and hardwood
CONTINENT: Asia

Namibia

CAPITAL: Windhoek
POPULATION: 1,622,328
MAJOR LANGUAGES: English (official), Afrikaans, German, Oshivambo, Herero, Nama, and various languages
AREA: 318,707 sq mi; 825,418 sq km
LEADING EXPORTS: diamonds, copper, gold, zinc, and lead
CONTINENT: Africa

Nauru

CAPITAL: Government offices in Yaren District
POPULATION: 10,501
MAJOR LANGUAGES: Nauruan and English
AREA: 8 sq mi; 21 sq km
LEADING EXPORTS: phosphates
LOCATION: Pacific Ocean

Nepal

CAPITAL: Kathmandu
POPULATION: 23,698,421
MAJOR LANGUAGES: Nepali (official) and 20 various languages divided into numerous dialects
AREA: 54,365 sq mi; 140,800 sq km
LEADING EXPORTS: carpets, clothing, and leather goods
CONTINENT: Asia

Netherlands

CAPITAL: Amsterdam
POPULATION: 15,731,112
MAJOR LANGUAGE: Dutch
AREA: 14,414 sq mi; 37,330 sq km
LEADING EXPORTS: metal products and chemicals
CONTINENT: Europe

New Caledonia

CAPITAL: Noumea
POPULATION: 194,197
MAJOR LANGUAGES: French and 28 Melanesian-Polynesian dialects
AREA: 7,359 sq mi; 19,060 sq km
LEADING EXPORTS: nickel metal and nickel ore
LOCATION: Pacific Ocean

New Zealand

CAPITAL: Wellington
POPULATION: 3,625,388
MAJOR LANGUAGES: English and Maori
AREA: 103,741 sq mi; 268,680 sq km
LEADING EXPORTS: wool, lamb, mutton, beef, fish, and cheese
LOCATION: Pacific Ocean

Nicaragua

CAPITAL: Managua
POPULATION: 4,583,379
MAJOR LANGUAGES: Spanish (official), English, and various languages
AREA: 50,000 sq mi; 129,494 sq km
LEADING EXPORTS: meat, coffee, cotton, sugar, seafood, and gold
CONTINENT: North America

Niger

CAPITAL: Niamey
POPULATION: 9,671,848
MAJOR LANGUAGES: French (official), Hausa, and Djerma
AREA: 489,208 sq mi; 1,267,000 sq km
LEADING EXPORTS: uranium ore and livestock products
CONTINENT: Africa

Nigeria

CAPITAL: Abuja
POPULATION: 110,532,242
MAJOR LANGUAGES: English (official), Hausa, Yoruba, Ibo, and Fulani
AREA: 356,682 sq mi; 923,770 sq km
LEADING EXPORTS: oil, cocoa, and rubber
CONTINENT: Africa

Niue

CAPITAL: (Free association with New Zealand)
POPULATION: 1,800
MAJOR LANGUAGES: Polynesian and English
AREA: 100 sq mi; 260 sq km
LEADING EXPORTS: canned coconut cream, copra, and honey
LOCATION: Pacific Ocean

Norway

CAPITAL: Oslo
POPULATION: 4,419,955
MAJOR LANGUAGES: Norwegian (official), Lapp, and Finnish
AREA: 125,186 sq mi; 324,220 sq km
LEADING EXPORTS: petroleum and petroleum products
CONTINENT: Europe

Oman

CAPITAL: Muscat
POPULATION: 2,363,591
MAJOR LANGUAGES: Arabic (official), English, Baluchi, Urdu, and Indian dialects
AREA: 82,034 sq mi; 212,460 sq km
LEADING EXPORTS: petroleum, re-exports, and fish
CONTINENT: Asia

Pakistan

CAPITAL: Islamabad
POPULATION: 135,135,195
MAJOR LANGUAGES: Urdu (official), English (official), Punjabi, Sindhi, Pashtu, Urdu, Balochi, and other languages
AREA: 310,414 sq mi; 803,940 sq km
LEADING EXPORTS: cotton, textiles, clothing, rice, and leather
CONTINENT: Asia

Palau

CAPITAL: Koror
POPULATION: 18,110
MAJOR LANGUAGES: English (official), Sonsorolese, Angaur, Japanese, Tobi, and Palauan
AREA: 177 sq mi; 458 sq km
LEADING EXPORTS: trochus, tuna, copra, and handicrafts
LOCATION: Pacific Ocean

Panama

CAPITAL: Panama
POPULATION: 2,735,943
MAJOR LANGUAGES: Spanish (official) and English
AREA: 30,194 sq mi; 78,200 sq km
LEADING EXPORTS: bananas, shrimp, sugar, clothing, and coffee
CONTINENT: North America

Papua New Guinea

CAPITAL: Port Moresby
POPULATION: 4,599,785
MAJOR LANGUAGES: English, pidgin English, and Motu
AREA: 178,266 sq mi; 461,690 sq km
LEADING EXPORTS: gold, copper ore, oil, logs, and palm oil
LOCATION: Pacific Ocean

Paraguay

CAPITAL: Asuncion
POPULATION: 5,291,020
MAJOR LANGUAGES: Spanish (official) and Guarani
AREA: 157,052 sq mi; 406,750 sq km
LEADING EXPORTS: cotton, soybeans, timber, and vegetable oils
CONTINENT: South America

Peru

CAPITAL: Lima
POPULATION: 26,111,110
MAJOR LANGUAGES: Spanish (official), Quechua (official), and Aymara
AREA: 496,243 sq mi; 1,285,220 sq km
LEADING EXPORTS: copper, zinc, and fish meal
CONTINENT: South America

Philippines

CAPITAL: Manila
POPULATION: 77,725,862
MAJOR LANGUAGES: Filipino and English (official)
AREA: 115,834 sq mi; 300,000 sq km
LEADING EXPORTS: electronics, textiles, and coconut products
CONTINENT: Asia

Poland

CAPITAL: Warsaw
POPULATION: 38,606,922
MAJOR LANGUAGE: Polish
AREA: 120,731 sq mi; 312,680 sq km
LEADING EXPORTS: intermediate goods
CONTINENT: Europe

Portugal

CAPITAL: Lisbon
POPULATION: 9,927,556
MAJOR LANGUAGE: Portuguese
AREA: 35,553 sq mi; 92,080 sq km
LEADING EXPORTS: clothing and footwear, and machinery
CONTINENT: Europe

Qatar

CAPITAL: Doha
POPULATION: 697,126
MAJOR LANGUAGES: Arabic (official) and English
AREA: 4,247 sq mi; 11,000 sq km
LEADING EXPORTS: petroleum products, steel, and fertilizers
CONTINENT: Asia

Romania

CAPITAL: Bucharest
POPULATION: 22,395,848
MAJOR LANGUAGES: Romanian, Hungarian, and German
AREA: 91,702 sq mi; 237,500 sq km
LEADING EXPORTS: metals and metal products, and mineral products
CONTINENT: Europe

Russia

CAPITAL: Moscow
POPULATION: 146,861,022
MAJOR LANGUAGES: Russian and various languages
AREA: 6,952,996 sq mi; 17,075,200 sq km
LEADING EXPORTS: petroleum and petroleum products
CONTINENT: Europe and Asia

Rwanda

CAPITAL: Kigali
POPULATION: 7,956,172
MAJOR LANGUAGES: Kinyarwanda (official), French (official), and Kiswahili
AREA: 10,170 sq mi; 26,340 sq km
LEADING EXPORTS: coffee, tea, cassiterite, and wolframite
CONTINENT: Africa

Saint Kitts and Nevis

CAPITAL: Basseterre
POPULATION: 42,291
MAJOR LANGUAGE: English
AREA: 104 sq mi; 269 sq km
LEADING EXPORTS: machinery, food, and electronics
LOCATION: Caribbean Sea

Saint Lucia

CAPITAL: Castries
POPULATION: 152,335
MAJOR LANGUAGES: English and French patois
AREA: 239 sq mi; 620 sq km
LEADING EXPORTS: bananas, clothing, cocoa, and vegetables
LOCATION: Caribbean Sea

Saint Vincent and the Grenadines

CAPITAL: Kingstown
POPULATION: 119,818
MAJOR LANGUAGES: English and French patois
AREA: 131 sq mi; 340 sq km
LEADING EXPORTS: bananas, and eddoes and dasheen (taro)
LOCATION: Caribbean Sea

Samoa

CAPITAL: Apia
POPULATION: 224,713
MAJOR LANGUAGES: Samoan and English
AREA: 1,104 sq mi; 2,860 sq km
LEADING EXPORTS: coconut oil and cream, taro, copra, and cocoa
LOCATION: Pacific Ocean

San Marino

CAPITAL: San Marino
POPULATION: 24,894
MAJOR LANGUAGE: Italian
AREA: 23 sq mi; 60 sq km
LEADING EXPORTS: building stone, lime, wood, and chestnuts
CONTINENT: Europe

São Tomé and Príncipe

CAPITAL: São Tomé
POPULATION: 150,123
MAJOR LANGUAGE: Portuguese (official)
AREA: 371 sq mi; 960 sq km
LEADING EXPORTS: cocoa, copra, coffee, and palm oil
CONTINENT: Africa

Saudi Arabia

CAPITAL: Riyadh
POPULATION: 20,785,955
MAJOR LANGUAGE: Arabic
AREA: 757,011 sq mi; 1,960,582 sq km
LEADING EXPORTS: petroleum and petroleum products
CONTINENT: Asia

Senegal

CAPITAL: Dakar
POPULATION: 9,723,149
MAJOR LANGUAGES: French (official), Wolof, Pulaar, Diola, and Mandingo
AREA: 75,752 sq mi; 196,190 sq km
LEADING EXPORTS: fish, ground nuts, and petroleum products
CONTINENT: Africa

Serbia and Montenegro

CAPITAL: Belgrade
POPULATION: 11,206,039
MAJOR LANGUAGES: Serbo-Croatian and Albanian
AREA: 39,436 sq mi; 102,350 sq km
LEADING EXPORTS: none
CONTINENT: Europe

Seychelles

CAPITAL: Victoria
POPULATION: 78,641
MAJOR LANGUAGES: English (official), French (official), and Creole
AREA: 176 sq mi; 455 sq km
LEADING EXPORTS: fish, cinnamon bark, and copra
CONTINENT: Africa

Sierra Leone

CAPITAL: Freetown
POPULATION: 5,080,004
MAJOR LANGUAGES: English (official), Mende, Temne, and Krio
AREA: 27,700 sq mi; 71,740 sq km
LEADING EXPORTS: rutile, bauxite, diamonds, coffee, and cocoa
CONTINENT: Africa

Singapore

CAPITAL: Singapore
POPULATION: 3,490,356
MAJOR LANGUAGES: Chinese, Malay, Tamil, and English
AREA: 244 sq mi; 633 sq km
LEADING EXPORTS: computer equipment
CONTINENT: Asia

Slovakia

CAPITAL: Bratislava
POPULATION: 5,392,982
MAJOR LANGUAGES: Slovak and Hungarian
AREA: 18,860 sq mi; 48,845 sq km
LEADING EXPORTS: machinery and transportation equipment
CONTINENT: Europe

Slovenia

CAPITAL: Ljubljana
POPULATION: 1,971,739
MAJOR LANGUAGES: Slovenian, Serbo-Croatian, and various languages
AREA: 7,837 sq mi; 20,296 sq km
LEADING EXPORTS: machinery and transportation equipment
CONTINENT: Europe

Solomon Islands

CAPITAL: Honiara
POPULATION: 441,039
MAJOR LANGUAGES: Melanesian pidgin and English
AREA: 10,985 sq mi; 28,450 sq km
LEADING EXPORTS: fish, timber, palm oil, cocoa, and copra
LOCATION: Pacific Ocean

Somalia

CAPITAL: Mogadishu
POPULATION: 6,841,695
MAJOR LANGUAGES: Somali (official), Arabic, Italian, and English
AREA: 246,210 sq mi; 637,660 sq km
LEADING EXPORTS: bananas, live animals, fish, and hides
CONTINENT: Africa

South Africa

CAPITAL: Pretoria (administrative), Cape Town (legislative), Bloemfontein (judicial)
POPULATION: 42,834,520
MAJOR LANGUAGES: Afrikaans, English, Ndebele, Pedi, Sotho, Swazi, Tsonga, Tswana, Venda, Xhosa, and Zulu (all official)
AREA: 471,027 sq mi; 1,219,912 sq km
LEADING EXPORTS: gold, other minerals and metals, and food
CONTINENT: Africa

Spain

CAPITAL: Madrid
POPULATION: 39,133,996
MAJOR LANGUAGES: Spanish, Catalan, Galician, and Basque
AREA: 194,892 sq mi; 504,750 sq km
LEADING EXPORTS: cars and trucks, and semifinished goods
CONTINENT: Europe

Sri Lanka

CAPITAL: Colombo
POPULATION: 18,933,558
MAJOR LANGUAGES: Sinhala (official) and Tamil
AREA: 25,333 sq mi; 65,610 sq km
LEADING EXPORTS: garments and textiles, teas, and diamonds
CONTINENT: Asia

Sudan

CAPITAL: Khartoum
POPULATION: 33,550,552
MAJOR LANGUAGES: Arabic (official), Nubian, Ta Bedawie, Nilotic, Nilo-Hamitic, and Sudanic dialects
AREA: 967,532 sq mi; 2,505,810 sq km
LEADING EXPORTS: gum arabic, livestock/meat, and cotton
CONTINENT: Africa

Suriname

CAPITAL: Paramaribo
POPULATION: 427,980
MAJOR LANGUAGES: Dutch (official), English, Sranang, Tongo, Hindustani, and Japanese
AREA: 63,041 sq mi; 163,270 sq km
LEADING EXPORTS: alumina, aluminum, and shrimp and fish
CONTINENT: South America

Swaziland

CAPITAL: Mbabane
POPULATION: 966,462
MAJOR LANGUAGES: English (official) and SiSwati (official)
AREA: 6,641 sq mi; 17,360 sq km
LEADING EXPORTS: sugar, edible concentrates, and wood pulp
CONTINENT: Africa

Sweden

CAPITAL: Stockholm
POPULATION: 8,886,738
MAJOR LANGUAGES: Swedish, Lapp, and Finnish
AREA: 173,738 sq mi; 449,964 sq km
LEADING EXPORTS: machinery, motor vehicles, and paper products
CONTINENT: Europe

Switzerland

CAPITAL: Bern
POPULATION: 7,260,357
MAJOR LANGUAGES: German, French, Italian, Romansch, and various languages
AREA: 15,943 sq mi; 41,290 sq km
LEADING EXPORTS: machinery and equipment
CONTINENT: Europe

Syria

CAPITAL: Damascus
POPULATION: 16,673,282
MAJOR LANGUAGES: Arabic (official), Kurdish, Armenian, Aramaic, Circassian, and French
AREA: 71,501 sq mi; 185,180 sq km
LEADING EXPORTS: petroleum, textiles, cotton, and fruits
CONTINENT: Asia

Taiwan

CAPITAL: Taipei
POPULATION: 21,908,135
MAJOR LANGUAGES: Mandarin Chinese (official), Taiwanese, and Hakka dialects
AREA: 13,892 sq mi; 35,980 sq km
LEADING EXPORTS: electrical machinery and electronics
CONTINENT: Asia

Tajikistan

CAPITAL: Dushanbe
POPULATION: 6,020,095
MAJOR LANGUAGES: Tajik (official) and Russian
AREA: 55,253 sq mi; 143,100 sq km
LEADING EXPORTS: cotton, aluminum, fruits, and vegetable oil
CONTINENT: Asia

Tanzania

CAPITAL: Dar Es Salaam
POPULATION: 30,608,769
MAJOR LANGUAGES: Swahili, English, and various languages
AREA: 364,914 sq mi; 945,090 sq km
LEADING EXPORTS: coffee, cotton, tobacco, tea, and cashew nuts
CONTINENT: Africa

Thailand

CAPITAL: Bangkok
POPULATION: 60,037,366
MAJOR LANGUAGES: Thai and English
AREA: 198,463 sq mi; 511,770 sq km
LEADING EXPORTS: machinery and manufactures
CONTINENT: Asia

Togo

CAPITAL: Lome
POPULATION: 4,905,827
MAJOR LANGUAGES: French, Ewe and Mina, Dagomba, and Kabye
AREA: 21,927 sq mi; 56,790 sq km
LEADING EXPORTS: phosphates, cotton, cocoa, and coffee
CONTINENT: Africa

Tonga

CAPITAL: Nukualofa
POPULATION: 108,207
MAJOR LANGUAGES: Tongan and English
AREA: 289 sq mi; 748 sq km
LEADING EXPORTS: squash, vanilla, fish, root crops, and coconut oil
LOCATION: Pacific Ocean

Trinidad and Tobago

CAPITAL: Port-of-Spain
POPULATION: 1,116,595
MAJOR LANGUAGES: English, Hindu, French, and Spanish
AREA: 1,981 sq mi; 5,130 sq km
LEADING EXPORTS: petroleum and petroleum products
LOCATION: Caribbean Sea

Tunisia

CAPITAL: Tunis
POPULATION: 9,380,404
MAJOR LANGUAGES: Arabic and French
AREA: 63,172 sq mi; 163,610 sq km
LEADING EXPORTS: hydrocarbons and agricultural products
CONTINENT: Africa

Turkey

CAPITAL: Ankara
POPULATION: 65,566,511
MAJOR LANGUAGES: Turkish, Kurdish, and Arabic
AREA: 301,394 sq mi; 780,580 sq km
LEADING EXPORTS: manufactured products, and foodstuffs
CONTINENT: Europe and Asia

Turkmenistan

CAPITAL: Ashgabat
POPULATION: 4,297,629
MAJOR LANGUAGES: Turkmen, Russian, Uzbek, and various languages
AREA: 188,463 sq mi; 488,100 sq km
LEADING EXPORTS: natural gas, cotton, and petroleum products
CONTINENT: Asia

Tuvalu

CAPITAL: Fongafale, on Funafuti atoll
POPULATION: 10,444
MAJOR LANGUAGES: Tuvaluan and English
AREA: 10 sq mi; 26 sq km
LEADING EXPORT: copra
LOCATION: Pacific Ocean

Uganda

CAPITAL: Kampala
POPULATION: 22,167,195
MAJOR LANGUAGES: English, Luganda, Swahili, Bantu languages, and Nilotic languages
AREA: 91,139 sq mi; 236,040 sq km
LEADING EXPORTS: coffee, cotton, and tea
CONTINENT: Africa

Ukraine

CAPITAL: Kiev
POPULATION: 50,125,108
MAJOR LANGUAGES: Ukranian, Russian, Romanian, Polish, and Hungarian
AREA: 233,098 sq mi; 603,700 sq km
LEADING EXPORTS: coal, electric power, and metals
CONTINENT: Europe

United Arab Emirates

CAPITAL: Abu Dhabi
POPULATION: 2,303,088
MAJOR LANGUAGES: Arabic, Persian, English, Hindi, and Urdu
AREA: 29,183 sq mi; 75,581 sq km
LEADING EXPORTS: crude oil, natural gas, re-exports, and dried fish
CONTINENT: Asia

United Kingdom

CAPITAL: London
POPULATION: 58,970,119
MAJOR LANGUAGES: English, Welsh, and Scottish Gaelic
AREA: 94,529 sq mi; 244,820 sq km
LEADING EXPORTS: manufactured goods, machinery, and fuels
CONTINENT: Europe

United States

CAPITAL: Washington, D.C.
POPULATION: 270,311,758
MAJOR LANGUAGES: English and Spanish
AREA: 3,618,908 sq mi; 9,372,610 sq km
LEADING EXPORTS: capital goods and automobiles
CONTINENT: North America

Uruguay

CAPITAL: Montevideo
POPULATION: 3,284,841
MAJOR LANGUAGES: Spanish and Brazilero
AREA: 68,041 sq mi; 176,220 sq km
LEADING EXPORTS: wool and textile manufactures
CONTINENT: South America

Uzbekistan

CAPITAL: Tashkent
POPULATION: 23,784,321
MAJOR LANGUAGES: Uzbek, Russian, Tajik, various languages
AREA: 172,748 sq mi; 447,400 sq km
LEADING EXPORTS: cotton, gold, natural gas, and minerals
CONTINENT: Asia

Vanuatu

CAPITAL: Port-Vila
POPULATION: 185,204
MAJOR LANGUAGES: English, French, pidgin, and Bislama
AREA: 5,699 sq mi; 14,760 sq km
LEADING EXPORTS: copra, beef, cocoa, timber, and coffee
LOCATION: Pacific Ocean

Venezuela

CAPITAL: Caracas
POPULATION: 22,803,409
MAJOR LANGUAGES: Spanish and various languages
AREA: 352,156 sq mi; 912,050 sq km
LEADING EXPORTS: petroleum, bauxite and aluminum, and steel
CONTINENT: South America

Vietnam

CAPITAL: Hanoi
POPULATION: 76,236,259
MAJOR LANGUAGES: Vietnamese, French, Chinese, English, Khmer, and various languages
AREA: 127,248 sq mi; 329,560 sq km
LEADING EXPORTS: petroleum, rice, and agricultural products
CONTINENT: Asia

Yemen

CAPITAL: Sanaa
POPULATION: 16,387,963
MAJOR LANGUAGE: Arabic
AREA: 203,857 sq mi; 527,970 sq km
LEADING EXPORTS: crude oil, cotton, coffee, hides, and vegetables
CONTINENT: Asia

Zambia

CAPITAL: Lusaka
POPULATION: 9,460,736
MAJOR LANGUAGES: English (official) and about 70 various languages
AREA: 290,594 sq mi; 752,610 sq km
LEADING EXPORTS: copper, zinc, cobalt, lead, and tobacco
CONTINENT: Africa

Zimbabwe

CAPITAL: Harare
POPULATION: 11,044,147
MAJOR LANGUAGES: English, Shona, and Sindebele
area: 150,809 sq mi; 390,580 sq km
LEADING EXPORTS: agricultural products and manufactures
CONTINENT: Africa

Glossary of Geographic Terms

basin
a depression in the surface of the land; some basins are filled with water

bay
a part of a sea or lake that extends into the land

butte
a small raised area of land with steep sides

▲ butte

canyon
a deep, narrow valley with steep sides; often has a stream flowing through it

cataract
a large waterfall; any strong flood or rush of water

◀ cataract

delta
a triangular-shaped plain at the mouth of a river, formed when sediment is deposited by flowing water

flood plain
a broad plain on either side of a river, formed when sediment settles on the riverbanks

glacier
a huge, slow-moving mass of snow and ice

hill
an area that rises above surrounding land and has a rounded top; lower and usually less steep than a mountain

island
an area of land completely surrounded by water

isthmus
a narrow strip of land that connects two larger areas of land

mesa
a high, flat-topped landform with cliff-like sides; larger than a butte

mountain
an area that rises steeply at least 2,000 feet (300 m) above surrounding land; usually wide at the bottom and rising to a narrow peak or ridge

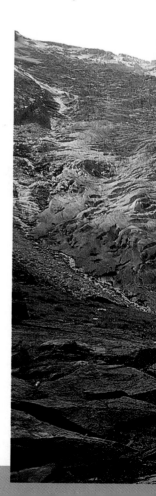

▶ glacier

◀ delta

mountain pass
a gap between mountains

peninsula
an area of land almost completely surrounded by water and connected to the mainland by an isthmus

plain
a large area of flat or gently rolling land

plateau
a large, flat area that rises above the surrounding land; at least one side has a steep slope

river mouth
the point where a river enters a lake or sea

strait
a narrow stretch of water that connects two larger bodies of water

tributary
a river or stream that flows into a larger river

volcano
an opening in the Earth's surface through which molten rock, ashes, and gasses from the Earth's interior escape

▶ volcano

Gazetteer

A

Amazon Rain Forest a large tropical rain forest occupying the drainage basin of the Amazon River in northern South America and covering an area of 2,700,000 square miles, p. 19

Andes Mountains (13°S, 75°W) a mountain system extending along the western coast of South America, p. 8

Argentina (35.3°S, 67°W) a country in South America, p. 12

Atacama Desert (23.5°S, 69°W) a desert in Chile, South America; the driest place on the Earth, p. 14

B

Bolivia (17°S, 64°W) a country in South America, p. 3

Brasília (15.49°S, 47.39°W) the capital city of Brazil, p. 76

Brazil (9°S, 53°W) the largest country in South America, p. 12

C

Canal Zone a 10-mile strip of land along the Panama Canal, stretching from the Atlantic Ocean to the Pacific Ocean, p. 101

Caracas (10.3°N, 66.58°W) the capital city of Venezuela, p. 148

Caribbean (14.3°N, 75.3°W) a part of the southern Atlantic Ocean, p. 9

Central America (10.45°N, 87.15°W) the part of Latin America that includes the seven republics of Guatemala, Honduras, El Salvador, Nicaragua, Costa Rica, Panama, and Belize, p. 9

Chile (35°S, 72°W) a country in South America, p. 14

Colombia (3.3°N, 72.3°W) a country in South America, p. 25

Condado a waterfront area of San Juan, Puerto Rico, p. 123

Copán (14.5°N, 89.1°W) a ruined ancient Mayan city in western Honduras, p. 36

Cuba (22°N, 79°W) an island country, the largest of the Caribbean islands, p. 11

Cuzco (13.36°S, 71.52°W) a city in Peru; capital of the Incan empire, p. 39

G

Guatemala (15.45°N, 91.45°W) a country in Central America, p. 36

H

Haiti (19°N, 72.15°W) a country in the Caribbean Sea, on the island of Hispaniola, p. 50

Hispaniola (17.3°N, 73.15°W) an island in the Caribbean Sea, divided between Haiti in the west and the Dominican Republic in the east, p. 11

J

Jamaica (17.45°N, 78°W) an island country in the Caribbean Sea, p. 11

L

Lake Maracaibo (9.55°N, 72.13°W) a lake in northwestern Venezuela, p. 13

Lake Titicaca (16.12° S, 70.33° W) the world's largest lake, in the Andes Mountains in South America, p. 13

M

Mexico (23.45°N, 104°W) a country in North America, p. 9

Mexico City (19.28°N, 99.09°W) the capital of and largest city in Mexico; one of the largest urban areas in the world, p. 36

Miami (25.45°N, 80.11°W) a city in southeastern Florida, p. 107

P

Panama (9°N, 80°W) a country in Central America, p. 53

Panama Canal (9.2°N, 79.55°W) an important shipping canal across the Isthmus of Panama, linking the Caribbean Sea (and the Atlantic Ocean) to the Pacific Ocean, p. 96

Paraguay (24°S, 57°W) a country in South America, p. 3

Patagonia (46.45°S, 69.3°W) a desert in southern Argentina; the largest desert in the Americas, p. 17

Peru (10°S, 75°W) a country in South America, p. 13

Port-au-Prince (18.35°N, 72.2°W) the capital city and chief port of Haiti, p. 113

Puerto Rico (18.16°N, 66.5°W) an island commonwealth of the United States in the Caribbean Sea, p. 11

R

Rio de Janeiro (22.5°S, 43.2°W) a major city in Brazil, p. 129

S

Salvador (12.59°S, 38.27°W) the capital city and major port of Bahia state, in northeastern Brazil, p. 130

San Juan (18.3°N, 66.10°W) the capital and largest city in Puerto Rico, p. 123

Santiago (33.26°S, 70.4°W) the capital city of Chile, p. 142

São Paulo (23.34°S, 46.38°W) the largest city in Brazil, p. 74

South America (15°S, 60°W) the world's fourth-largest continent, bounded by the Caribbean Sea, the Atlantic Ocean, and the Pacific Ocean, and linked to North America by the Isthmus of Panama, p. 9

T

Tenochtitlán Aztec metropolis covering more than five square miles near modern Mexico City; originally located on two small islands in Lake Texcoco, it gradually grew; one of two Aztec capitals, its name means "stone rising in the water," p. 37

Tikal (17.16°N, 89.49°W) the largest Mayan city in the northern part of Guatemala, p. 36

Trinidad and Tobago (11°N, 61°W) republic of the West Indies, on the two islands called Trinidad and Tobago, p. 3

V

Valley of Mexico the area in Mexico where Lake Texcoco, Tenochtitlán, and modern Mexico City are located, p. 36

Venezuela (8°N, 65°W) a country in South America, p. 12

W

West Indies (19°N, 78°W) the islands of the Caribbean, p. 3

Glossary

A

altiplano [al tih PLAH noh] a high plateau region; a region of high plateaus in the Andes, p. 135

aqueduct a pipe or channel used to carry water from a distant source to dry areas, p. 41

B

bauxite a mixture of minerals that is the main ore aluminum is made of; looks like clay, p. 23

boom a period of increased prosperity during which more of a product is produced and sold, p. 149

C

cacao a tree that grows in the American tropics and produces seeds used to make chocolate and cocoa, p. 23

campesino [kahm pe SEE noh] a poor Latin American farmer, p. 58

canopy a dense mass of leaves forming the top layer of a forest, p.129

Carnival an annual celebration in Latin America with music, dances, and parades, p. 72

caudillo [kow DEE yoh] a military officer who rules strictly, p. 54

citizen an individual with certain rights and responsibilities under a particular government, p. 121

commonwealth a self-governing political unit with strong ties to a particular country, p. 121

communist having an economic system in which the government owns all large businesses and most of a country's land, p. 109

conquistador [kon KEES ta dor] 16th-century conquerors working for the Spanish government who were in charge of gaining land and wealth in the Americas, p. 44

constitution a statement of a country's basic laws and values, p. 123

coral a rock-like substance formed from the skeletons of tiny sea animals, p. 11

Creole a person, often of European and African descent, born in the Caribbean or other parts of the Americas, whose culture has strong French and African influence; a dialect spoken by Creoles, p. 115

criollo [kree OH yoh] a person born of Spanish parents born outside Spain; often among the best-educated and wealthiest people in the Spanish colonies, p. 50

D

dialect a version of a language that is spoken in a particular region, p. 115

dictator a ruler of a country who has complete power, p. 109

diversify to add variety; to expand, p. 27

diversity variety, p. 64

E

economy the ways that goods and services are produced and made available to people, p. 55

elevation height of land above sea level, p. 17

El Niño [el NEEN yoh] a warm ocean current that flows along the western coast of South America; this current influences global weather patterns, p. 14

emigrate move out of one country into another, p. 67

encomienda [en KOH mee en duh] the right to demand taxes or labor from Native Americans; this right was granted to American settlers by the Spanish government, p. 47

ethnic group a group of people who share the same ancestors, culture, language, or religion, p. 70

exile a person who leaves or is forced to leave his or her homeland for another country, p. 110

H

hacienda [hah see EN duh] plantation owned by the Spanish settlers or the Catholic Church in Spanish America, p. 47

hieroglyphics [hy ur oh GLIF iks] a system of writing using signs and symbols, used by the Maya and other cultures, p. 36

hydroelectricity [hy droh ee lek TRIS ih tee] electricity produced by rushing water, p. 23

I

illiterate unable to read or write, p. 112

immigrant a person who has moved into one country from another, p. 67

import to bring products into one country from another to sell, p. 76

indigenous [in DIJ uh nus] describes people who are descendants of the people who first lived in a region, p. 64

injustice lack of fairness, p. 65

invest to spend money to earn more money, p. 55

isthmus narrow strip of land that has water on both sides and joins two larger bodies of land, p. 11

L

ladino [luh DEE noh] in Guatemala, a mestizo, p. 90

Line of Demarcation an imaginary line from the North Pole to the South Pole (at about 50° longitude) set forth in the 1494 Treaty of Tordesillas; Spain had the right to settle and trade west of the line and Portugal had the right to settle and trade east of the line, p. 44

lock a section of waterway in which ships are raised or lowered by adjusting the water level, p. 96

M

maize both the plant and the kernel of corn, p. 36

maquiladora [ma kee la DOR a] a U.S.-owned factory in Mexico that is located close to the U.S.-Mexico border, p. 66

mestizo a person of mixed Spanish and Native American ancestry, p. 46

migrant farmworker a laborer who travels from one area to another, picking crops that are in season, p. 86

moderate a climate that is mild and without extremes in temperature or weather; also known as temperate, p. 178

montaña in northeast Peru, large stretches of tropical forests on the lower slopes of mountains, p. 136

P

pampas [PAHM puhs] flat grassland regions in the southern part of South America; a region similar to the Great Plains in the United States, p.12

pesticide [PES tuh syd] a chemical used to kill insects and diseases that can attack crops, p. 147

photosynthesis [foht oh SIN thuh sis] the process by which green plants and trees produce their own food using water, carbon dioxide, and sunlight; oxygen is released as a result of photosynthesis, p. 133

plateau [pla TOH] large raised area of mostly level land, p. 11

plaza public square at the center of a village, town, or city, p. 85

political movement a large group of people who work together to defend their rights or to change the leaders in power, p. 93

privatization [pry vuh tih ZAY shun] a policy by a government to sell its industries to individuals or private companies, p. 152

Q

quipu [KEE poo] a knotted string used by Incan government officials and traders for record keeping, p. 41

R

revolution a political movement in which people overthrow the existing government and set up another, p. 50

rural having to do with the countryside, p. 59

S

sierra a group of mountains, such as the one that runs from northwest to southeast Peru, p. 136

squatter a person who settles on someone else's land without permission, p. 84

strike work stoppage; a refusal to continue to work until certain demands of workers are met, p. 93

subsistence farming the practice of growing only as much food as a group of people needs to survive, p. 75

subtropical a climate that occurs in regions next to the Tropics, and is hot and humid although less so than in tropical climates, p. 178

T

treaty an agreement in writing made between two or more countries, p. 44

Treaty of Tordesillas [tor day SEE yas] the 1494 treaty setting up the Line of Demarcation, giving Spain the right to settle and trade west of the line and Portugal the same rights east of the line, p. 44

tributary [TRIB yoo tehr ee] river or stream that flows into a main river, p. 13

tropical a climate that is very hot and humid, p. 20

tundra a cold region with little vegetation; in mountains, the area above the tree line, p. 138

U

urban having to do with cities, p. 59

Index

L

soil, 12, 23, 25, 58
Sonoran Desert, 14, *p 14*
South America, 9, *m 10,* 12, *p 12,*
   m 24, 63, 69, 73–77,
   128–153, *m 128,* 185–189,
   m 196, m 197, 217
   ancestry of, 73
   Andes, 8, *p 8,* 9, 12, 14, 39, 73,
      74, 143–144, 145
   art of, 75
   climate of, 17
   colonization of, 73
   culture in, 73–77
   export crops of, 75
   farming in, 12, 17, 25, 75–76
   independence in, 52–54, *m 52*
   landforms of, 9, 12
   language of, 73
   Native Americans in, 73
   natural resources of, *m 24,* 25
   population growth in, 77
   Regional Data Bank, 185–189
   religion in, 73
   urbanization in, 75, 77
   women in, 77
Soviet Union
   and Cuba, 109, 111
   government in, 111
   and United States, 109
Spain, 43–47, 52–54, 73, 212
Spanish, 40, 92
   in Chile, 144
   colonies, 108
   colonization, 46–47, 73
   culture, 123, 125
   empire, 46, *m 46*
   explorers/conquistadors, 43–47,
      m 44, 137
   government, 46, 51
   Harlem, 123
   influences in Chile, 144
   influences in Peru, 137
   influences in Puerto Rico, 122
   language, 10, 64, 70, 73, 125, 148
   missionaries, 64
   social classes 46–47
Spanish-American War, 108
squatter, 84, 220
strike, 93, 220

subsistence farming, 75, 220
sugar cane, *p 16,* 114, 123
Suriname, *m 15, m 18,* 74, *m 128,*
   187, 212
surveyor, 30, *p 31*

T

tables, foreign debt, 56
Tenochtitlán, 37, 38, 217. See
   also Mexico City
Tikal, 36, 217
time lines, 48–49
tin, *m 24*
Tlaloques, 11
Tobago, 72, 184, 213
Topa Inca, 40
tortora reed, 139
trade
   Colombian Exchange, 47
   in Cuba, 108–109
   in Latin America, 57
treaty, 44, 220
Treaty of Tordesillas, 44, 220
tributary, 13, 217, 220
Trinidad, 213
   Carnival in, 72
   economy of, 27
   natural resources of, 23
   oil in, 27
   Regional Data Bank, 184
tropical, 220
Trujillo, Peru, 136
tundra, 138, 220
Turrini, Hector, 133
Tzoc, Justina, 92

U

United States, 128, 129, 213
   and Chile, 147
   and Cuba, 107, 108–109, 111
   culture of, 123
   and Haiti, 113, 116–117
   immigration to, 67
   and Mexico, 66
   and Panama, 99, 101
   petroleum imports, *c 151*

   population growth in, *c 65*
   and Puerto Rico, 121, 122,
      124–125
   and the Soviet Union, 109
   Spanish-American War, 108
uranium, *m 24*
urban, 59, 220
   versus rural, *c 83*
urbanization
   in Brazil, 131
   in Central America, 66–67
   in Latin America, 59
   in Mexico, 66, 67, 83–88
   in Peru, 139
   in South America, 75, 77
   in Venezuela, 150
Uros, 74, 135, *p 135,* 138, 139
   Lake Titicaca, 135, 139
   totora reeds, 135, 139
Uruguay, 12, *m 15, m 18,* 74, 75,
   m 128, 189, 213, 217
   climate of, *m 15,* 17, 19
   economy of, *c 56*
   farming in, 75
   natural vegetation of, *m 18,* 19
Uruguay River, 13

V

Valley of Mexico, 36, 217
vegetation, *m 5,* 14–19, *m 18,*
   c 179
   in the Atacama Desert, 19
   and elevation, *c 17,* 19
Venezuela, 12, 52, 53, 74, *m 128,*
   148–153, 213, 217
   agriculture in, 150
   barrios in, 77
   cities in, 150
   Country Profile of, 149
   culture in, 150–151
   diversification in, 27, 152
   economy of, 27, *c 56,* 148–149,
      150, 152–153
   employment in, 148–149, 150
   farming in, *p 152*
   Germany and 151
   government of, 148, 152
   Lake Maracaibo, 149, 151

Acknowledgments

Cover Design

Bruce Bond, Suzanne Schineller, and Olena Serbyn

Cover Photo

Jon Chomitz

Maps

MapQuest.com, Inc.
Map information sources: Columbia Encyclopedia, Encyclopaedia Britannica, Microsoft® Encarta®, National Geographic Atlas of the World, Rand McNally Commercial Atlas, The Times Atlas of the World.

Staff Credits

The people who made up the **World Explorer** team—representing editorial, editorial services, design services, on-line services/multimedia development, product marketing, production services, project office, and publishing processes—are listed below. Bold type denotes core team members.

Barbara Bertell, **Paul Gagnon, Mary Hanisco, Dotti Marshall,** Susan Swan, and Carol Signorino.

Additional Credits

Art and Design: Emily Soltanoff. Editorial: Debra Reardon, Nancy Rogier. Market Research: Marilyn Leitao. Production Services: **Joyce Barisano.** Publishing Processes: **Wendy Bohannan.**

Text

30, "Where the Flame Trees Bloom," by Alma Flor Ada. Text © 1994 Alma Flor Ada. Reprinted with the permission of Atheneum Books for Young Readers, an imprint of Simon & Schuster Children's Publishing Division. **110,** Excerpt from "Finding My Father," by Lydia Martin, The Miami Herald, June 18, 1995. Reprinted with permission of The Miami Herald. **158,** Poem LXXII (Question Book) by Pablo Neruda. Spanish original reprinted from Libros de las Preguntas, by Pablo Neruda. © Pablo Neruda and Fundación Pablo Neruda, 1974. English translation from Late and Posthumous Poems 1968–1974, by Pablo Neruda, translated by Ben Belitt. © 1988 by Ben Belitt. Used by permission of Grove/Atlantic, Inc.

Photos

1 TL, TR, © Chip & Rosa María de la Cueva Peterson, **1B,** © Mark Lewis/Tony Stone Images, **5,** © Mark Thayer, Boston, **7,** © Photri, **8, 11,** © Chip & Rosa María de la Cueva Peterson, **12,** © Bryan Parsley/Tony Stone Images, **13,** © Will & Deni McIntyre/Tony Stone Images, **14,** © Robert Frerck/Odyssey Productions, **15,** © William J. Hebert/Tony Stone Images, **16,** © Martin Rogers/Tony Stone Images, **19,** © Wolfgang Kaehler/Wolfgang Kaehler Photography, **22,** © Chip & Rosa María de la Cueva Peterson, **23, 25,** © Robert Frerck/Odyssey Productions, **26 L,** © Erik Svenson/Tony Stone Images, **26 R,** © Chip & Rosa María de la Cueva Peterson, **31,** © Photri, **32, 35,** © Chip & Rosa María de la Cueva Peterson, **36 T, BL, BR,** © Robert Frerck/Odyssey Productions, **38 L,** © Chip & Rosa María de la Cueva Peterson, **38 R,** © Robert Frerck/Odyssey Productions, **39,** © Chip & Rosa María de la Cueva Peterson, **40,** © Ed Simpson/Tony Stone Images, **41,** © Robert Frerck/Odyssey Productions, **42,** © Wolfgang Kaehler/Wolfgang Kaehler Photography, **43,** © Daniel Aubry/Odyssey Productions, **45,** © Stock Montage, **49,** © David Young-Wolff/PhotoEdit, **50,** © North Wind Picture Archives, **51,** © Robert Frerck/Odyssey Productions, **53,** © Chip & Rosa María de la Cueva Peterson, **55,** © Robert Frerck/Odyssey Productions, **57,** © Mark Segal/Tony Stone Images, **58,** © Elizabeth Harris/Tony Stone Images, **59,** © Chip & Rosa María de la Cueva Peterson, **62,** © Robert Frerck/Odyssey Productions, **64,** © Sheryl McNee/Tony Stone Images, **66 L,** © Robert E. Daemmrich/Tony Stone Images, **66 R,** © Tom Benoit/Tony Stone Images, **68,** © Jason Laure'/Laure' Communications, **70,** © SuperStock International, **71 L,** © Corbis-Bettmann, **71 R,** © Photri, **72,** © Doug Armand/Tony Stone Images, **73,** © Alex Irvin/Alex Irvin Photography, **74,** © Ed Simpson/Tony Stone Images, **75,** Untitled, by Yhaninc Puelles Enriquez, age 12, Peru. Courtesy of the International Children's Art Museum, **85,** © Demetrio Carrasco/Tony Stone Images, **87,** © David R. Frazier/Tony Stone Images, **88, 89,** © Robert Frerck/Odyssey Productions, **91 L,** © James Nelson/Tony Stone Images, **91 R,** © James Strachan/Tony Stone Images, **92,** © Chip & Rosa María de la Cueva Peterson, **94–95,** © David Young-Wolff/PhotoEdit, **99,** © Chip & Rosa María de la Cueva Peterson, **100 L, R,** © Odyssey Productions, **107,** © Shepard Sherbell/SABA Press Photos, **109,** © Corbis-Bettmann, **110,** © Alyx Kellington/D.D. Bryant Stock Photo, **111,** © Miami Herald/Miami Herald Publishing Co., **112,** © Mary Altier/Mary Altier Photography, **113, 115 L, R,** © Corbis-Bettman, **116,** Untitled, by Cange Walthe, age 12, Haiti. Courtesy of the International Children's Art Museum, **117,** © Corbis-Bettman, **120,** © Benno Friedman, **123,** © Lawrence Migdale/Tony Stone Images, **124 L,** © Robert Frerck/Odyssey Productions, **124 R,** © Wolfgang Kaehler/Wolfgang Kaehler Photography, **125,** © Suzanne L. Murphy/D.D. Bryant Stock Photo, **129,** © Jacques Jangoux/Tony Stone Images, **131,** © Sylvain Grandadam/Tony Stone Images, **132,** © Ary Diesendruck/Tony Stone Images, **135,** © Wolfgang Kaehler/Wolfgang Kaehler Photography, **137,** © D.E. Cox/Tony Stone Images, **138 L, R,** © David Mangurian/David Mangurian Photography, **139,** © Robert Frerck/Odyssey Productions, **140,** © David Young-Wolff/PhotoEdit, **142,** © Photography by S.R.H. Spicer, Vermillion, South Dakota, U.S.A., **144 L,** © Rhonda Klevansky/Tony Stone Images, **144 R,** © Robert Frerck/Odyssey Productions, **145,** © Chip & Rosa María de la Cueva Peterson, **146,** © Charles Philip/Photri, **148,** © Photri, **150,** © Chip & Rosa María de la Cueva Peterson, **152,** © Jacques Jangoux/Tony Stone Images, **153,** © Julie Marcotte/Tony Stone Images, **156,** © David Young-Wolff/PhotoEdit, **159 L, R,** © Francois Gohier/Francois Gohier Pictures, **160, 163,** © Mark Thayer, Boston, **164 I,** © Steve Leonard/Tony Stone Images, **164 B,** © Robert Frerck/Odyssey Productions, **165 T,** © Wolfgang Kaehler/Wolfgang Kaehler Photography, **165 BL,** © John Elk/Tony Stone Images, **165 R,** © Will & Deni McIntyre/Tony Stone Images, **175,** © G. Brad Lewis/Tony Stone Images, **177,** © Nigel Press/Tony Stone Images, **204 T,** © A & L Sinibaldi/Tony Stone Images, **204 B,** © John Beatty/Tony Stone Images, **205 T,** © Hans Strand/Tony Stone Images, **205 BL,** © Spencer Swanger/Tom Stack & Associates, **205 BR,** © Paul Chesley/Tony Stone Images.